EDUCATION TODAY: LANGUAGE TEACHING

*Applied Linguistics
and the Teaching of English*

For a full list of titles in this series, see back cover.

Applied Linguistics and the Teaching of English

A Collection of Papers edited by

HUGH FRASER
English Department, Jordanhill College of Education

W. R. O'DONNELL
English Department, Moray House College of Education

With a Foreword by

ANGUS McINTOSH
*Forbes Professor of English Language
University of Edinburgh*

HUMANITIES PRESS · NEW YORK

First published in the United States of America 1969 by
HUMANITIES PRESS INC
303 Park Avenue South, New York, N.Y. 10011

© *Longmans, Green and Co. Ltd 1969*

Published throughout the world except the United States of America, by Longmans, Green and Co. Ltd., London and Harlow.

Printed in Great Britain by William Clowes and Sons, Limited, London and Beccles

Foreword

What is poetry and if you know what poetry is what is prose enquires Gertrude Stein in a neglected paper called 'Poetry and Grammar'. One might add: 'and just to *know* even what both are, would that be enough?' Certainly from the point of view of the present volume any kind of private knowing is not enough: we are concerned here rather with the *attainment* of certain kinds of knowledge, and how to pass these on and inculcate them.

The focus in this book is mainly upon problems encountered (whether they always fully realize it or not) by native speakers of English in handling their own language, and the means of tackling these. Many of them are problems about which applied linguistics —with due assistance from other disciplines—has something significant to contribute. But it can do nothing but harm in this context to attribute to applied linguistics the miraculous properties of some revolutionary new science. It is more realistic to speak of it as an 'approach' rather than as a science and to pay some regard to its limitations as well as to its value. Something must therefore be said about the kind of part it has to play in tackling such problems of attainment and inculcation as are here under scrutiny.

A good deal of misunderstanding about this matter has arisen in the following way. Applied linguistics has developed in the main in connection with teaching people a language other than their mother tongue, and its insights have been highly fruitful in this direction. Its very succcess here has led the more readily to an often unquestioned assumption that the same approach must surely therefore be proper when one is dealing with young people who are developing their capacity to handle their own language. In fact this second situation is so unlike the other that a radical difference of approach to it is necessary. For in certain ways an English-speaking child's knowledge of English is always in advance of what we can teach him, whereas this is in no way true of his knowledge of (say) Russian. In his own language he can handle at an early age things that no grammarian has yet succeeded in fully accounting for structurally.

For example, I have been struggling for a long time with a tangle of problems all connected in one way or another with the deceptively simple question: 'Why can I say "I hate to get up early" and "I like to get up early" but not "I dislike to get up early"?' Now a full explanation of this and similar things (supposing it were available) would have little relevance to the everyday problems of the young native English speaker as such, because in many such matters he is not likely to go wrong anyhow. Why this is so is itself an interesting matter, since he is in some ways like a child at the wheel of an Aston Martin; and so also is the question: 'Why does he make the kind of mistakes he does?'

But even supposing he does say or write: 'I dislike to get up early', then a simple factual correction, comparable to one bearing on the mistaken understanding of the meaning of some noun or on a misspelt word, is likely to be less confusing and altogether more beneficial than an involved theoretical explanation. The question is of course of very considerable *grammatical* interest and an adequate answer, which covered in one sweep a number of apparently separate pitfalls, could be incorporated with advantage in an English grammar for foreign learners. Other similar answers connected with problems which do bother the native speaker will naturally be directly relevant to him also; however by no means all his difficulties, lexical or grammatical, can be met with profound 'scientific' elucidations of this kind.

The English student approaching Russian is in a quite different position and he requires help of a far more elementary kind; so much less can be taken for granted. So there is an obviously stronger case for teaching him in a much more systematic and 'overall' way about its structural characteristics; almost everything is a potential pitfall. In this way he is brought the more easily to see how some of the surface realities of Russian—all hitherto unfamiliar to him—are made up and interrelate. This is not of course the only way of approaching a foreign language. And though it can be made to work very effectively it would be misleading to maintain even then that *everything* can be made to seem orderly and logical. As Henry Sweet said long ago: 'there are some grammatical constructions, some methods of expression in special languages, which all foreigners—as well as unprejudiced natives of a philosophical mind—would agree in considering irrational.'*

It is often overlooked that the success of a carefully systematized approach to a foreign language rests in no small measure on the student's already developed ability to handle his own language. Much is written about the way a knowledge of one language interferes with the acquisition of an idiomatic control of another. Less is said about the appalling difficulties likely to arise if learners had *no* previously acquired native language at all and so lacked, if not fundamental linguistic insights, at least the linguistic experience which this has given them. For this reason it is not the least of the arguments in favour of an approach which will enable young native speakers to deepen their understanding and control of English, that it will give them some added insights into the problems they face when they tackle a second language. Inadequate attainment in foreign language learning, no less than that in many other fields of study, may often be attributed to inadequate enlightenment about the native language.

In all this I do not wish to lose sight of some of the differences which I began by stressing. To oversimplify, one might say that applied linguistics attempts to expound Russian grammar in a way best suited to help an (e.g.) English-speaking learner to acquire a knowledge of the Russian language. Whereas in the native-language situation there is some danger—sometimes entirely unperceived—that a linguistic enthusiast will in fact expound 'the facts of English' in such a way that it helps the student rather to acquire a knowledge of English grammar than to improve his command of the language itself. It is part of the task of *applied* linguistics, as this book will show, to ensure that the main attack is made in the other direction. Otherwise it is as if, in helping a normal child to run further and faster, we were to delude ourselves into thinking that our techniques of anatomy, dietetics, applied physiology and the rest were in some way more

* Henry Sweet, *The Practical Study of Languages*, Dent, London, 1899, p. 56.

indispensable in our training programme than another factor—the child's already considerable ability to run. And as if we then subordinated our real objective—better running—to the inculcation of information about the techniques themselves.

It would be easy at this point to carry the analogy too far, and to fall into the opposite error of recommending that all approaches to the development of native-language ability should be devised in such a way as merely to 'unwrap' some skill that was there anyhow. I can speak with no authority on the debates that rage around discovery-oriented learning, but I am struck by the presence of some verbal confusions here. What one is trying to 'unwrap' and encourage is certainly not so much knowledge in the ordinary sense as the innate ability to extend and develop that knowledge. And so, with English, one must attempt to tap this *ability*. This is the heart of the problem. It is not a new one but it must continually be re-approached with whatever improved resources and techniques are available. And on top of this, there *is* a need to inculcate knowledge; 'Let your language (or your child's) alone' is a silly sort of slogan which has outlived any use it once had.

Needless to say, the directions in which one must try to move are many. There is the question of taking in, of understanding and evaluating, written and spoken English in a bewildering variety of modes. There is on the other hand the related but distinct matter of personal performance, of helping the child to develop his own ability to write and speak adequately in what, as he grows older, will usually be an ever-extending range of situations and circumstances. And since the successful tapping of abilities always requires some motivation, the whole pedagogical business of developing the ability to handle English in either direction involves far more than a neatly packaged kit of applied linguistic devices, however 'scientifically' these may be based.

It is not therefore without reason that the present volume contains a number of papers which explore beyond the limits of applied linguistics in the narrow sense, and among other things the problem of how to provide adequate stimuli and incentives is not ignored. It is all too easy to invent a 'discipline' and then to limit the problems to precisely those which that discipline can handle, no matter how arbitrary and meaningless such a limitation may be from the human point of view. But the applied linguistic approach does not so isolate itself and it is not difficult to demonstrate its value, both to teachers and to pupils, for the conveying of certain insights of modern linguistic theory which have a direct bearing on the goals we have been considering.

For one thing it helps to clear away numerous current misconceptions and fallacies which would not matter so much were it not that so many people cling to them like grim death and allow them to affect their own linguistic attitudes and behaviour. For another it helps to demonstrate the fascinating and sometimes unsuspected possibilities of the language for performer and recipient alike; in this way it can be discovery-oriented in the best sense, and for the generality of learners nothing else can achieve anything comparable.

The papers in the present volume as a whole underline the importance of relating relevant linguistic insights, insights about the language, to the learning situation; under 'learning situation' is included the nature of the learning child and the possibilities and limitations of the classroom. They owe a great deal to workers in many fields of education and it is hoped that they will stimulate and encourage, without cramping or fettering, those many teachers who are already wrestling with the kind of problems here considered.

Edinburgh, 1968　　　　　　　　　　　　　　ANGUS McINTOSH

Preface

One of our principal obligations in this brief preface is, we feel, to make clear to prospective readers just what is implied by the term 'Applied Linguistics', so that no one may either mistake the aims of the papers or be in any doubt as to what they may be expected to contain.

We see this discipline not as a sub-department of Linguistics, but as one which, though historically and otherwise related to Linguistics, exists in its own right. It would be wrong to think of its proper function as being that of discovering practical applications for Linguistics; this would imply that we should begin with certain theoretical answers and work back towards such subsequently defined problems as fitted these answers. Applied Linguistics is in essence a problem-centred discipline. It starts, that is, by asking not how this or that insight into language might be employed, but rather how this or that practical language problem might be solved, whether the theoretical answers are ready to hand or not.

Applied Linguistics has a relevance to a very wide range of problems, such as may arise in foreign language teaching, machine translation, speech pathology or any one of several other areas where the study of language has an important contributory role. It is impossible, in fact, to specify at this time all those fields where Applied Linguistics has an immediate or potential contribution to make. The papers in the present collection, however, deal, directly or by implication, with one set of problems only, those which arise in the teaching of English to the native speaker.

There are two main categories into which the papers fall. On one hand there are those which concern themselves with areas of linguistic or other knowledge relevant in a more or less general way to the solution of language-teaching problems; on the other, there are those which concern themselves with classroom problems of a specific nature. Each of the contributors has a specialist knowledge of the subject on which he was invited to write, and all have borne in mind that the aim of the collection is to be informative rather than impressive, and to offer all the assistance that is possible in this compass and at this time to teachers involved in real-life language-teaching situations.

It remains only to add that the contributors to this volume, including the Editors, wish to thank most sincerely all those colleagues and friends who were kind enough to read and comment upon earlier drafts of these papers.

Hugh Fraser
Glasgow and Edinburgh, 1968
W. R. O'Donnell

Contents

	FOREWORD		v
	PREFACE		xi
1	SOME APPROACHES TO THE STUDY OF LANGUAGE		1
	Donald Macaulay	Head of Department of Celtic, University of Aberdeen	
2	LANGUAGE DEVELOPMENT IN CHILDREN		21
	Elisabeth Ingram	Lecturer, Department of Applied Linguistics, University of Edinburgh	
3	LINGUISTICS AND CHILDREN'S INTERESTS		38
	Richard Handscombe	Associate Professor of English, York University, Toronto	
4	PROGRAMMED LEARNING		54
	Anthony P. R. Howatt	Lecturer, Department of Applied Linguistics, University of Edinburgh	
5	ANALYSING CLASSROOM PROCEDURES		73
	John Pride	Lecturer, School of English, University of Leeds	
6	LINGUISTICS AND THE TEACHING OF LITERATURE		88
	Alex Rodger	Senior Lecturer, Department of English as a Foreign Language, University of Edinburgh	
7	THE TEACHING OF READING		99
	Julian Dakin	Lecturer, Department of Applied Linguistics, University of Edinburgh	
8	THE TEACHING OF WRITING		121
	Hugh Fraser	Lecturer, English Department, Jordanhill College of Education	
9	THE TEACHING OF MEANING		140
	S. Pit Corder	Head of Department of Applied Linguistics, University of Edinburgh	
10	THE TEACHING OF GRAMMAR		159
	W. R. O'Donnell	Lecturer, English Department, Moray House College of Education	
11	LINGUISTIC FORM AND LITERARY MEANING		176
	Alex Rodger	Senior Lecturer, Department of English as a Foreign Language, University of Edinburgh	

ACKNOWLEDGMENTS

We are indebted to John Wiley & Sons Inc. for their permission to reproduce copyright material from *On Human Communication* by C. Cherry.

1

Some Approaches to the Study of Language

DONALD MACAULAY

The appeal to linguistics—indeed to 'modern, scientific linguistics'—which has been such a feature of the conversations of teachers of English in recent years has seldom been attended by anything like reasonable precision in the use of these terms. So imprecisely have they been used, in fact, that unless one knew better one might easily infer that linguistics covered, directly, everything from Johnny's stammer to the quality of Mr Prufrock's domestic arrangements.

Clearly, this is an unsatisfactory state of affairs. On the one hand, the implied extension of its domain does no service to linguistics; and linguists are no more happy than other people at finding themselves occupying a false position. On the other hand, it does not benefit teachers who are denied whatever real help linguistics has to give them. One might go further and say that if teachers are misled into regarding it as co-extensive with their own very diverse range of interests the effect that 'linguistics' will have on their work is likely to be harmful rather than helpful.

If the teacher of English were not engaged in vital work, or if linguistics had nothing to offer which would, in some sense, help him it might be possible to tolerate the situation. But the first of these conditions is obviously false: and it is the conviction of the writer that the second is false also. Accordingly, this paper seeks to do two things. Firstly, it sets out to discuss some of the lines of enquiry which have held the attention of linguists and which teachers may have difficulty in coming to terms with because they lack the necessary background. Obviously, only a limited number of topics can be dealt with, and those only cursorily; an attempt has therefore been made to confine the discussion to those areas which have some relevance—real or imputed—to the teaching of English. Secondly, it tries to indicate, again very briefly, what attitudes the teacher of English should properly have to linguistics.

We may begin by putting the question 'What is linguistics?'. The apparently widespread belief that the answer to this question is 'self-evident' or will 'become clear as we go along' is unfortunately not borne out in experience. At the same time we do not raise the question in order to offer a satisfactory, simple answer: it is necessary to point out that the question is a complex one. Thus, if we suggest a somewhat circular answer such as 'Linguistics is the study of language', we are led to the further question 'What is language?' And it can fairly be said that all linguistic enquiry is directed to finding answers to this question. But, clearly, our answer to the original question is inadequate. If we relate to it another circular answer 'Linguistics is what linguists do', we find that there is in fact considerable disagreement among those who regard themselves as linguists about what constitutes 'doing linguistics'. They disagree both about goals and about methods. They disagree about the meaning of 'language', of 'scientific' and even of 'modern'. And if there is disagreement among linguists themselves about what linguistics is, a simple, short answer to our original question is unlikely to be of much value.

The point is, of course, that there is nothing to be gained by simply invoking terms like 'scientific', 'modern' and 'linguistics' in support of argument. They provide no magic answers to the teacher's problems and they should not be used without proper definition, or outside the contexts in which they are appropriate.

Caution is made all the more necessary by the curious attitudes to language one finds and the bizarre forms which statements about the nature of language sometimes take. The following is a startling—but genuine—example: 'Language is somewhat like a domesticated dog, manageable when on the leash but inclined to be wild or even promiscuous when free.' It is true that one might be inclined to dismiss this sort of thing out of hand—or regard it as no more than a good sermon against uncontrolled vividness of expression. After all, everyone knows there is a vast difference between language and dogs! But there are statements which may not be so obviously dismissible; for example: 'Language is communication.' The fine aphoristic ring and the insidious technological appeal of this statement should not be allowed to conceal the fact that as it stands it fails to distinguish language from the honey-gathering activities of bees or the mating rituals of penguins, both of which involve communication systems. Using technical terms in a loose and inappropriate way merely adds pretension to confusion: the first of our quotations above cannot, in other words, be redeemed by rewriting it as 'Linguistic behaviour patterns correlate in some degree with the behaviour patterns of canines modified by lengthy exposure to human-controlled environments; they are predictable when the range of potential responses is rigorously curtailed by artificial sanctions but etc. . . .'

The present interest of English teachers in linguistics dates, to a degree, from the publication of Paul Roberts' *Patterns of English* (1956).[1] This book, based mainly on the work of C. C. Fries, made what they have come to call 'structural grammar' available to teachers of English on their home ground, as it were. Fries's own book *The Structure of English* (1952)[2] had a considerable influence on attitudes to linguistics and to language teaching; Fries was actively interested in both of these fields.

It is common knowledge that one of the strongest selling points of the work of Fries and his followers was their attack on the failings of traditional grammar. One finds these listed in the literature of the movement; for example, S. R. Levin[3] discusses them under such headings as 'the semantic fallacy', 'the normative fallacy', 'the logical fallacy', 'the Latin fallacy' and so on.

The 'semantic fallacy' refers to the practice of definition in terms of meaning; for example, the definition of a 'noun' as 'the name of a person, place or thing . . .'. If one defines a noun in such terms, then the definition has to be extended in order to include words like 'happiness', 'charity', 'retreat', and then further extended to include other items until all generality is lost. Furthermore, it was said, the parts of speech have nothing to do with *meaning*; they are distributional classes defined by their possibility of occurrence in certain formal environments. For establishing these classes semantic notions were regarded as irrelevant.

'The normative fallacy' involved the prescription of 'standards of correctness' which had no factual contemporary basis. Prescription of this kind, it was held, derived from the view that the language was in a state of decadence and that continual vigilance and strenuous rear-guard action were necessary to prevent verbal chaos.

This view of language has, of course, a long history. In the eighteenth century there grew up a strong movement to establish the canons and arrest the backsliding of the English tongue, and such works as Dr Johnson's Dictionary were projected to do just this—to 'preserve the purity' and to 'correct or proscribe' 'improprieties and absurdities' of the language. It is interesting to note that Johnson would not go so far as to support the establishing of an Academy, which he thought the sense of liberty of the English people would speedily disestablish. However, despite such early misgivings about following them to their logical conclusions, notions of absolute correctness in language behaviour have persisted in English school grammars down to the present day. We refer to the favourite section headed 'Common Errors' with its proscription of split-infinitives, and prepositions ending sentences.

Such proscriptions have no sanction whatsoever, in so far as we gain any insight into the matter from linguistic study. Indeed they frequently appear to have very little justification of any kind. However, because of persistent misunderstandings, it should be reiterated that no linguist would expect teachers to resign their right to impose standards. The proper conclusion to be drawn from arguments about the 'normative fallacy' is that standards should be based upon realistic criteria reflecting contemporary usage rather than upon attitudes reflecting social intolerance. And this is not 'linguistics' at all, but simply good sense. Teaching grammars are by their very nature prescriptive or normative, but the norms which they seek to inculcate must be realistic ones.

'The logical fallacy' concerns the extension of certain laws to the study of language on the presumption that they are universally applicable. A favourite example of this particular fallacy is the attempt to analyse all languages as having tense systems consisting of three terms, 'past', 'present' and 'future', by analogy with the time continuum. For English, and for many other languages, this analysis is inadequate.

The so-called 'Latin fallacy' involves the presumption of the essential rightness of grammars devised for Latin and an attempt to describe the grammar of, say, English entirely in identical terms. That obvious differences between the two languages (Latin being highly inflected; English relatively uninflected) make such a description unrealistic is ignored.

The objections to these fallacies stressed, in the first place, the necessity for regarding language as a subject worthy of study in its own right, not necessarily governed by the same laws as other subjects, and requiring, in its analysis, a particular methodology. In the second place it stressed the necessity for studying each language independently without assuming that it had the kind of similarities to other languages which would make possible the transfer of categories from one to another. The problems with positions like this arise in turn when people assert, e.g., that tense has nothing to do with time, or that there are no such things as linguistic universals.

However, the contribution of the structuralist school was not entirely negative, despite the vigour of their attack on traditional notions. We therefore propose to look briefly at two of the proposals to be found in Fries's *The Structure of English*. It must be borne in mind, however—in the same way as we must remember that there are different kinds of 'traditional' grammar, e.g. 'scholarly' and 'school' grammars—that Fries was only one protagonist, and that others, such as Hockett[4] and Harris,[5] developed some basic ideas of 'structural' linguistics to a degree of sophistication well beyond that attained in *The Structure of English*.

The first of the proposals we will consider is concerned with the notions of 'Immediate Constituents' (I.C.). Basically, I.C. analysis is a device for analysing sentences. The usual practice has been to operate in terms of binary cuts. In the sentence 'The sailors loved the girls', we get our first cut between 'sailors' and 'loved', giving us two immediate constituents: (*a*) 'the sailors' and (*b*) 'loved the girls'. The second cut comes between 'loved' and 'the', dividing constituent (*b*) into its two immediate constituents. The next cuts come between 'the' and 'sailors' and between 'the' and 'girls'; both cuts being regarded as belonging to the same layer. And finally we have cuts between 'sailor' and 's', between 'love' and 'd' and between 'girl' and 's'; the three cuts being regarded as on the same layer. The process may be represented in the form of a diagram.

| the | sailor | s | love | d | the | girl | s |

Other forms of diagram have been used, but they are, by and large, equivalent in purpose, and potentially equivalent in their representational resources, though they may arbitrarily select the amount of structure they wish to represent.

Cutting into constituents, or bracketing, may be supplemented by 'labelling'.[6] Labelling involves naming the types of constituents and the types of relationships between them. The first cut in the example above, for instance would yield two constituents; 'subject' and 'predicate'. The phrases 'the sailors' and 'the girls' would yield constituents 'head' (sailors, girls) and 'modifier' (the). However, the usage in labelling constituents varies considerably among its exponents and, at this stage, goes very little beyond representing fairly well-established traditional notions.

The second Fries proposal concerns the so-called 'substitution in frame' technique for assigning parts of speech to 'form classes' according to their ability to occur in the same formal environments (given certain conditions). In the example below the sentence provides the frame or formal environment and all words that can be substituted for the 'blank' to give an acceptable English sentence belong to the same form class:

(The) ... is/are good.

This particular frame was supplemented by seven other criteria.[7]

The relevance of frames of this kind to certain kinds of formal exercise in language teaching, e.g. substitution exercises, is obvious; but they have, in fact, been shown to be a rather dubious theoretical device, in that the claims of objectivity made for them can hardly be sustained. Operationally, the frame given above does classify together many of what are called 'nouns' in English. But, for example, neither the frame nor the additional criteria appear to exclude the word 'other' from the same class, and this is surely an unsatisfactory result.

Fries in rejecting the traditional parts of speech also rejected the names given to them, and gave his form classes such designations as Class 1, Class 2, Group A, Group B, etc. This he justified on the grounds that, for example, the class 'noun' and the class 'Class 1' did not coincide. It might be argued, however, that by jettisoning the insightful parts of the traditional notion of 'noun' more was lost than was gained. Moreover, this approach would seem to take the idea of labelling too literally. Provided one has the safeguard of distributional criteria (i.e. knows what items operate in what places in frames) there seems little danger in retaining the term 'noun', especially since a significant sub-set of Class 1 words are in fact the names of 'persons, places or things'.

One must, however, see this movement in the context of its time. The enthusiasm for renaming can be ascribed to the drive for objective criteria in language study, which follows from the desideratum of 'linguistics as a science' laid down by Leonard Bloomfield,[8] regarded by many as the father of American structuralist linguistics.

Bloomfield's own work had been subject to the influence of (among others) Ferdinand de Saussure,[9] whom he credited with giving a 'theoretic foundation to the newer trend in linguistic study'. Indeed, the remainder of this paper could be devoted with profit to an exegesis of de Saussure's difficult *Cours de Linguistique Générale* (1916) and a study of the influence of his ideas on modern linguistic thought. We shall confine ourselves, however, to a passing reference to some of his basic notions.

De Saussure, in discussing language, distinguished between *langage*, *langue* and *parole*. *Langage* is the 'heterogeneous mass' of human language. *Langue* is the language system—a system of 'concrete entities' called 'signs' which consist of 'the unison of a meaning and a sound image—both parts being psychological'. The system is held in common by the speakers of a given language: it 'resides in the collectivity'; and it makes communication in language and classification in linguistics possible. Finally, *parole* is the 'executive' side of language. *Actes de parole*, or speech acts, are always controlled by the individual. The system, the *langue*, is what de Saussure would have linguists study.

Bloomfield selected from de Saussure's ideas and adapted them to his own purposes, as is clear from the relative importance given to them. And he, and his followers, can hardly be said to be following de Saussure entirely in their emphasis on physicalism, and in resisting appeals to meaning or introspection. But these notions, inherent in Bloomfield's writings, became a central feature of the so-called 'neo-Bloomfieldian' school.

Presumably a major motivation for their attitude was the success enjoyed by the physical sciences, which operated with supposedly objective criteria; and certain philosophical ideas concerning the unity of the sciences and the feasibility of verifying experimental results once one's data are observable.

There were, however, some unfortunate consequences of this attitude. One of these was an over-concentration on methodology, on procedure and method of analysis, to the extent that methodology, in some cases, became an end rather than a means to an end, and goals of linguistic enquiry were obscured. Another consequence was the narrowing of the field of linguistic study by the attempt to exclude from consideration those areas not accessible to immediate observation. This led to the elevation of the status of the phoneme as 'the basic element' or 'the most stable element in language' and to the practice of 'doing linguistics' as if this consisted of simply analysing strings of basic units combined into larger ones. Accordingly, while redirection towards a closer attention to the 'facts' of language is, in general, desirable, facts tended to be confused with data, and this resulted in some cases in an obsessive concern with the analysis of texts. Slogans such as 'text signals structure' proved a disincentive to formulate generalizations or look for underlying regularities in language, or to seek principled explanations beyond the immediately obvious. All that was deemed necessary was to classify elements and label the classes. In its extreme form this becomes a cryptic game involving such non-speculations as how to devise a grammar for a language one does not know. It is on such scores as these that the kind of approach to language study we have been discussing has been criticized by later linguists.

In linguistics as in other fields new developments follow from dissatisfaction with previous ideas. M. A. K. Halliday,[10] for example, has listed the sins of 'Bloomfieldian' linguistics in much the same way as its exponents listed their objection to the fallacies of traditional grammar.

Halliday was concerned with setting up a homogeneous theoretical framework which would make possible effective total descriptions of languages. In this he was building upon and reinterpreting the work of J. R. Firth[11] whose teaching and writings have been a major influence in the field of linguistics in Britain since the early 1930s. Firth was himself greatly influenced by his association with the anthropologist Malinowski,[12] whose work on the culture of the Trobriand Islanders and his attempts to render their language into intelligible English had convinced him of the shortcomings of those traditional notions of language which saw it simply as a vehicle for 'ideas' or as a 'countersign of thought'.

To Malinowski, language was a 'mode of action', a special mode of social co-operation. This view led him to rehabilitate types of language generally considered inferior to the philosophical and literary kinds which were the traditional concern of students of language. Thus, he saw language study as embracing even such stereotyped forms as greetings 'How do you do?', 'How are you?', 'Isn't the weather awful!', which enable people to establish social contact and avoid uncomfortable silence. The meaning of a piece of language was for Malinowski related to the situation or typical situation in which it occurred; it was a function of a 'situation' which embraced both language and non-language events.

Firth followed Malinowski in holding that the investigation of language necessitated the study of all kinds of language. His view was that all of us speak many languages, 'restricted languages', each performing its own function in enabling people to live their lives and act out the different roles which this demands of them.

Again, he held that all language study was the study of 'meaning'. It was this principle that unified linguistic study, and he suggested various categories in terms of which he proposed to investigate language from this point of view. Since language was a complex phenomenon, he advocated that it should be studied at various 'levels of analysis': phonological, morphological, situational, etc. This diversity in approach was unified for Firth by the fact that investigation at every level was concerned with meaning; he spoke of situational elements in a context of situation, morphological elements in a context of morphology and phonological elements in a context of phonology, and of situational, morphological and phonological meaning.

Firth's theory of meaning has been criticized in at least some of its aspects, in particular the implications of his all-embracing use of the term 'meaning'. But through his followers it has had a considerable influence both on linguistic thought and on attitudes to language teaching.[13] In the teaching of English this influence is to be seen most clearly in the emphasis on the notion of 'situation' in the construction of teaching materials and in the concern with language varieties (or 'register studies'). It certainly cannot be claimed that the study of either 'situation' or 'register' is in a very satisfactory theoretical state, but perhaps it has led teachers to a realization of some of the complexities of human language and, however vaguely, to a consideration of some of the implications of these complexities for their own work.

Halliday, as we have said above, followed on from and

reinterpreted Firth's work. He too sets up a system of linguistic levels. Language, Halliday says, is 'patterned activity', and each level deals with a basically different kind of pattern. The three basic levels are 'form', 'substance' and 'context'.[14]

The level of 'form', which is central, consists of two sub-levels: 'grammar' and 'lexis'. These sub-levels are concerned with describing the way in which 'language is internally structured to carry contrasts of meaning'—'to account for all those places in the language where there is a possibility of meaningful choice' (i.e. grammatical choice or lexical choice). They are concerned with the placing of what are called 'formal items'; a formal item being any meaningful stretch of language, of any extent, like, for instance, 'the' or 'chair' or 'I've thrown it away'.

The crucial notion here is that of 'meaningful choice'. Very simply, in a sentence such as 'I saw the chair' we can substitute alternative items for 'the' and 'chair'; for example, 'a' and 'table' respectively: there is a choice. And since, if we do substitute in this way, we produce a sentence which means something different from 'I saw the chair', the choice is meaningful.

We can regard 'the' and 'chair' as instances of different grammatical classes: 'a' and 'the' are instances of the class 'deictic' and 'chair' and 'table' of the class 'noun'. Furthermore, 'the' and 'a' are to be regarded as different from 'chair' and 'table' in that the former are 'fully grammatical'; that is to say the choice here is from a finite restricted set, or 'closed system', whereas the choice of items which may replace 'chair' and 'table' is from a very large, unrestricted set, an 'open set'. This difference in the range of possible choices constitutes, in Halliday's theory, the basic differences between grammar and lexis.

'Class' and 'system' are two of the four theoretical 'categories' set up by Halliday to account for language. The other two are 'unit' and 'structure'. 'Theoretical category' here means universal; i.e. applicable to all languages, although the term universal is avoided. Opposed to the term 'theoretical category' we have the term 'descriptive category'; i.e. categories, such as 'preposition', 'passive' and so on, which apply to particular languages being studied, but do not necessarily have universal application. For example, all languages will make use of units, but the particular kinds of unit found in one language will not necessarily be found in others—all languages have units, but we should not assume that all languages have, say, clauses. 'Unit' is the term used to refer to stretches of language which carry patterns, and 'structure' defines the kind of pattern carried by a particular unit.

In addition to these abstract 'categories': unit, structure, system and class, Halliday makes use of three 'scales' (hence the name 'Scale and Category Grammar'). These are the scales of 'rank', 'delicacy' and 'exponence'.

The rank scale is the scale which relates the units to one another. Theoretically, each unit consists of one or more than one member of the unit next below on the rank scale. Descriptively, in English, the units are sentence, clause, group, word and morpheme and every sentence consists of one or more clauses, every clause consists of one or more groups, and so on down to morpheme, the lowest unit on the rank scale in English. For example, if we analyse the sentence 'The girls loved the sailors also', we get a sentence which consists of one clause. The clause in turn consists of four groups—'the girls', 'loved', 'the sailors' and 'also'. Each group consists of one or more than one word, and so on. We may provide a partial representation of the analysis by a diagram.

||| The − girl + s | love + d | the − sailor + s | also |||

(||| = sentence boundary marker; | = group boundary marker − = word boundary marker and + = morpheme boundary marker.)

It should be noted that utterances such as 'yes', 'the postman' and 'John did' are regarded as sentences in this theory. That is, a sentence may consist of one morpheme, by consisting of one clause consisting of one group consisting of one word consisting of one morpheme; e.g. 'Yes'. We have no utterance which is less than a sentence.

Also, we may have, for instance, a clause operating in the structure of a group, e.g. the clause 'I saw yesterday' in the group, 'the girl *I saw yesterday*'. This is called 'rankshift', and it allows units to operate in the structure of other units of equal or lower rank.

The 'scale of delicacy' is concerned with depth of descriptive detail. For example, in the group 'the big boy', at primary delicacy we can say that both 'the' and 'big' belong to the class 'modifier', but more delicately we can assign 'the' to the secondary class 'deictic' whereas 'big' is assigned to the secondary class 'epithet'.

The 'scale of exponence' enables us to, for example, relate a class to an instance of that class; e.g. 'noun' to 'chair'.

It has not been possible to do more here than touch very briefly on some of the basic notions of 'Scale and Category' theory. However, enough has been said, perhaps, to indicate some of the complexity involved. This is not meant to dissuade teachers from studying the theory in detail should they wish do do so, but rather to warn them against any naive assumption that this can be done to good effect without expending considerable time and effort on it. We have already referred them to works which they may consult. Teachers who are anxious to introduce linguistics into the classroom would do well to reflect on these difficulties. They should also, of course, give lengthy consideration to their motivation for doing so in terms of the goals they hope to achieve.

The most radical, and probably the most fruitful, recent departure in the study of language, is to be found in what has become known as 'Transformational-Generative (T-G) Grammar'.[15] Here again, though certain aspects of this grammar are clearly developments of earlier notions of structural grammar, we find that it constitutes a strong reaction against some basic structuralist tenets. Writers on T-G grammar, both explicitly and by implication, call into question many of the fundamental premises of structural grammar. They do not deny that the rigorousness it introduced into language study was desirable, or that it provided some new insights into the nature of language, but they consider that many of the innovations introduced were misguided.

They hold that concern with objectivity has led to means being allowed to determine ends; that the belief that linguists should concern themselves only with what is directly observable has narrowed the scope of linguistics to the extent that proper fields of enquiry are ignored or considered irrelevant and aims are distorted. Furthermore, they maintain that some linguists continue to employ, in the name of being 'scientific', notions such as 'objectivism', 'physicalism' and the 'verification principle' which are philosophically suspect and which have long been discredited by philosophers of science.

T-G grammarians believe that linguistics has to do with principled explanations of the underlying regularities of language; not simply with the classification of surface features. Data, they say, must not be confused with facts, and to them linguistic theory consists of provisional hypotheses about the facts of language which may be tested empirically by seeing how well they account for the data. Accordingly, they see the process of beginning with a mass of data and abstracting structure from surface signals as an exercise of doubtful value.

Appeal is sometimes made in T-G grammar to traditional grammar, many of the aims of which, e.g. the search for universals, are accepted as basically correct. The objection to traditional grammar is that it was not formulated explicitly and that it was too concerned with irregularities at the expense of the regular forms to which they constitute exceptions. Traditional grammars left most of the basic regularities to be inferred by the reader of the grammar in the light of his own intuitive knowledge of the language in question. And, they assert, it is precisely this intuitive knowledge, the 'native speaker's' knowledge of his language that a grammar must attempt to characterize.

A T-G grammar, then, attempts to characterize or represent in some way the speaker's knowledge of his language. This is what is referred to as his language 'competence'. It is to be understood as different from his knowledge *about* his language; many people whose knowledge *about* their language is infinitesimal are yet able to speak it perfectly adequately. It is the 'knowledge' which enables the native speaker to do this that primarily concerns the T-G grammarian.

The question is: how is a grammar to characterize this knowledge? There are certain things it must be able to do. A native speaker's knowledge enables him to distinguish between strings of words which are sentences and strings which are not; e.g.

between 'the sailors loved the girls' and 'girls the the loved sailors'. And the native speaker is able to distinguish one sentence from another; e.g. 'the sailors loved the girls' from 'the girls loved the sailors' or from 'do the sailors love the girls?' An adequate grammar must therefore be able to do both these things. Again, the native speaker can produce and understand an infinite number of sentences which he has never heard before. He does not in any sense 'remember' these sentences (the sentences in this paper, for instance, have almost all never been written before, and will probably never be duplicated). And so a grammar must be constructed in such a way that it accounts for this ability of the speaker/listener. We say that a grammar must 'generate' all possible sentences of the language and none that are non-sentences; 'generate' here meaning 'represent explicitly and assign structural descriptions in an explicit way' to these sentences.

For these and other reasons it is concluded that what the speaker/listener knows cannot be represented adequately as an inventory of elements; not, that is, as de Saussure's 'system of concrete entities', but rather as a system of 'rules'. The speaker/listener's competence consists in his ability to handle what these rules represent.

Competence, as a technical term, must be distinguished from 'performance', which, in general, correlates with what de Saussure calls the 'executive' side of language. This is concerned with the actual selection and application of rules in the production of actual sentences in particular situations. A grammar of the kind we have been discussing, therefore, does not produce actual sentences or recognize them. It is a representation or model of the speaker/listener's intuitive knowledge of his language: it is not a model of his 'use' of language. Performance entails psychological and sociological features as well as linguistic ones.

It is very important to understand this; that T-G grammar is not simply dealing in a different way with the same thing as Scale and Category and structural grammar but is dealing with, in a sense, something quite different. They, generally speaking, handle what the language user produces, once he has produced it: they process the data; T-G grammar attempts to describe the knowledge of the language—as distinct from knowledge of its use—which makes production possible.

A complete T-G grammar has three components: syntactic, semantic and phonological. The syntactic component consists of two sub-components: a base and a transformational sub-component. The base in turn consists of context-free (see below) 'categorial' rules (of the type 'Sentence → Noun Phrase + Predicate Phrase') together with a lexicon. The base generates the 'deep structures' of sentences, which are given a semantic interpretation by the semantic component. The transformational rules of the syntactic component convert deep structure into 'surface structure', which is given a phonetic interpretation by the rules of the phonological component. The syntactic component is thus central and the other two have an interpretive function.

The point of the distinction between deep and surface structure is that it can be shown by such examples as 'I like flying planes', that text does not always unambiguously signal structure. This example may be paraphrased as either 'I like to fly planes' or 'I like planes that are flying'. In other words one surface structure may have two (sometimes more) deep structures, and hence two meanings. These examples are admittedly obvious but they serve to make the point. Again, the same deep structure may be realized in different ways, e.g. 'I often fly planes', 'I fly planes often'.

The notion of 'rule' is in itself fairly simple. For example, $2 + 2 = 4$ may be regarded as an arithmetical rule. Again, $a + b = c$ is a similar rule which differs from the first in that each of the symbols may refer to a range of values. An example of a grammatical rule would be: Sentence → Noun Phrase + Predicate Phrase, where the arrow is interpreted as 'is rewritten as'. Such rules are referred to as 'rewrite rules'. Certain fairly restrictive conditions are necessarily placed upon grammatical rules, and it is these conditions which are liable to cause difficulty rather than any inherent difficulty in the notion itself.

Grammar rules may be either context-free or context-restricted. Context-free rules are not restricted to any particular environment. The example given above is context-free. Context-restricted rules are confined to particular environments. For example,

SOME APPROACHES TO THE STUDY OF LANGUAGE 17

$a \to b + c \mid X - Y$ may be interpreted as: a is rewritten as $b + c$ provided it is preceded by X and followed by Y.

Transformational rules make possible for example the deletion and reordering of items; e.g. $a + b + c \to b + c$, or $a + b + c \to b + c + a$. Such rules are involved in the generation of elliptical utterances such as 'John did'. Transformational rules are governed by stringent conditions in their application.

If we take as an example 'The sailor loved the girl' this sentence can be generated by means of a set of rules:

$$S \to NP + Pred\ P$$
$$Pred\ P \to Tense + VP$$
$$VP \to V + NP$$
$$NP \to D + N$$
$$Tense \to pt$$
$$V \to love$$
$$N \to sailor,\ girl$$
$$D \to the$$

These rules also of course generate 'The girl loved the sailor'. That is to say they have a certain generality; they do not represent simply the description of our example. If we wanted to illustrate the structure generated we could represent it in the form of a tree diagram:

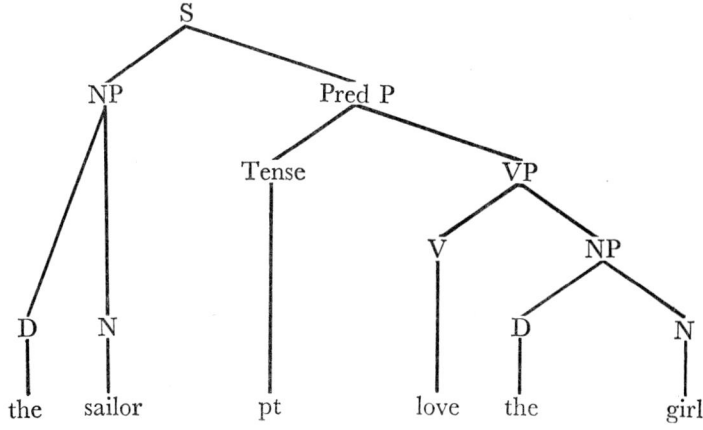

This representation defines for us which NP is the subject and which is the object of 'love'; 'pt' would be combined with 'love' by means of a transformational rule eventually producing *loved* when phonological rules are applied.

It is readily admitted that the above discussion gives only a very superficial and greatly simplified account of T-G grammar, but perhaps two things at least will be clear. In the first place, natural language is a complex phenomenon, and this simple fact is often overlooked. Nevertheless an adequate grammar must account for it. Secondly, any grammar which confines itself to the description of surface structure alone will not be adequate.

Reasonably accessible treatments of T-G grammar are available[16] and teachers who wish to pursue the subject are recommended to consult these works both for relevant explication of the theory and for examples of simple T-G grammars.

It remains for us to say something, briefly, about what the attitudes of the teacher of English might sensibly be to 'modern, scientific linguistics'. We ought to point out once more that linguistics is not an easy subject to master. It employs advanced theoretical constructs and rigorous methodology. Moreover it is a subject which does not in the present circumstances lend itself easily to simplification—it is in many ways 'unestablished', with different schools of thought each promoting its own particular point of view with regard to aims and methods. A synthesizing textbook of basic principles is badly needed.

The teacher of English, therefore, cannot be expected to master the field minutely and indeed should not seek to do so, for it is not his field. But, at the same time, he should not ignore it. There is no reason why he should not try to absorb as much of it as will assist him, for example, in evaluating classroom materials and methods which are presented to him under the blanket description 'linguistic'.

Linguistics has had a fairly long association with language teaching both in this country and in the United States, but one is led to the conclusion that neither has served the other very well. The reason may be that in neither discipline was there to be found much understanding of the other. The teacher must realize that linguistics is concerned with finding answers to the question 'What is the nature of human language?' and that this does not necessarily entail answers to the further questions 'How is language learned?' or 'What is the best way of teaching a language?' or 'How does a poem achieve its aesthetic effect?' Such questions, it is true, may, some of them, be closely related questions; they may take account of linguistic findings among other things; but they are essentially questions about special areas of the psychology of learning, of teaching methodology and of aesthetics respectively. The linguist, for his part, must not assume that his special knowledge about language qualifies him as an expert in language teaching—any more than it qualifies him as an expert in aesthetics.

What the teacher must do is seek access to the most reliable linguistic information available. Initially, he may find this difficult for the reasons mentioned above: he will find it difficult to assess its reliability. It is in this way, however, that he will become well-informed about the nature of language and develop realistic attitudes towards it. This should be his primary objective. The knowledge gained he must then use to his own ends. Some of the ways he may set about doing this are dealt with specifically in other articles in this volume.

Finally, the teacher must not lose sight of the fact that the only valid testing-ground for teaching materials and methods, whatever their provenance, is the classroom. If he keeps this in mind and is aware of, for example, some of the ambiguities in the term 'grammar' he will treat with caution those who claim that their special version of grammar is the best one for him to use in his work. They are in fact claiming to present a pedagogical grammar and they may not have the experience to judge its pedagogical value. In other words, if linguistics is seen to help the teacher to achieve what he is convinced are his proper pedagogical goals in a particular case then he should make use of it; in any other case he should obviously not do so, however 'modern' or 'scientific'—or, indeed, adequate in its own right or useful in other circumstances—it may be. This view envisages the kind of co-operation between linguists and teachers where each learns sufficient about the other's problems to make the co-operation effective and where particular judgments of merit are made by those best qualified to make them.

NOTES

1. Paul Roberts, *Patterns of English*, Harcourt Brace, 1956.
2. C. C. Fries, *The Structure of English*, Harcourt Brace, 1952.
3. S. R. Levin, 'Comparing Traditional and Structural Grammar' in *Readings in Applied English Linguistics*, ed. H. B. Allen 2nd edn, Appleton Century Crofts, 1964.
4. C. F. Hockett, *A Course in Modern Linguistics*, Macmillan, New York, 1958.
5. Zellig S. Harris, *Structural Linguistics*, Phoenix, 1960.
6. H. A. Gleason, *Linguistics and English Grammar*, Holt, Rinehart & Winston, 1965, ch. 7.
7. C. C. Fries, *op. cit.*
8. Leonard Bloomfield, *Language*, Holt, 1933.
9. Ferdinand de Saussure, *Course in General Linguistics* (trans. Wade Baskin), Peter Owen, 1960.
10. M. A. K. Halliday, 'Categories of the Theory of Grammar' in *Word*, Vol. 17, No. 3, December 1961.
11. J. R. Firth, *Papers in Linguistics 1934–1951*, Oxford U.P., 1957.
12. Bruno Malinowski: Supplement 1 of *The Meaning of Meaning*, Ogden & Richards, Routledge and Kegan Paul, 1946.
13. M. A. K. Halliday, A. McIntosh and P. Strevens, *The Linguistic Sciences and Language Teaching*, Longmans, 1964.
14. A diagrammatic representation of the levels is given on p. 18 of *The Linguistic Sciences and Language Teaching*.
15. N. Chomsky, *Aspects of the Theory of Syntax*, M.I.T., 1965.
16. Paul Roberts, *English Syntax* (Teachers' edn), Harcourt, Brace & World, 1964; Owen Thomas, *Transformational Grammar and the Teacher of English*, Holt, Rinehart & Winston, 1965.

2

Language Development in Children

ELISABETH INGRAM

The study of language development in children has to be divided up in various ways. The first distinction to make is between the pre-language period, lasting roughly from birth to around a year, and what may be called the language-learning period, which lasts from about a year until the child has approximated in important respects to the language that is spoken by the adults around him, at perhaps five or six years. This is a division in terms of time, of chronological sequence.

In the language-learning period one must distinguish between the child's ability to *pronounce* the sounds of the language he hears, his ability to produce utterances that have a reasonably stable *structure*, and his ability to use these utterances *meaningfully*. The distinction between pronunciation, structure and meaning bears some relation to the distinction that some linguists make between phonology, grammar and context.

Though nothing that we can properly call language occurs during the first year, there are a number of preliminary stages that the child goes through, without which he would not be able to go on to the language-learning stage, as far as we know. All babies cry; this is the first vocalization of human infants. Later, usually within a month or two, the infant begins to make vocal noises other than crying. M. M. Lewis[1] distinguishes between comfort noises and discomfort noises. Somewhere between four and six months the baby will seem to respond selectively to the sound of the human voice. It will turn its head in the direction of the speaker, or freeze in a listening attitude. This response will rarely follow noises from other sources. From this time onwards the vocalizations will vary enormously in pitch—the baby will indulge in everything from squealing to growling.

Somewhat later the utterances become increasingly syllabic. This is the so-called stage of babbling. It has been reported that babies who are born deaf vocalize in roughly the same pattern up to six to eight months, but become progressively more silent after that. The difference would seem to be that babies with normal hearing receive the stimulus of the spoken voice of adults, certainly they increasingly engage in 'conversations'. There has been a great deal of speculation about whether the child imitates the adult's language. It seems much more usually the case that it is the parent who imitates the child at this stage. When the child utters its syllabic noises: da-da-da, ma-ma-ma, na-na-na, or whatever, the adult intervenes in the babbling by producing the same syllables as the baby. The baby responds by continuing his own babble. This is highly satisfactory both to the parent and child, and out of this co-operation reasonably stable two-syllable sections gradually become isolated out of the stream.

It is obviously useful for the child to have his vocal apparatus exercised and under some control, so that when he is ready to begin to apply syllabic utterances in a more or less consistent way to persons or objects, he has already practised how to produce these syllables. The child from eight to ten months onwards understands increasingly more complex remarks made to it. Most babies will have a consistent response to such commands as 'Wave bye-bye', 'Come to Mama', 'Stand up', 'Upsy-daisy', and so on. The pre-language stage comes to an end when the child utters his first few single words. The one word 'Mama' (or exceptionally 'Dada') is not by itself a reliable indicator. Parents are perhaps too ready to discover that the child can say this word. For developmental assessment one needs evidence of some other word.

Pronunciation

A great deal of work has been done on the speech of children since the advent of the tape-recorder, that is since the end of the second world war. D. C. Irwin and his associates[2] studied in great detail the actual noises made by infants from birth until about the age of two. They showed that the range and variety of vocal noises increase steadily with age, and also of course that the noises gradually become more 'human'—that is to say, more like the noises of the adults round them. These studies were important in many respects, perhaps chiefly because they exploded the old myth that infants begin by making *all* the speech sounds of *all* the languages in the world, and that they gradually learn to limit themselves to the sounds they hear around them.

But perhaps the most fundamental contribution was made by the linguist and phonetician, W. F. Leopold.[3] He described the development of his four daughters, particularly the two younger ones, who were brought up to speak both English and German. He found that he could not always tell whether in a given instance they were speaking English or German. For example, the German for 'book' is 'Buch'. In both languages you start with /b/. Then there is a back rounded vowel, short in English, longer in German, but made in roughly the same way. Then there is /k/ in English, and the sound of *ch* in Scottish *loch* in German, but even German children do not learn to make this sound until quite late. Leopold discovered that what came out of the mouths of his 2½-to-3-year-old children saying the word for 'book' did not allow him to tell which language they were speaking. This made him look not for the exact nature of the noises his children were making, like Irwin, but for the *contrasts* they operated. This is not, of course, a new concept in the study of speech sounds. It was first fully formulated by de Saussure.[4] In language it does not matter what the exact noises are; what matters is that the different noises which make up different words are systematically distinguished from one another. When a Scot says 'bit', his vowel may well sound rather like the vowel of a Southern English person saying 'bet', but when a Scot says 'bet' you can hear that he is not saying 'bit' because the vowel sounds he makes are systematically different for these two words (and for all other words which necessitate the same contrast).

These systematically contrasting speech sounds which distinguish one word from another are called phonemes. Phonemes operate in closed systems; adults speaking German or English operate vowel systems which have a fixed number of phonemes for each dialect. For instance, J. C. Catford[5] describing Scots dialects (using the same criteria for all) established systems with nine stressed vowel phonemes for many of the Central and Eastern dialects, and systems with up to twelve vowel phonemes elsewhere. The position for other dialects of English and for German dialects is similar. Leopold showed that very young children operate with very much simpler systems. He believes that at the stage where one can begin to analyse his speech sounds at all a child may have a vowel system with as few as three significant contrasting sounds or phonemes:

1 A front high vowel, covering all the noises of adult short and long /i/ (bit, beet), short /e/ (bet), perhaps as far as the sound of adult 'man' (as spoken by R.P.[6] adults).
2 A low back vowel, covering the vowel sounds of adult 'father', 'saw', 'pot' and perhaps 'sun'.
3 A high back rounded vowel, covering the vowel sounds in adult 'pool', 'pull' and sometimes 'sun'.

It is not so much the details of this that matter as the point that children seem to make fewer and cruder systematic distinctions when they speak than adults do. Sounds which to adults would be meaningfully different may be the same to very young children. This is important in the study of the grammar of child language. It is often impossible to decide whether a child has said 'it's' or 'that's'; what comes out is a general front vowel + 'ts'. Later children may use, say, a five-point distinction and go on from there to the full adult system.

There is great tolerance, at least among speakers of English, of variation in the vowel sounds, which is not surprising in view of the great regional and class variations in the pronunciation of vowel sounds. But when it comes to consonants people do not have the same tolerance. All the published studies on the development of child speech known to the writer produce statistics on the sequence of the acquisition of acceptable consonant sounds, but none concern themselves greatly with vowels.

The Medical Research Council sponsored project on the speech development of children, which is based in Edinburgh, is, at the time of writing, incomplete but offers interesting qualitative suggestions.[7]

1 Stops *p b t d k g*, nasals *m n ng* and semi-vowels (*y* as in yellow, *w* as in way) are mastered early.

2 Among the stops, front sounds, *p b t d*, are mastered before back or velar stops, *k g*.

3 When two consonants occur together (consonant clusters), complicated things happen:

   (*a*) s + C (C = any consonant).

   (i) One thing that can happen is that the *s* is simply omitted: *spoon* becomes *poon*, *stand* becomes *tand*, and so on.

   (ii) Though the *s* is omitted, the second sound is lengthened and takes on some of the features of the *s*; for example, in *smoke* the child of $2\frac{1}{2}$ or 3 may say not only *moke* but *hm-moke*, substituting a voiceless *m* (i.e. by blowing through his nose with his lips closed). The voiceless *m* is an approximation to *sm* in that the voiceless characteristics of the *s* are 'carried' by the labial.

   (iii) When the initial *s* is pronounced it may be unusual. It may be a fronted or lisped *s*, or a palatalized (or hissing) *s*. This is very like what Leopold found. Adults reject hissing as well as lisping substitutes for *s* but the child does not initially distinguish these variants. They are intelligible, so it is not absolutely essential that he should do so yet. (There is a close parallel here to the demands made of foreigners—minimally they should be intelligible, maximally they should produce sounds satisfying to the native ear.)

   (*b*) In clusters where the second sound is *l* or *r*, the second element is at first omitted or reduced; *pane* for *plane*, *paam* or *pwam* for *pram*.

   (*c*) When both elements of a cluster are produced, there is often a lengthening of the second element. This happens mainly with newly-acquired clusters. It is perhaps difficult to imagine how a child could lengthen the *t* in *stand*; in fact he just stops for a moment, *st . . . and*.

The general trends, then, are fairly clear:

1 Sounds are omitted.
2 Sounds are substituted: The child produces some of the features of the adult sound—voiceless *m* for a preceding voiceless *s*; front stop *d* for back stop *g*, etc.
3 There is a wider range of tolerance of acceptable noises: various lisps and hisses are as acceptable as adult *s*.
4 When clusters appear, they show very clearly that speech is also a matter of temporal organization. At the stage when a cluster is represented by a single sound, this sound is often lengthened. When the cluster is (more or less accurately) represented by two sounds, the second sound may be long. The child seems to approximate to adult requirements by slow yet perhaps surprisingly systematic stages.

Grammar

The utterances of the first few simple words are not of great interest to the grammarian. These single utterances, which are closely tied to a single person—the mother—or a single event—eating or potting—are not in their nature different from the signals that many kinds of animals make to each other. Grammatically, there is very little one can say about one-word utterances. It is, strictly speaking, incorrect to describe these first utterances either as words or as sentences. From a grammatical point of view, all that one knows about them is that they cannot usefully be divided into units smaller than themselves, nor do they form part of larger linguistic structures. In adult language, grammatical units such as words or sentences are defined in terms of their hierarchical relationships to one another. When one has only one kind of utterance, therefore, it is meaningless to describe examples either as words or sentences, or even one-word sentences. Recent workers on child language have introduced a special name for them—'the holophrase'.

For a linguist the crucial distinction is between the holophrase, or one-word utterance, and the two-word utterance. There are, of course, difficulties in determining what constitutes a word in practice, but in principle it is quite clear. The point is whether a child makes a meaningful utterance which can be analysed into two separate units. Two separate units—let us call them words— are established when each can be uttered in combination with at least one other word. Only then is it possible to begin to talk in terms of grammatical structures which have grammatical constituents. (In the interests of simplification we are ignoring the problems raised by such items as 'cats'— i.e. 'cat' + 's'.)

When a significant number of the child's utterances consist of two-word sentences the grammarian can start investigating the child's language. The first and most important problem is to try to establish the child's grammar—the grammar according to which he produces his utterances. A great many observations and quite a few systematic studies have been made on the development of children's language in the last sixty to eighty years but the earlier descriptions were always made on the assumption that the child's grammar is a primitive and faulty version of adult grammar. The investigators described the utterances of the child in terms of adult grammar. If a child said 'Mama', it was classified as a word because it is a word in adult grammar. It was, further, called a noun, because that is its classification when used by adults, and so on. It is only in the last ten years or so that the realization has come that one must endeavour to discover the child's own grammatical rules, and describe his utterances in terms of these. These rules may, of course, be simplified versions of the adult rules, but quite often they seem not to be. Some are makeshift rules which the child has constructed for himself. They may not be useful in the long run, so they are eventually discarded in favour of more serviceable ones. As he develops, the child's rules increasingly approximate to those of the adults round him.

The description of child grammar presents a number of practical problems. To begin with, children pass through stages of language acquisition very quickly. But in order to establish a structure one must collect a significant number of utterances exemplifying the same pattern. And if the examples are not collected quickly enough the child may have grown out of one stage and into the next, and the pattern in question may be lost. Then again, apart from variations over a period of time, there may be variations occurring at the same time, for children's language patterns are not particularly consistent. Almost all children, for instance, go through a period of saying 'mines'. This tends to co-exist with the alternative form 'mine', for quite a long time. The problem is how to interpret these variations.

Consider, for example, the sentences ''s a man' and ''s man'. The adult expansions of both are 'that's a man' or 'it's a man'. There are various possibilities of interpretation:

1 Both sentences are classified as ungrammatical according to adult grammar. This is not illuminating.
2 The second sentence ''s man' is classified as an error in terms of the child's own grammar. This is a very reasonable procedure, as even adults make a surprisingly large number of casual grammatical mistakes when they speak; one has only to listen to recordings of conversation to realize this.
3 The child may be in a transitional stage, having discovered the existence of the indefinite article and being engaged in experimenting with its correct distribution. (This is the formulation of an adult writing for adults; I do not mean to imply that the child symbolizes to itself what it is doing, in grammatical or any other terms.)
4 The child may be operating with two equally valid grammatical variants. The one nearest to the adult pattern will be reinforced, the other one will drop out in time.
5 The child may be treating the variants as identical from the point of view of structure, and varying only in pronunciation. This may be a slightly startling suggestion, but it is not unreasonable to suppose that certain phenomena which in adult language would be accounted for in grammatical terms might be better accounted for in child language in phonological terms.[8]

Trying to describe the child's grammar leaves one open to two kinds of error. Suppose that one has a sample of 1,000 utterances from a child aged three years, collected over a month or so. One sets out to discover the rules which govern the production of the structures that the child commands. The corpus will contain utterances of varying length, from one-word utterances to sentences of, say, ten words. There will undoubtedly be examples of variants, such as 'mines' and 'mine', ''s a man' and ''s man'. There will probably be types of structures exemplified by only one utterance. Perfect grammars would contain rules which would account for all acceptable utterances obtained and which would disallow any utterances which would never have been made. In practice this is impossible. Either one writes a few cautious rules, which do not imply a whole lot of types of utterance not actually obtained, but which leave quite a few observed utterances unaccounted for; or one writes rules which account for nearly all the data actually obtained, with the drawback that they imply that the child is capable of producing all sorts of structures for which there is no evidence. By testing comprehension as well as recording utterances, the discrepancies may be reduced, but the testing of understanding of purely grammatical features is a difficult business which has hardly received any systematic attention.

This is a problem for all grammarians, but it is particularly acute for the grammarian of child language. People opt for various compromises, depending on their view of unobtained utterances. If there is no example of a particular structure in the data, that does not mean that the child is necessarily unable to produce the structure: it simply means that since it has not occurred one does not know whether he can use it or not.

Here Chomsky's well-known distinction between competence and performance is indirectly helpful.[9] Chomsky means, by competence, the ideal speaker/hearer's knowledge of his language; that is, the rules which will generate an infinite number of grammatical sentences. Someone would need to describe completely the grammar of English—or any other language—in order to describe the competence of the ideal speaker/hearer. By performance, on the other hand, Chomsky means—and here we must simplify—not all possible sentences, but the actual utterances produced and understood by speakers and hearers. Performance is governed not only by the grammatical rules, but also by what the speaker wants to say, the situation he is in, his intelligence, memory, state of health, degree of attention, etc.

Chomsky and his followers are interested mainly in competence. Some of them are interested in child language in order to understand the nature of linguistic competence in the child. But no direct observations can be made of competence. All utterances—including child utterances—are examples of performance; the data are performance data. Discovering competence—the perfect statement of the absolute knowledge of the ideal speaker/hearer—may be a logician's delight, but it is obviously limited in application. By formulating the distinction so uncompromisingly, Chomsky has made it clear that competence is by no means the only concern of those who are primarily concerned with children's language behaviour and development.

There is however one aspect of competence in the broader sense which is centrally important. This is the question of 'potential performance',[10] which confronts us as an aspect of the sampling problem. The first sampling problem is concerned with the child's actual performance. We can observe and record only a small proportion of the utterances that a child produces (and of only a handful of children). But, further, the total utterances that a child produces do not necessarily exhaust the utterances that he might have made, if the appropriate situation had occurred. By potential performance we mean the utterances that the child might have made at a given stage of his development, if the situation had demanded it. From this point of view observed and recorded utterances are a sample of actual performance, and actual performance is never more than a sample of potential performance.

The earlier, psychologically oriented studies of child language are fully reported by McCarthy.[11] They were mostly cross-sectional, and attempted to correlate indices of child language with other indices of general development. Several have used the technique of recording and analysing fifty consecutive utterances, first used by McCarthy. Their grammatical analysis was primitive, and the most useful single result was probably the discovery that the mean sentence length—average number of syllables, morphemes or words per utterance—is an extremely useful and reliable index of general language maturity.

The following table shows the results of two of the investigations on the average length of utterances of children of various ages.

Age	1½	2	2½	3	3½	4	4½	5
McCarthy 1930	1·2	1·8	3·1	3·4	4·3	4·4	4·6	
Ann Mason 1965			3·7	4·9	5·8	6·4	7·2	7·6

Mean length of fifty utterances at ages $1\frac{1}{2}$ to 5.

McCarthy[12] was the first to use fifty consecutive utterances, recorded in conversation with an adult. Ann Mason[13] is probably the most recent. McCarthy studied twenty children at each age level, one hundred and forty in all, chosen to be representative of the population. Mason's study is longitudinal, the same children being studied at half-yearly intervals. The investigation is not yet complete, so there are fewer children at the top age levels. Mason has recorded about fifty children at ages 2½, 3 and 3½, about thirty children at ages 4 and 4½; and nineteen children aged 5. The children are not representative of the population as a whole, as they are mainly the offspring of university parents.

The children, then, are not comparable, but the methods of investigation and scoring are the same in both studies. The important point is that in both the average length of utterance increases steadily with age. Williams[14] showed that the correlation is not so much with age as with mental age. She got a correlation of ·78 between mental age and sentence length (N = 38). Mason's highly selected group (average I.Q. 133) scored considerably higher than the representative group, which is a further indication of the close relationship between mental age and language development.

Another very interesting finding is that children who are not much spoken to by adults develop language more slowly. There are many studies on various aspects of this. Miller,[15] for instance, found that children whose mothers had proper two-way conversations with them at mealtimes scored higher on a composite language test than children whose parents did not talk to them much except for giving orders. This notion of the quality of the communication as well as the amount of communication has recently been taken up vigorously by Basil Bernstein.[16]

Bernstein's 'restricted' and 'elaborated' codes are not described in linguistic terms but in terms of the purpose of communication. The chief difference between the codes is that the elaborated code is appropriate to exchanging information, whereas the restricted code is the language in which everyday personal wishes, orders, plans are conveyed. Bernstein's main thesis is that development of an elaborated code is a matter of social class; it is middle-class parents, on the whole, who are in the habit of exchanging information unrelated to immediate needs and desires at home and so accustom their children both to this kind of behaviour and to the appropriate language.

There are still only a few linguistically oriented studies of child language. Brown and Bellugi,[17] Susan Erwin[18] and Braine[19] are probably the best known. Recently a group was set up in Edinburgh at the instigation of Dr T. T. S. Ingram, supported by the Nuffield Foundation. These studies are longitudinal, concentrating on sampling adequately the utterances of a very few children. None of them is complete, and their contributions so far are only suggestive. Perhaps one of the most important tentative conclusions is that children have usually learned to handle what we might loosely call the basic grammatical categories of English by about $3\frac{1}{2}$ to 4 years of age (provided that they start at or before about eighteen months). This view results from looking at the patterns that the child commands, instead of searching for 'errors' which may be accidental or a matter of detail, such as overgeneralizing the formation of participles, producing e.g. 'catched' instead of 'caught'.

Another characteristic of the recent studies is the interest in the relationship between the input—what the child hears, and his output—what he says. Roger Brown[20] has pointed out that children often initially ask questions simply by putting a *wh-*question word in front of an ordinary declarative sentence:

'Where it is?'
'What he did?'

and suggests that 'echo-prompt' questions from parents:

'It is where?'
'He did what?'

encourage and help the child to produce this intermediate pattern of *wh*-questions. The Edinburgh study has been unable to confirm this suggestion so far, but that is not important. What matters is that hypotheses about the input-output relationships are put forward and investigated.

Ruth Weir,[21] who recorded her son's monologues in bed at night, was probably the first to demonstrate that children engage in what might be called 'pattern practice' or drill, both in pronunciation and structure. Her son frequently produced sequences such as: *what colour*; *what colour blanket*; *what colour mop*; *what colour glass*. He also produced slightly looser sequences: *up there: over there; here; Bobo there; go up there*. That this kind of activity is general has been confirmed over and over in studies of other children by the investigators concerned.

Meaning

Most linguists now take it to be axiomatic that the grammatical structure of an utterance can be determined only when one knows the meaning of that utterance. When adults understand each other they agree, at least implicitly, about which features of the situation are involved. But we do not know which features of a situation, if any, are relevant to a child. And in the early stages of language development we cannot infer this from the form of his utterance. An eighteen-months-old girl said, within five minutes: 'No dolly' and 'No bumps'. But 'No dolly' was said as she looked vaguely around the room and apparently meant something like 'Dolly isn't here' or 'Dolly's gone', whereas 'No bumps', which came after the child had been joggled on somebody's knees, probably meant something like, 'Don't bump me any more' or 'I don't want to be bumped'.[22]

The task is then to interpret, from what the child says, and from his total behaviour within the situation, what are to him the relevant features. Obviously the study of the general development of the child is important here. The trouble is that most of the work on the mental growth of children uses language as an indicator of stages of development. In the period which grammarians of child language are interested in, up to ages 4–4½, the language indices used are very coarse, such as Gesell's 'phrases by three, sentences by four, years of age'. The very interesting observations and investigations on children's thinking carried out by Piaget and his followers mostly concern children of at least 4½–5 years of age, by which time they use more or less adult grammar.

Piaget, however, makes the very illuminating point that it is necessary for the child to distinguish between himself and his environment before language learning proper can start. He must see himself as subject, so to speak. Later, he is capable also of seeing other people as distinct from the environment, as subjects in their own right. It is very tempting to see this as perhaps related to reciprocal use of personal pronouns.[23]

The early studies of child language dealt with meaning of words only. Estimating the size of vocabulary of children has been a popular game for some time. Vocabulary tests may be arbitrary in their selection and give only quantitative information, but like counts of sentence length they give very useful information about language and mental development.

It has taken investigators a long time to realize that meaning relates not only to isolated words but also to grammatical structures and categories. The current studies on child language are trying to develop techniques for deciding whether children understand the meaning of contrasted grammatical features. Space and time concepts are obvious examples: at what stage does the child understand 'over' and 'under', 'in' and 'on'; when does the child understand the difference between past and present tenses; how are these things related to his understanding of adverbs of time and space, and what is the relationship between comprehension and production, and so on.

Theoretical and academic studies, though fascinating in themselves, are often difficult to relate to practical school problems. I believe that the recent and current studies on the course of child language development, incomplete and tentative as they are, have already made several important contributions:

1 There is evidence against the often-held view that children learn their first language 'unconsciously' or 'automatically' or in some other mysterious way different from all other learning.[24]

2 Children learn the basic sentence patterns of their language well before school age. Perhaps the only thing teachers of reading agree about is that it is pretty useless to try to teach children to read before they have a reasonable command of the spoken language. So far this has chiefly manifested itself in concern about pronunciation; schools that can choose are reluctant to admit children with so-called speech defects. There has been no way of assessing the equally important factor of command of structure, but this must have been seriously underestimated, judging from the sort of sentence found in many introductory readers: 'This is Pet.' 'Pet is a dog.' 'Come, Pet, come.' I know that the habit of using very simple sentences is strongly defended on pedagogical grounds, but if the tacit assumption of grammatical immaturity turns out to be ill-founded, perhaps the time has come to re-examine the position. If authors in this situation were encouraged to use sentences suitable for five- to six-year-old children, rather than three-year-olds, they would find it easier to make the stories more interesting, so that the most powerful of all incentives for reading—wanting to know what happens next—could be brought to bear.

3 Conversely, if children are handicapped in the pre-school language-learning period, for any reason whatever, this may seriously influence their ability to read and write and express themselves intelligibly. This, of course, is not a new idea, particularly as far as pronunciation is concerned, but recent findings give it more substance. Ann Mason[25] in an early stage of a follow-up study of speech-retarded children found that of eleven children aged seven and eight who had been speech retarded, seven underachieved in reading (by more than fifteen points in comparison with the I.Q.) and six in spelling; whereas out of a control group of twenty normal children only one underachieved in reading and three in spelling.

Also, more subtly, children who are not used to conducting two-way conversations or who are, in Bernstein's terms, trained only in the 'restricted code', have more difficulty in expressing themselves in speech and writing at school than those who have practised more extended modes of communication at home. The discrepancy cannot be accounted for by differences in intelligence alone.

Since some of these difficulties seem to result from inadequate exposure to language, it is natural to suggest that the cure lies in more exposure.[26]

I am not implying that all difficulties in reading and writing and communication in the school situation are necessarily due solely to linguistic factors. I am suggesting that when dealing with the problems of learning and using language skills it would be no more than reasonable to pay attention to the ideas and knowledge of linguists.

Even so, it is safe to say that a great deal more research, both academic and educational, is needed before we can get over the hit-and-miss stage of describing, diagnosing and treating those who fail, and perhaps no less importantly, of enabling those who merely get by to do even better.

NOTES

1 M. M. Lewis, *Infant Speech*, 2nd edn, Routledge & Kegan Paul, 1951.
2 D. McCarthy, 'Language Development in Children' in *Manual of Child Psychology*, 2nd edn, Wiley, 1954.
3 W. F. Leopold, *The Speech Development of a Bilingual Child*, 4 Vols., North-Western University Press, 1949.
4 Ferdinand de Saussure, *Course in General Linguistics* (trans. Wade Baskin), Peter Owen, 1960.
5 J. C. Catford, 'Vowel-Systems of Scots Dialect', *Transactions of the Philological Society*, 1957.
6 Received Pronunciation (R.P.) is the name given to that English pronunciation which has the greatest social prestige in England.
7 Personal communication: Sandra Hutcheson and Jody Riggs,

M. R. C. Speech Project, Dept. of Child Life and Health, Edinburgh.
8 Suggested by P. Van Buren, Nuffield Language Project, Edinburgh.
9 N. Chomsky, *Aspects of the Theory of Syntax*, M. I. T., 1965.
10 A term emerging in discussion with students at the Department of Applied Linguistics, Edinburgh.
11 D. McCarthy, *op. cit.*
12 D. McCarthy, *op. cit.*
13 Ann Mason, M. R. C. Speech Project, Interim Report, Edinburgh University.
14 Reported in McCarthy, *op. cit.*
15 Reported in McCarthy, *op. cit.*
16 B. Bernstein, 'A Socio-linguistic Approach to Social Learning, in the *Penguin Survey of the Social Sciences*, 1965.
17 Brown and Bellugi, 'Three Processes in the Child's Acquisition of Syntax' in Vol. 34, No. 2, *Harvard Educational Review*, Special Edn.
18 Susan Erwin, 'Imitation and Structural Changes in Children's Language' in *New Developments in the Study of Language* (ed. Lenneberg), M. I. T. 1964.
19 M. Braine, 'The Ontogeny of English Phrase Structure', *Language*, 1963, 39, pp. 1–13.
20 R. Brown, Lecture to the Spastic Society, Study Group on Speech and Communication, London, May, 1966.
21 Ruth Weir, *Language in the Crib*, Mouton, The Hague, 1962.
22 This point was made by Renira Huxley of the Nuffield Child Language Study at the Psycholinguistics conference in Edinburgh, 1966.
23 A suggestion made by Ruth Clark of the Nuffield Child Language Project.
24 See, for example, Ruth Weir, *op. cit.*, on the child's use of repetition and structural drill.
25 Ann Mason, Preliminary Analysis, M. R. C. Language/Reading Project, Edinburgh.
26 Selected schools in the United States have tried so-called 'enrichment programmes' for language underachievers, but it is still too early to assess results.

3

Linguistics and Children's Interests

RICHARD HANDSCOMBE

> 'Do you think of yourselves as children?'
> 'Well, not exactly . . . but our parents call us children.'

The world children live in seems to be a self-contained unit impinged upon by adults at well-defined places and times. It might not now be a world of gnomes and fairies, if it ever was, but it has its own viewpoint. One nine-year-old girl says:

> I used to have a guinea-pig when I was in Class I, but it died with its legs crossed.

An adult, even a primary-school teacher, would probably summarize this with some such statement as 'Brenda's guinea-pig died a year ago': what has impressed the child, however, is neither the time of the animal's death nor the fact of its dying, but that it died *with its legs crossed*. Here is a significant shift of emphasis, one of a type that usually passes quite unnoticed. In some ways this is understandable because detailed information about such definitive aspects of children's interests is hard to come by.

Of course it is not difficult to discover that the guinea-pig is a common pet among young children, and questioning those adults who meet children commercially—pet-shop keepers, record-retailers, stamp-dealers, tailors, booksellers, hairdressers, travel-agents—can lead to a very accurate assessment of current interests. Parents and teachers, less impersonal, more closely connected with physical and mental development, are able to supplement this with individual lists of past as well as present enthusiasms. University departments, often obtaining their information by means of questionnaires, can deal with selected areas in depth. Little of this evidence, however, is obtained from sources easily recognizable as language: sales returns are probably the most frequent indirect means of showing where interests lie and these are usually in the form of figures or graphs. Even the replies to questionnaires are limited to one or two words, where indeed language is used at all. Investigations today into what children find interesting need hardly involve children, and can get by with the minimum of language.

There is no doubt that sources such as those described above can and do provide important evidence about all manner of topics, from the way children spend their pocket-money to the kind and number of library-books they read, from the relative popularity of dance-steps and hair-styles to the reasons why they start, and stop, smoking. Some of the information is directly relevant to the construction of new curricula and methodologies, particularly those being composed with a certain age-group in mind: children's interests can and, surely, should be integrated wherever possible into the syllabus, and remain one of the reasons for its continual modification. But the collection and classification of interests has only a limited application in education; it is only part of the picture.

A second reason why adults so often fail to grasp the essence of the child's interest—that the guinea-pig died *with its legs crossed*—stems from the fact that the information is often either misheard or misinterpreted. The adult's much longer exposure to and familiarity with the language leads to his employment of what might be called a conversational 'filter'. This device admittedly makes a great contribution to the comfort of living, and without it much of present-day life would be intolerable. To see it operating at its most efficient, at maximum information-exclusion rate, one need only go to a formal party and observe the number of people who are talked at rather than with, while at the same time engaging in all the physical movements associated with deep and interested conversation. In order actively to profit by a knowledge of children's interests, this filter must be dropped: what the children really say and write is what must first receive attention. Only then can the business of using interests constructively be entered upon.

The focus, then, must be on the children's language, and that person whose concern is with actual or potential language events is the linguist. In order to be able to speak with authority, he must start his investigations from a very broad base. It is not merely upon isolated responses that he can make his deductions, but rather on the running texts of spoken and written children's language, from which interest-information is one of the many possible abstractions. For him, interests are inseparably intertwined with their own grammar and vocabulary: his concern, then, is not only with the interests of children but also with the grammatical, lexical, phonological and graphological choices that their selection involves. What advantages has the linguist over other users of the language? Mainly these are revealed when one piece of language has to be described and related to other spoken or written language events.

Every native speaker of English is competent to make *ad hoc* comments on the 'form' and 'content' of a passage which in many cases may well afford valuable insights into the construction of an utterance and its implications. Considerable difficulties arise, however, when these extempore classifications are applied to longer and more varied stretches of text. Inconsistencies occur, and other *ad hoc* classes are then set up to accommodate them. The complex patterns of language are also deceptive; stretches of text which look identical may often be different, whereas other stretches, the surface appearance of which would suggest no similarity, may be basically of very similar pattern with differences of minimal importance. The native speaker, working his way through a series of texts, is unlikely to be able to preserve throughout his examination an entirely consistent classification of his material, and it is in the end only by employing a *consistent* description that we are able to make valid observations about contrasts or similarities in the texts we study.

How can the linguist help the teacher to make further, constructive use of his pupils' interests? In some cases the information he can supply will only be of marginal importance to the teacher. Where crafts and allied interests are concerned there may not be much difficulty in incorporating them into a school subject, at least in the beginning. An eight-year-old boy painting a picture, for instance, is not primarily concerned with being linguistically explicit about what he is doing. In this case, his new language-needs may be limited to a small additional vocabulary of colour-names.

But the exploitation of other interests may depend on a much more detailed knowledge of how children verbalize their environment, which concepts they choose and understand, and in what terms these are discussed. The matching, in other words, of a private interest with a school subject now becomes very largely a linguistic matter; a course on photography must teach not only the practical manipulation of cameras and equipment but also the grammar and vocabulary of the photographer's 'field'. A comparative study of the language of the interest, on the one hand, and the technical language of the subject, on the other, will reveal those areas where confusion and misunderstanding are likely to arise on mainly linguistic grounds. For many of the arts subjects the language itself is the most important, and in some cases the only, medium by which information is transferred. In history, for example, the child learns most of the subject through language, with visual aids and real objects playing a secondary role, while poetry depends upon language for its very existence.

The idea of the comparative study of varieties within a language brings out a further point. In a pioneering study of children's interests, Jersild Tasch[1] suggested that

> it is important ... to raise the question whether the kind of replies children give, the language they use, the mode of expression they employ actually are characteristic of children at different age levels and in various groups.
>
> (pp. 3–4)

The effect of such information would be widespread throughout the whole sphere of education: being specific about the features characteristic of ten-year-olds' language might be very useful in devising scales of attainment for backward twelve-year-olds; knowledge of those areas in which eight-year-old girls are articulate in speech might cause yet further revision of their reading and writing syllabus—the list is endless. But such an enquiry first requires the setting up of language norms for the various age-groups. Where an interest is acknowledged by a child, a test would then show to what extent its grammar and vocabulary had been absorbed; reference to the norm would show where the child stood linguistically in relation to his fellows. One of the difficulties here is that this sort of comparative study is still not practicable. There are as yet no norms against which a child's language may be measured.

During 1964, the Nuffield Child Language Survey was established. Its terms of reference are broad. It is to gather a corpus of children's language, written and spoken, from which these norms might possibly be deduced. The Survey's main allegiance, however, is to the Nuffield Foreign Languages Teaching Materials Project, which is concerned with the production of foreign language courses for British primary and secondary school children; its main aim, therefore, is to collect information on the grammar, vocabulary and centres of interest of these children so that it can be exchanged with similar material from abroad. So far, the material has been collected from 320 children, 80 in each of the age-groups 9–12 inclusive.

The children were usually recorded in groups of three, so that their speech would be intelligible for transcription purposes, and each group was recorded for about an hour. Most boys and girls of these age-groups are familiar with tape-recorders and being recorded, and their language after the first few minutes was generally easy and spontaneous. For the written section of the corpus, an examination of the tapes had shown which topics the children had talked of and which they had found interesting. A list of thirty appropriate composition titles was then drawn up, six under each of five headings, and then all the children who had already been recorded were asked to choose one topic from each heading and write about it, five topics in all from each child and a total of some 2,000 pages.

At one point, the compilers of the Nuffield French Course found themselves in need of detailed information about the actual topics talked about by the secondary-school children, together with some indication of where their interests lay. As there was at that time no written work available, the Survey undertook the examination of some forty hours of recorded material and the abstraction and classification of each individual topic as it occurred. (The findings of the Survey with regard to the interests of nine-year-old children are appended to this article.) Those that were mentioned most often were judged to be interests. Further, however, the compilers wanted to know how best such material could be utilized in making up the situations that formed the basis of their method. It was obvious that any solution to this problem would go far towards meeting the Survey's original terms of reference. It is evident that where a language is being taught through situations, grammatical and vocabulary frequency-lists based on the language as a whole are not in themselves sufficient to furnish the teaching items upon which to base the course: consideration must also be shown to the linguistic demands of the actual topic chosen for the situation. In their contribution to *Linguistics and Style*,[2] Michael Gregory and John Spencer have defined the 'field' of a text as its 'subject-matter and the linguistic features which may be associated with it'. The Survey is convinced that this concept, the concept of 'field', furnishes a means of systematically relating interest-information to the needs of the classroom. It is concentrating, therefore, on collecting grammatical and lexical information in the various fields selected for discussion by the various age-groups.

This information need not be used exclusively for the production of foreign language materials: wherever language is the medium of instruction the teacher might find it helpful to devise topic-paragraphs of contextualized material. The Nuffield Survey is only a pilot one, however, and the principles involved would need to be validated by the analysis of a greater variety of texts before the 'small languages' of, say, science and geography were being thus presented.

Of course, that both topic and language are appropriate still carries no guarantee that the children will be interested. In the first place there is the danger of being too dogmatic in the use of what has been found to be of general interest. The individuality of children is without question. Television cartoons are popular with certain groups, but there is a scattering of well-formed criticism:

> I think cartoons are the worst things imaginable. I think they're ever so silly and stupid ... I think if they're going to have any films on at all at television, you ought to have real characters in. I mean, some of the characters they portray on these cartoons, they look so ridiculous, like monkeys all dressed up in clothes and speaking ... I don't know how the producers of these cartoon films expect people to like them, because they haven't got any set meaning and there's just a lot of jabber ... you can't understand one thing they're talking about because they try to make them into real people without real voices ... And they do such silly things like crashing through roofs and going down chimney pots and landing in the fire and not getting burned, and having nails stuck through them and nothing happening, and things like that ...
> I've heard of a cat having nine lives, but they have about fifty-nine ...

An adult would have to exert considerable effort to change these ten-year-old girls' opinions, even supposing he wanted to.

Nor is it enough to establish that a particular topic is interesting to a particular age-group. In devising a situation for foreign-language teaching, it is possible to have all the right ingredients—a real and potentially interesting topic, natural and appropriate language—and still have no success with it as far as the children are concerned. It is certainly a step in the right direction to use material firmly based in reality, and in some cases it may be sufficient: the children may be intelligent, the motivation for learning may be elsewhere, and the presentation may therefore be entirely successful. But in many others it will be disastrous. Understanding and, subsequently, learning do not take place until there is a positive reaction between the pupil and the material. In what way may this vital spark be added?

Sometimes it will be the singer rather than the song that will capture and hold the children's imagination—'Art's ever so nice, because we've got Miss X and she's ever so nice ...'—and where children are intrigued and beguiled in this way it is possible to teach them almost anything.

But more often than not it is some curious aspect of a topic that attracts. These two examples are taken from written material in the Survey's collection of nine-year-olds' language; they contain some of the characteristic linguistic markers of the field of interest itself:

> Then I think I like English next because it helps you to speak the Queens english without any hesitation and also it helps you to learn words of the dictionary. English also helps you to write and to spell correctly but when you don't concerntrat you loose valuable marks. When words crop up and you don't know what they mean and you cann't spell them that is where your english comes in or look in a dictionary. English is very usefull in more ways than one ...

> I like prehistoric life because it tells you about how man came from the speck of life. My favourite part is about the dinesaurs The first thing when any one wants to learn about dinosaurs, is that when you think about them you must think big ...

The creation of teaching materials based on situation stands a general chance of success if some element of the unusual, perhaps even the bizarre or the fantastic, can be included occasionally without distorting either the general pattern of development or the seriousness of purpose behind the course. This is not to suggest that a vast quantity of expendable material should be allowed entry, but it may be useful to remember that many interests are legitimately outgrown and the necessity for some aspects of their language superseded. If impermanence is a feature of the interests of a certain age, then one could include certain topics whose features were not all to be subject to later recall. Some of the most permanent aspects of language would remain, especially, of course, grammar, whose patterns in childhood correspond fairly closely to those in adult usage. In this way the common-core features of the language could be continually reinforced.

Many people have worked to discover what constitutes the

essence of interest, some of them using formal linguistic criteria as an aid to their investigation. In *Structure and Direction in Thinking*, Berlyne[3] describes the experiments of Morozova, who set up passages variously dealing with latitude and longitude and then measured the degree of interest each of these aroused, by criteria which included the number of utterances (from the reader) like 'How interesting!' and the number of questions asked about the material. The most popular version, she discovered, was one where a young hero is obliged by circumstances to find out where he is.

Hints towards the use of problem-solving techniques to elicit language can be deduced from the children's own speech. During the last twenty minutes of each hour of recording, both the primary and secondary groups in the Survey imagined themselves to be in a situation of their own choosing. They then acted out the incidents of it as if they were taking part in a sort of radio drama. In one such 'free-play' episode, as these were called, two nine-year-old girls start by simply going on a picnic. Within a few minutes they hear a mewing:

> Oooh . . . look up there . . . there's a little cat on . . . on that tree . . . oh . . . w . . . I hope . . . help, Beth's going after it . . .
>
> Come on I think we'd better go now . . .
>
> I think it must be injured otherwise it would have moved or something . . .
>
> Let's . . .
>
> It looks as if it's stuck . . .
>
> Let's go and see . . .
>
> Hm . . .
>
> The girls go next door to see if the cat i . . . the kitten is really stuck . . . they find that its paw is bleeding badly . . . so Stella and Jean climb up . . . hm . . . to see it . . .
>
> Oh poor thing . . . I think we'd better get this kitten to the vet or something . . .
>
> Hm . . . I'll carry it down . . . oh gosh that's bleeding badly I think we'd better patch it up once we get down . . .

LINGUISTICS AND CHILDREN'S INTERESTS 47

> Yes . . . well I . . . I've got a big hanky here perhaps that would do it but . . .
>
> We'd better clean it first . . . let's go back to the stream . . .
>
> Yes . . .
>
> It's a nice clear one . . .
>
> The girls go back to the stream and though the kitten is mewing m . . . piteously . . . they . . . they hold it carefully and i . . . and it doesn't cry any more and soon it settles down to sleep . . . Jean and Stella bandage up its paw and then . . . they walk off to the vet's . . .

What has stimulated the language is an imagined incident, itself posing small but important problems about what to do and, therefore, in this situation, what to say. Certain linguistic selections make it obvious that the girls are involved with the kitten's plight: there is a different mode of speech used to distinguish action itself from commentary on the action, and there are markers of concern that are, at this age, not necessarily sentimental.

Not all the free-play situations produce such material, however: random, but entirely appropriate, utterances occur in many. Here three boys are out cycling. Their conversation turns to weights and measures:

> We . . . we have . . . I have been . . . doing . . . hm . . . measuring . . . it's great fun . . . we go . . . hm . . . racing round the classroom measuring things . . . I found out that I . . . er . . . my height was four feet eight inches and an eighth . . .
>
> Oh mine's five foot . . . er . . . three . . . three inches . . . I . . . I weigh . . . hm . . . five stone nine . . . I think . . .
>
> Mm . . . my sister weighs nearly . . . er . . . ten stone I think . . .
>
> Well I wonder what Sonia M. weighs . . .
>
> Yes . . . surprising . . . her bike holds her . . .
>
> Yeh . . .
>
> Spect the spr . . . springs of her saddle are all bent and crunched up . . .

Hm...

Surprising though... she eats very small dinners in comparison with me...

Hm... and me...

I expect she eats more slowly and they all sort of swell up an'...

Hm...

Spect she eats a lot of air with it... I mean you've got more air and water inside you than you have... hm... food and flesh and things...

Yes...

Well I'm getting hot... I'm going to take my pullover off...

The linguist cannot pretend to be able to supply the teacher with a foolproof answer to the problem of how to arouse children's curiosity or stimulate their imaginations. What some of us can now supply is an adequate description of the language used by children of a particular age about certain topics—a description based on as large a sample as possible. In a very limited survey of nine-year-old children talking about their brothers and sisters, for example, the following points became clear:

1. The hierarchy in the family is most definitely insisted upon: the items *age*, *birthday*, *year*, *old*, *older* habitually occur.
2. *Eyes* and *hair* are frequently described.
3. The brothers and sisters are talked of in their usual environment (*house/home*, *table*, *tea*, *teatime*, *sleep*).
4. The family and the home are seen within the confines of the day—*day*, *morning*, *night*—whereas favourite sports, for example, are seen in terms of seasons—*summer*, *winter*.
5. Communication is important in this topic, with the frequent use of *say*, *tell*: reported speech is usually handled directly, ('He said "Go away"').
6. Items selected to describe brothers and sisters include *terror*, *menace*, *cheeky*, *horrible*, *naughty*, *pest*, *scallywag*, *silly*: a related set, notably smaller, includes *cute*, *generous* and *nice*.

What linguistic items characterize a particular interest can thus be deduced to some extent from the evidence afforded by surveys of this nature.

In putting forward the case that, in using children's interests in teaching, attention must first be focused on the language, it is not suggested that children's language is superior to that of adults, neither is the ideal state envisaged as one where everybody speaks like an eight-year-old. No matter how much adults try to confuse the child with their own special languages, he will adapt his own language to his adult needs as he grows up. In a special way, however, his language is superior: it is superior *as far as he is concerned*. A language develops with every generation: that parents and children so often disagree may partly at least be due to unnoticed changes that have taken place in the language. The failure of mere prescriptivism in the past has shown us that no one can lay down a generation's usage. How much more efficiently, therefore, will children learn if the teacher begins with the language they know and expands his subject as he expands their linguistic competence in it. Children can only create linguistically if they have the tools. The language of their interests is evidence of fields wholly or partially acquired, and is thus a potentially powerful source of material. Linguistics can help the teacher select those tools which can be used most effectively to mould this material to his and the children's best advantage.

NOTES

1 Jersild Tasch, *et al.*, *Children's Interests and What They Suggest for Education*, Teachers College, Columbia University, New York, 1949.
2 J. Spencer, M. Gregory and N. Enkvist, *Linguistics and Style*, Oxford U.P., 1964
3 D. Berlyne, *Structure and Direction of Thinking*, Wiley, 1965.

NUFFIELD FOREIGN LANGUAGES TEACHING MATERIALS PROJECT—CHILD LANGUAGE SURVEY

Relative Popularity of Topics of Conversations of nine-year-old Children

AMOUNT OF TEXT: Each occurrence of a topic is measured in points, with 0–¼ page of transcription = 1 point, ¼–½ page = 3 points, ½–1 page = 5 points, 1–2 pages = 10 points, 2–3 pages = 15 points, and over 3 pages = 20 points.

This information is collected from approximately 400 pages of transcription.

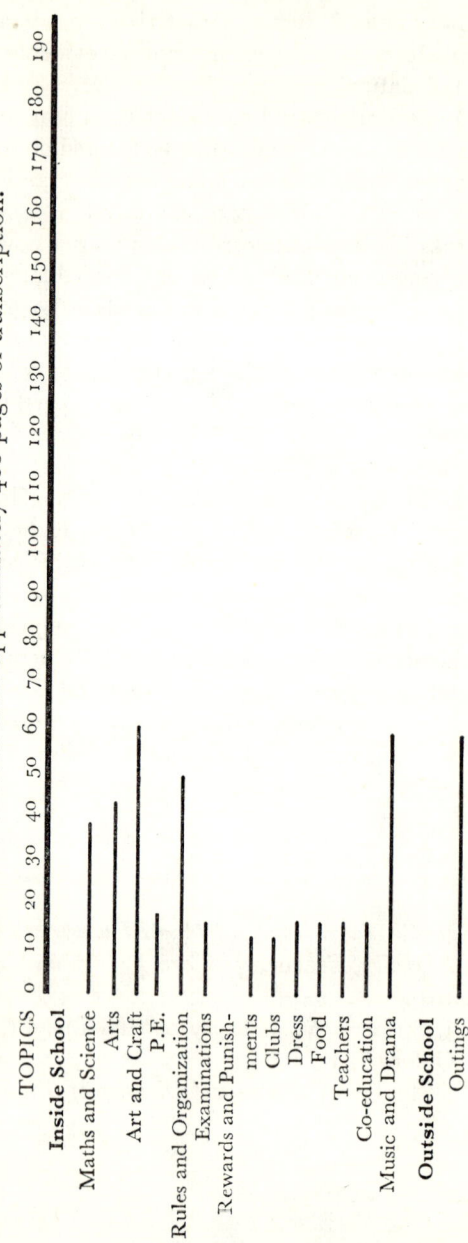

TOPICS

Inside School
- Maths and Science
- Arts
- Art and Craft
- P.E.
- Rules and Organization
- Examinations
- Rewards and Punishments
- Clubs
- Dress
- Food
- Teachers
- Co-education
- Music and Drama

Outside School
- Outings

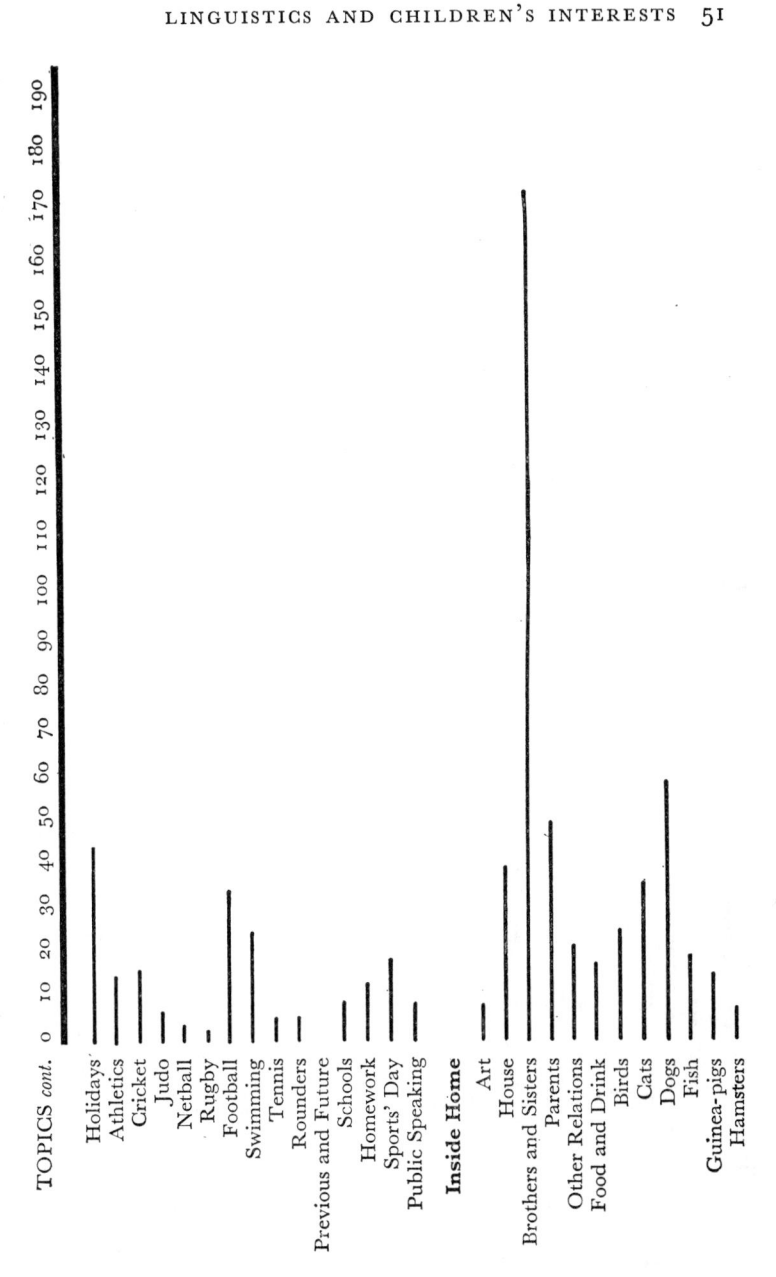

LINGUISTICS AND CHILDREN'S INTERESTS 51

TOPICS *cont.*

- Holidays
- Athletics
- Cricket
- Judo
- Netball
- Rugby
- Football
- Swimming
- Tennis
- Rounders
- Previous and Future Schools
- Homework
- Sports' Day
- Public Speaking

Inside Home

- Art
- House
- Brothers and Sisters
- Parents
- Other Relations
- Food and Drink
- Birds
- Cats
- Dogs
- Fish
- **Guinea-pigs**
- Hamsters

52 RICHARD HANDSCOMBE

TOPICS *cont.*

Topic	
Hedgehogs	
Rabbits and Hares	
Tortoises and Terrapins	
Other Pets	
Bedtime	
Chess	
Boxing	
Listening to Music and Stars	
Television	
Reading	
Collecting	
Making Models	
Making Clothes	
Writing	
Performing Music	
Photography	
Housework	
Mods	
Rockers	
Fashion	
Outside Home	
Nature and Minerals	
Transport	
Outings	
Cinema	
Church etc.	
Football Matches	

LINGUISTICS AND CHILDREN'S INTERESTS 53

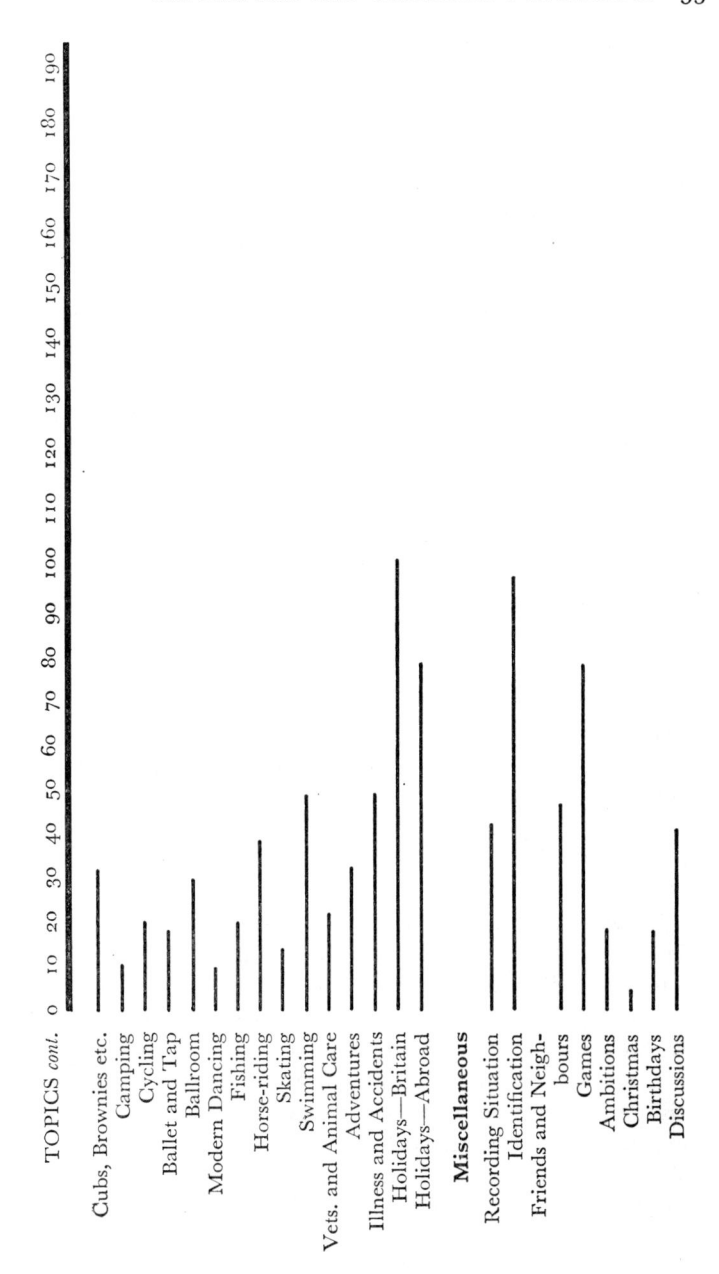

TOPICS *cont.*

Topic	Value
Cubs, Brownies etc.	~30
Camping	~10
Cycling	~20
Ballet and Tap	~20
Ballroom	~30
Modern Dancing	~10
Fishing	~20
Horse-riding	~35
Skating	~15
Swimming	~50
Vets. and Animal Care	~30
Adventures	~50
Illness and Accidents	~100
Holidays—Britain	~95
Holidays—Abroad	~75

Miscellaneous

Topic	Value
Recording Situation	~40
Identification	~75
Friends and Neighbours	~45
Games	~20
Ambitions	~5
Christmas	~15
Birthdays	~35
Discussions	

4

Programmed Learning

ANTHONY P. R. HOWATT

It is, I suppose, commonplace to observe that the teaching of the mother-tongue envisages as its aim organized creativity. Fashion and the varying temperaments of individual teachers lead to lesser or greater emphasis on the two aspects of organization and creativity, but both are relevant. A child may be let loose to perform feats of splendid creativity, but without the pressure of a conscious system of organization, without rules of a kind, the bowl on the potter's wheel may refuse to take any recognizable—and therefore communicable—shape. Conversely, a too narrow insistence on the rules of the game may destroy interest. In fairness one could say that both approaches may be shown to work, possibly because in the former case the child discovers a system for himself (which asks much of his intelligence) whereas in the latter case he succeeds in expressing himself despite a rigid teaching system (which demands a great deal of his personality). In other words, the pupil equalizes at half-time, so to speak.

The point of this introduction is to state that if the child is to adapt his language usefully to life, he plainly needs both to whip up his enthusiasm and to know how and when to bridle it. The store of memories and images, of emotions and thoughts which feed his imaginative inner life is built from his personal experience, from his contact with others, from art and design and so on: it is not in dispute that deprivation of this faculty requires compensation from the teacher's personal vision, direction and insight. However, it is a complex road from thought and feeling to externalized speech or writing which may usefully connect the pupil with the social context—and hence regenerate his sense of personal achievement.

Programmed learning has sometimes been treated with caution on the grounds that it is in some way antipathetic to such humanistic intentions in teaching. It has itself to blame in a sense because of the connotations of 'mechanized instruction' that are attached to it by its association both with teaching machines and with a theory of learning that can be easily misunderstood. This theory, usually referred to as the behaviourist theory of learning, stands on the basic principle of demanding overt, observable behaviour as evidence for theoretical statements. Therefore, it cannot handle 'internal, mental processes' except by inference. In addition, much of the experimentation is performed with animals, such as Professor Skinner's famous pigeons (of which more later), and the findings are then extrapolated into the human context. The result of all this is obvious—behaviourist psychology appears to be a surface psychology, excessively preoccupied with measurement and dangerously willing to equate human and sub-human learning. The criticism is at its sharpest where language is concerned because of the obvious fact that no animal has ever been taught speech.

What Skinner found in his experiments with animal learning was—briefly—that if a hungry animal is reinforced (i.e. fed) immediately after responding correctly (i.e. performing an action designated by the investigator as relevant), the animal is more likely to respond correctly in similar stimulus conditions in the future. The reader will be familiar with procedures of this kind from descriptions of animal training and the like. Having noted that the significant point of the experimentation is the immediate reinforcement of a correct and relevant response, we can move on to the human situation.

Broadly speaking, Skinner's theory says that a human being learns if he responds (i.e. answers a question, carries out an instruction, etc.) and is then immediately reinforced (i.e. allowed to know that his answer is correct). Obviously, there is the problem of wrong answers and Skinner has suggested that in general, mistakes are 'punishing'. This is difficult to accept entirely since mistakes which we can ourselves rectify or which may be turned to good account by a teacher are potentially a source of enlightenment. However, in the context of a written programme, with no recourse to a teacher, there is no way of ensuring that a mistake will be clarified, and the pupil should therefore not make mistakes in a programme. It is on this point that there is disagreement between the different approaches to programming—the school of 'branching' programming believes that a mistake is an indication that the pupil needs help and the programme refers him to a subsidiary page (or frame) where the problem can be discussed in more detail.

The next point is that a response does not exist in a vacuum—it is one of a system of responses and to programme means to organize the material presented to the learner in such a way that he can 'enter into' the learning operation by being asked to solve a series of problems, all of which are related both to each other and to the ultimate aim of the programme (or, the terminal behaviour). He is at all times allowed access to the correct answers.

Skinner refers to this process of solving intermediate problems on the road to an ultimate aim as 'shaping the organism's behaviour towards a desired terminal behaviour by successive approximations'. So long as we admit the pupil's *own* contribution, the word 'shaping' is a reasonable metaphor. However the 'mechanistic' overtones of programming derive sustenance from a misunderstanding of this notion. A programmer in the human situation, it might be pointed out, is *not* a sort of 'reinforcement-artisan', operating on a passive subject to 'control' or mysteriously 'shape' the subject's 'behavioural repertoire', however realistic this attitude may be with the pigeons. On the one hand a pigeon can only be communicated with instrumentally by means of food, clicks or flashing-lights (it cannot be told what to do, in other words) and on the other hand, because it is unaware of the intention of the investigator, it is inevitably a non-co-operative, passive subject going through a series of activities, not in order to learn them, but in order to get its meal. But to introduce a human learner is to introduce an interactive agent who can both know what the teacher has in mind (i.e. acquire an internalized image of the terminal behaviour as a whole) and also interact with the programme by translating the programmer's aim as his own personal intention (i.e. he can adapt his behaviour to achieve an aim he can consciously apprehend).

In practical terms, an animal trainer is forced to break the total behaviour down into a chronological, linear sequence of small 'steps' because he has no way of telling the animal what to do and the animal is in no position to co-operate in order to adapt its behaviour to the image. It is from animal training that the programming idea of 'small stages' is derived but the 'smallness' is beside the point. What a human teacher has to do is announce an aim to engage the intention of the learner in achieving this aim. It may be possible for the learner to reach this goal 'in one go', in which case a programme is intended to refine a skill already acquired in a crude form. Or the teacher may decide to set up a series of intermediate goals (problems) which are, of course, the 'steps' in the programme, the main significance of each step being not so much its size as its relevance to the ultimate aim of the programme. The question of size, or difficulty, is impossible to decide in advance since it depends on feedback from the users of the programme, but the rule-of-thumb notion that there should be as few steps as necessary would be a useful one.

Some proponents of behaviourist programmed learning have, therefore, tended to create the impression that learning is a simple matter of hooking responses on to stimuli by some magic 'association', and that all the teacher is really doing is helping the pupil to make daisy-chains of behaviour in a 'mechanistic' sense. This is an over-simplification of Skinnerian psychology and it misinterprets as ignorance the behaviourist hesitation to talk without evidence. And the second feature of the 'image' that programming has presented to the world (the emphasis placed on the miniaturization of learning into sequences of very small units) obscures a more fundamental idea behind programming, which is the concern to discover and apply the principles of organization that contribute to the success of a teaching operation. This is a large ambition.

Nobody would disagree that 'organization' is a basic concept, because this proposition is vague enough to be acceptable, but there is plenty of disagreement about what it means. The most general interpretation of the word 'organized' would be something like 'clear, concise, coherent, logical', etc. If these words are taken in the context of teaching materials, they would imply, say, 'a good well-written textbook'. There is no doubt that the current preoccupation with the problems and principles of programming will spill over into textbook writing, and, one hopes, result in 'better-written textbooks', but nobody would yet refer to a well-written textbook as 'programmed' for reasons elaborated below.

Taken one step further, an 'organized' textbook is one which communicates effectively with the reader-learner. If in the classroom situation you want to make sure that the learner is following you, you presumably ask him a question occasionally. If he answers correctly, you continue with the next bit; if he makes a mistake, you take time off to explain the point in more detail. Furthermore, the usefulness of the pupil's answer as a diagnosis of whether or not he has understood depends on how relevant the question is. Good questions obviously give valuable information. Textbooks arranged in this way—arranged to ask occasional questions in order to diagnose whether the learner is healthily 'in touch' and to explain difficult points in greater detail if he is having trouble—seem an eminently sensible idea. They are usually known as branching programmes (or as intrinsic programmes) and have been developed principally by Norman A. Crowder. Sometimes programmes of this kind are presented in the type of teaching machine that looks like a TV set and costs at least twice as much. But in normal circumstances the textbook format is perfectly adequate.

The final step is obvious. Instead of asking an occasional 'check-up' question as a branching programme does and switching the learner to extra information if he needs it, why not ask questions all the time? If the interrogation is astute enough and exquisitely graded, every pupil ought to learn and they can all go through the same material. This last type of programming (known as linear programming since it does not recognize the need for branch-lines—on the hypothesis that if the train stops at all the stations on the main-line, i.e. if the pupil answers many simple questions correctly, branch-lines can be dispensed with) is of course the Skinnerian programming mentioned earlier.

It will be clear that the textbook is the written version of the classroom talk (with much the same restrictions as a lecture) and that a branching programme is a printed classroom discussion. A linear programme reproduces a difficult classroom technique—close, intricately structured interrogation leading to control over a new behaviour pattern. A classroom procedure that can be transferred to print (or any other 'mock up' such as pictures, devices, etc.) is *ipso facto* available to each pupil individually. This is the second fundamental idea behind programming: allowing each pupil the undivided, continuous and patient attention of the 'teacher-in-the-programme'.

It is usual to adduce two further principles of programming: (*a*) The principle of the active response. (This condition appears to rule the ordinary textbook out of court as a 'programme' since silent reading is not 'active'. This is an arguable assumption which, it seems to me, confuses active with overt.) (*b*) The principle of small steps. This has already been alluded to.

Both these principles have occasioned considerable research, most of it inconclusive, as to the merits of overt/covert responses, large/small steps and so on. I should, therefore, like to make two comments.

Firstly, it would appear that the value of eliciting an active response from the pupil and the value of eliciting such a response often (i.e. by dissecting the material into steps) lie principally in their effect of arresting and focusing the pupil's capacity to concentrate. Most linear programmes force the learner to concentrate by their technique of dividing the page into separate 'frames' and by their constant questioning. Branching programmes are usually less tightly controlled and the pupil reads a full page at a time. A chapter in a textbook is one long stimulus and plainly demands much greater concentration and a much greater capacity on the pupil's part to process and master the information contained in it. The linear, small-step technique predicts success with weaker pupils because it goes more slowly, demands less prolonged attention and concentrates the pupil on a series of questions. Experiment has on the whole substantiated this prediction—linear programming helps the less bright pupil. Ultimately the ability of the learner to grasp a given amount of information (or acquire a given level of skill) is related principally to (*a*) his intelligence and (*b*) his previous experience. An introductory programme on, say, punctuation which was broken down into 100 steps might be right for one pupil, but infuriating for a brighter one and also for a pupil who already knew something about the subject. At the other end of the scale, one pupil might be able to read a whole chapter of a book and process the salient features with no difficulty, whereas another would be greatly helped by a technique which broke down the load of information that had to be dealt with. It is important, therefore, to notice what pupils the programmer has in mind if you are considering using a programme (what their assumed entry behaviour is, to use the term complementary to terminal behaviour mentioned earlier).

Secondly, an active response is not, as we have seen, activity in vacuo. There is not only activity, but also, in some form or other, feedback. This may come from the confirmation of the correct answer (the reinforcement), or it may come from a later part of the programme, or from the relationship between what the pupil is learning in the programme and what he already knows. As was stressed before, a human learner is not a passive 'subject' whose behaviour is being 'shaped' in a mechanistic sense, he is a partner in a two-way process. This is obvious in the pupil–teacher relationship; it is implicit even when the pupil is simply reading a book; with a programme it is, albeit in a very simplified way, explicit. To put it briefly—a programme is a conversation; hence, there is every reason for it to look and sound like a conversation.

These points underline a basic idea in this paper—that a programme is essentially a 'mirror-image' of a classroom lesson, presented in such a way as to direct the teaching to each pupil individually. The form of presentation (sometimes a teaching machine, more usually a printed text, with or without devices) will obviously impose its restrictions on the content of the programme. However, everything that can be organized in some way can be programmed; but not everything can be reproduced in a distributable form—so there are limitations on the technique.

Let us now revert to our original topic—the tension between those language-teaching activities that are aimed at developing the pupils' imaginative responses to life and literature, and those which are intended to provide the norms and rules of language which make expression comprehensible and therefore communicable. The ideas of programmed learning are not obviously applicable to the former aim. However, in an oblique sense, it is part of the teacher's intention to direct the pupils' imaginative experience, and the close interaction that exists between a learner and the teacher-in-the-programme would—if sensibly and sensitively used—promise a valuable means of communication. One might keep an open mind about this.

The second aspect of English teaching (the Highway Code aspect) has obvious relevance for programming purposes. So far, programmes have on the whole concentrated on teaching such 'traffic signals' as punctuation, spelling and the formal rules of grammar. Such programmes are useful and relieve the teacher of routine work and simultaneously lighten the pupil's learning burden (since it is the intention of a programme to be as easy as it can legitimately be).

I should like to go a little further and repeat a remark made earlier—that the path from thought and feeling to word is a complex one. As the Soviet psychologist L. S. Vygotsky put it:

> Thought and word do not coincide. Thought unlike speech does not consist of separate words. If I want to communicate the thought that today I saw a bare-footed boy in a blue shirt running down the street, I do not see everything concerning that separately: the boy, the shirt, the blue colour, his running, the absence of shoes. I see all this in one act of thinking but in transferring it into speech I put it in separate words. A speaker very often unfolds one and the same thought in the course of several minutes. In his mind the thought is there simultaneously, but in speech it has to be developed successively. A thought can be compared to a cloud which sheds a shower of words.

In this connection one remembers the injunction to 'think clearly and write simply'. The difficulty pupils experience is that they think all too 'clearly'—images and memories rush into consciousness—but once there they tumble around and the child's expression of them in words is quite inadequate to his intention. Vygotsky stresses one reason: a thought or image is an experience where many 'elements' are present simultaneously, but its expression requires a conscious dissection and structuring of the 'elements' in a linear order. The other reason is plain and related: the child's ability to express his image is dependent on the meaningful distinctions he can make and also on the names he has at his disposal for his distinctions, i.e. his vocabulary.

Programming has a special function in this connection. A programme can give a child something to think about and *control* the way and speed with which this thought is split into inter-related 'elements' which may later become paragraphs and then sentences and then words. This is particularly so if the thought is presented non-linguistically, i.e. by means of a picture, cartoon, film etc. For example, suppose a child were asked to look at a postcard of a scene and to describe it as if he were sending the postcard to a friend, what strategy would the teacher-in-the-programme adopt in order to control the pupil's response to this single thought, the image of the scene? Clearly, teachers are aware of many possible strategies (e.g. dividing the scene into components—the castle, the hill, the sea; taking an imaginary walk along the shore; inventing an imaginary episode, etc.). The point is that the strategy adopted should generalize to other pictures and to mental pictures, that the child should have a technique for dividing up his unitary images into those smaller components that language can convey to the external world. Of course, there is nothing new here; teachers have always tried out such strategies. But a programme is more controlled and more explicit, and also allows the teacher to experiment with different strategies, to see how they differ with different pupils, to see how people learn.

The appended example of a (linear) programme requires a word or two of introduction. The prime reason for including it is to exemplify the idea that a programme may be regarded as a 'conversation' between the learner and the teacher-in-the-programme. The reader should note that the overall plan of the programme is to start from the picture and, having made the ultimate aim of the exercise explicit ('suppose you were to send this postcard to a friend, how would you describe it, what would you say?'), to take each 'element' of the picture separately (the bridge, the river and the village) in order to discuss in increasing detail the features it represents. Thus the plan takes the pupil from the 'whole' to the 'parts'. However, at the same time, the programme, in its recapitulation frames, moves in the opposite direction—from the 'parts' of the description to the 'whole', which is given in the final frame. It presents, therefore, one of the possible strategies which a pupil could adopt in order to solve the problem of how to organize what he wants to say. Afterwards, he can try a similar description for himself.

(It should be said that the following programme is intended primarily for foreign learners of English of intermediate standard. It is for this reason that the overall strategy is very straightforward, and, furthermore, the closeness with which the programme focuses the learner's attention on specific vocabulary distinctions (e.g. between 'small', 'tiny' and 'low') is a necessary aspect of teaching English to foreigners—although it is a valid principle in mother-tongue teaching as well. In general, therefore, the programme (pp. 64 ff.) may be regarded as an example of principle and technique which might require modifications in application to other teaching situations.)

THE BRIDGE OVER THE RIVER

1 This is a postcard, the kind of postcard you send to your friends when you are away on holiday.

Suppose you wanted to send this postcard, and you wanted to tell your friend about the scene in the picture.

What would you say?

First of all, you would have to describe the most important things in the picture. Here is a list of things. Choose the three most important:

    the gardens   the clouds
    the roofs   the sailing boats
    the bridge   the river
    the traffic   the trees
    the village

2 Yes, the three most important things are probably the bridge
the village
the river

As you perhaps already know, this is a real bridge. It is called the Forth Road Bridge and is one of the longest bridges in the world.

Why is it called a 'Road Bridge?'

Because it carries .... across the river.

3 You can see some of the traffic—some of the cars and lorries—in the picture.

It crosses the River Forth near Edinburgh in Scotland.

Which of these words describe the river:

    wide   small   winding   calm

4 Yes, it is a very wide river, and it is calm in the picture, too.

What colour do you think the river is?

I think it is ____ because ....

5 Yes, it is blue because you can see that the weather is fine. The sky is blue and the sun is shining. The water reflects the colour of the sky.

It is also calm. If it were not calm (if it were rough), you would be able to see waves on the water.

Can you see waves?   Yes/No.

6 No, you can't. Well, there are a few very small waves at the edge, but not many.

Is it a windy day?   Yes/No.

7 No, it isn't. It is a fine, calm, sunny day.

What season of the year is it? Look at the picture carefully.

8 Yes, it's summer. People are sailing on the river.

We've looked at the bridge and the river. Can you remember what we said about them?

Choose the right words:

I hope you like this postcard. It is of the Forth Road Bridge —one of the shortest / longest bridges in the world. It carries trains / cars across the River Forth. As you can see, it is a fine, sunny / dull, wet day in summer / winter and there are a few boats sailing on the rough, calm, blue / grey water. It must be difficult to sail today because there is so much / so little wind.

9 If you want to, you can check your answer now:

I hope you like this postcard. It is of the Forth Road Bridge —one of the longest bridges in the world. It carries cars across the River Forth. As you can see, it is a fine, sunny day in summer and there are a few boats sailing on the calm, blue water. It must be difficult to sail today because there is so little wind.

10 We shall look at the bridge again in a minute, but first let's have a look at the village.

It is called South Queensferry. What do you think the village on the other side of the river is called?

11 Yes, that was very easy—North Queensferry.

So in the picture we are looking towards the north / south / east / west of Scotland.

12 Towards the north, yes.

Can you see the Highlands of Scotland in the picture? No, the hills at the back of the picture are all very _____.

PROGRAMMED LEARNING 67

13 Yes, they're very low.
Now, let's take the village out of the picture and look at it specially:

It is a $\genfrac{}{}{0pt}{}{\text{big}}{\text{small}}$ village and the houses are built of $\genfrac{}{}{0pt}{}{\text{brick}}{\genfrac{}{}{0pt}{}{\text{stone.}}{\text{wood}}}$

14 The small village is very picturesque with its grey stone houses.

There are also a few $\genfrac{}{}{0pt}{}{\text{flats}}{\text{cottages}}$ among the houses.

15 Yes, the small houses are called cottages.
What do you think the people in the village do?
Look at this:

What is it? A h____.

16 A harbour. And a very small one, a tiny one.
   There are a few boats in the harbour. What sort of boats are they?
       sailing boats   rowing boats   steamers   fishing boats

17 Fishing boats.
   So, what do you think some of the people in the village do for a living?
   They ——.

18 They fish — yes.

19 Now look at the whole village again. Choose the words which you think describe the village: and write them in the spaces in Frame 20.

   It is a(n) {pretty, little, mining / ugly, big, fishing} village with {a lot of / a few} stone houses and cottages. The village has a {huge / tiny} harbour where {the steamers / the fishing boats} lie.

20 South Queensferry, which lies on the south bank of the River Forth is a ____, ____, ____-ing village with ____ ____ stone houses and c-____. The village has a ____ h-____ where the ____ boats lie.

21 You can check your answer if you want to:
   South Queensferry, which lies on the south bank of the River Forth, is a pretty, little fishing village with a few stone houses and cottages. The village has a tiny harbour where the fishing boats lie.

22 Now let's have one more look at the bridge itself:

We have already said that it is very____-ng, but it is also very ____ because the ships must be able to pass underneath it.

23 A long, high bridge.
Of course it is a very strong bridge built of steel and concrete—but from a distance the steel and wires look like lace. Three of these words describe it quite well:
      elegant   ugly   low   graceful   strong

24 Yes, the bridge seems to fly elegantly across the river like a strong graceful bird. Like an eagle, perhaps. You can see eagles in Scotland sometimes.

Now let's look at the whole picture again and see what we can say about it.
Choose the right words. (If you want to check your answers, look at the words in capitals in Frame 26.)

This is a postcard of the Forth Road Bridge—one of the longest/lowest bridges in the world. It carries cars and lorries over the River Forth. South Queensferry, the little village which you can see in the foreground of the picture, lies on the south bank of the river. It is a pretty/ugly little mining/fishing village with a few brick/stone houses and cottages. Behind the village you can see the tiny harbour where the fishing boats lie, and outside the harbour the fishing boats/sailing boats are sailing on the rough, blue/calm, grey water of the river. The sun is shining and the weather is fine;/windy; it is a beautiful winter/summer afternoon and the bridge looks like lace—very ugly/elegant and graceful, like a strong bird flying north.

25 Now see if you can remember everything you have learnt about the picture:

Dear John,

I hope you like this postcard. It is of the ____ ____ ____ in Scotland, one of the ____ bridges in the world. It carries road traffic (____ and ____) across the River Forth.

South Queensferry, the charming little ____ you can see in the foreground of the postcard, lies on the ____ bank of the river. It is a ____ little ____ village with a few ____ houses and ____ . If you look, you can see the ____ behind the village. I went there a few days ago to look at the ____ ____. I didn't see any sailing boats, though. But there are one or two in the postcard—sailing on the ____, ____ water of the river. It really is a beautiful day, isn't it? The sun is shining, the weather is fine and the water reflects the blue of the sky. Scotland is often like this in the ____, but in the winter it looks very grey and cold.

What do you think of the bridge? It reminds me of a strong ____ bird flying ____-ly across to the north, to the Highlands. Like an eagle. You must come and visit Scotland some day. Perhaps we shall be able to go north and we might even be lucky and see an eagle.

With best wishes,
Yours,
Jimmy.

26 You can check your answers here. (The words in capitals are the answers to Frame 24).

I hope you like this postcard. It is of the Forth Road Bridge in Scotland—one of the LONGEST bridges in the world. It carries road traffic (cars and lorries) across the River Forth.

South Queensferry, the charming little village you can see in the foreground of the postcard, lies on the south bank of the river. It is a PRETTY little FISHING village with a few STONE houses and cottages. If you look, you can see the harbour behind the village. I went there a few days ago to look at the fishing boats. I didn't see any SAILING BOATS, though. But there are one or two in the postcard—sailing on the CALM, BLUE water of the river. It really is a beautiful day, isn't it? The sun is shining, the weather is FINE and the water reflects the blue of the sky. Scotland is often like this in the SUMMER, but in the winter it looks very grey and cold.

What do you think of the bridge? It reminds me of a strong ELEGANT bird flying gracefully (OR It reminds me of a strong, graceful bird flying elegantly) across to the north, to the Highlands. Like an eagle.

27 Now here is another postcard of Scotland. It shows the small village of Kyleakin in the Isle of Skye.

See if you can describe this picture using some of the words and phrases you have learnt, as if you were sending it to a friend of yours.

The difference between this picture and the other one is that here the people do not cross the water by a bridge, but by a FERRY. You can see the ferry in the harbour. And the water is not a river. It is the sea—remember Skye is an island.

Perhaps you know the famous song about this island:

OVER THE SEA TO SKYE

This would be a good title for your story.

5

Analysing Classroom Procedures

JOHN PRIDE

The drift of my remarks may appear rather exclusively to concern the teaching of second languages. Examples are certainly taken from recent experience in the State University of the Mongolian People's Republic. I believe, however, that several of the questions raised pose interesting common problems for the teacher of the native language as well as of a second language.

No one will ever be able to declare, with conviction, 'These are the best procedures for teaching second languages'. He would have to add 'so far, for this type of locality or school, this age-group, this sex, these teachers', and many more qualifications. But even then it will probably still be the case that some other set of procedures, founded on apparently alien principles perhaps, could prove equally effective for the given job. This itself is of course an interesting question, because the comparative evaluation of teaching procedures demands an equivalent yardstick for measuring performance, and if agreement can be reached on *testing* methods then it can scarcely be far away where *teaching* methods are concerned. Both teaching and testing procedures will certainly vary as they are informed by different schools of linguistic thought. One approach, for instance, may have developed out of the notion that the real difficulties facing the learner are those which relate to formal (grammatical and suchlike) differences between the second language (L2) in question and the native language (L1)—and indeed other L2s, such as Russian in Mongolia or Arabic in Somalia with respect to English. Another, in contrast, may be based on the premise that the all-important problems are cultural, social and even personal: what languages does and will the learner use at home, at work, and who with, and why, what attitude does he display towards these languages, and so forth? The force of the first approach is initially to select formal features to teach and then, as a secondary consideration, to situationalize them. The second seems to require that learning situations be first selected and then formalized.

It is a natural temptation, for teacher and linguist alike, to make more or less committed choices between or among such apparently contradictory principles. Form 'versus' situation, rules (not only formal rules) versus patterns, prescriptive versus descriptive, social versus individual, translation versus no translation, and there are others. But the impulse to choose one thing *or* the other may, at least in some cases, mislead. Language itself is a kind of perpetual compromise, a form of behaviour which could be thought of in some senses as metaphorical, a happening which results from forces pulling in different directions. It is, for example, both formal *and* situational in character.[1] Tendencies toward committed choice, even in this respect, are well revealed by how much of the current—and considerable—linguistic interest in the problem of infant language acquisition puts the child in the role of a detective building up a set of formal rules from the scrappy formal clues provided by those around him. We are told that our unique ability, as human beings, to master languages, is fundamentally a formal ability. Scant attention in linguistic circles is yet paid to the child's concern to note under what circumstances (and what happens when) such and such an utterance occurs. Yet it seems more helpful to reflect, as the layman well might, that no normal infant would give twopence for the gift of language if it were not rather important for getting him what he wanted, than to settle for the implications of total commitment to a formal view of language behaviour. The situational experience of the individual ensures what most of us feel we know very well to be the case, that linguistic profiles are not uniform.

The second language learner, in this respect, is placed in a similar position. It pays therefore to think in terms of teaching procedures which are both situational and formal at the same time, and (more immediately realizable perhaps) of those which may be said to be broadly situational on the one hand and broadly formal on the other.

Situational procedures are those which involve the learner in communicating something to somebody (he will not be doing this for example when converting strings of sentences from active to passive). They might take the form of the use of objects in the classroom, parts of the room itself, pictures, dramatizations, games, conversation, monologue.... Linguistics will, or could, contribute to the development of situational teaching in at least four ways: by helping *first* to characterize the notion of situation itself, *second* to locate and outline some aspects of some characteristic 'real life' situations of given learners, *third* to set up classroom-centred situations, and *fourth*, more directly, to indicate how formal features correlate in each case. The following discussion aims to cover all four functions.

In talking about the level of situation in general, how far is it possible and desirable to establish theoretical categories? Dimensions such as social dialect, field of discourse, participant relationship, and so on, admittedly more closely specified than this but still (in most linguistic treatments) at a fairly high level of generality, will certainly provide a fairly broad grid or organizing scheme through which we may look at language in action. Yet it may be timely, perhaps, to make two points. First, if we do wish to structure situation, then it is essential to draw on the insights of at least several other disciplines. Second, it is a mistake to aim exclusively at a final systematic picture or at intermediate 'hypothetical constructs': there is reason, that is to say, to give close attention to more particular or *ad hoc* questions which quite recognizably belong to the everyday use of language.

Both observations can be illustrated by reference to some of the concerns of sociology. Bernstein, for example, it is now well known, first suggested some time ago that children from lower working-class homes in Britain, deprived at an early age of the opportunity of listening and responding to 'educated' English, find themselves in consequence at an educational disadvantage in having to 'translate' the language of their teachers (and textbooks) into their own language. More fortunate pupils manage to 'switch codes' according to circumstances, therefore do not have to translate, and so stand a better chance of prospering academically. One might say that 'interference' at several levels takes place between teacher and pupil. It is the *exact nature* of such interference, sociological, psychological and educational, as well as formally linguistic, that constitutes part of these children's learning *situation*. Linguistics, here as so often, is only at an advantage over other disciplines in so far as it may (sooner or later) be agreed to provide the best forum for discussion.

In this connection it is necessary to realize that there is a real distinction to be recognized between 'situation', in the rather wide sense used here, and neo-Firthian 'context', which is the (inter-)level of linguistic analysis at which formal variety in the use of language is surveyed by the linguist and corresponding 'varieties' propounded. 'Context' is not a multi-disciplined concern, and the language teacher should not feel obliged to restrict his attention to theories of context at the expense of situation.

In the study of situation different levels of abstraction are possible. One might aim to systematize the total communicative habits of a speech community; or, alternatively, to point out the mechanisms of typical 'speech events' within the community. In either case some degree of theoretical exhaustiveness seems ultimately to be called for. But again, one can isolate rather more particular situational factors for study, having made the assumption that they are relatively deeply involved in the kind of language behaviour one is interested in. For example, in the study of language-learning behaviour, it is possible to arrive at 'common types of language-learning situations' in this way:[2] there will be such variables as the degrees of formal difference between L_1 and L_2, levels of attainment expected in the L_2, degree and type of contact with the L_2 outside the school, type of motivation (intrinsic, extrinsic; instrumental, integrative; etc.), opportunities to learn the L_2 in school, mode of learning (formal, situational), and so on. This type of investigation (the comparative survey) is still extremely schematic, however, and does not really answer the need for approaches which work outwards from the more particular detail as opposed to inwards from the hypothetical generalization.

Two aspects of situation, social group and subject-matter, will have to suffice for exemplification. If one chooses to study the language of managers of large industrial concerns, or of urban school children, or even of infants, as social groups, it is necessary to realize that the problem has still to be further restricted to convenient proportions. Linguistics is not poised to offer a series of monographs on 'registers' of this sort, even if there were linguists enough prepared to work on such lines. It is not simply that too much is going on in terms of formal contrasts; equally, and perhaps more fundamentally, there is too much going on situationally. There are the different circumstances in which managers (say) are placed throughout the day, the different roles they play, commanding, requesting, advising, praising, reprimanding, planning, reporting, a rather large list it would seem of nevertheless recurrent, conventional, activities. And there may be various unforeseen complicating factors to consider in each individual case. Professor Burns (Edinburgh) found some years ago, for example, in sociological investigations into a group of electronics firms that a surprisingly large proportion of written commands passed from management to staff were interpreted on receipt as advice or suggestions. Nobody should be blind to the dangers in assuming that terminological judgments of this sort faithfully reflect the 'effects of the verbal action', yet such findings reinforce what one suspects about the everyday use of (even the native) language—that small but influential (and often largely situational) forms of interference are at work all the time. If so, then these are dimensions of situation relevant to all types of language teaching.

The need for closer specification of situational problems has been suggested too by a Leeds School of English postgraduate dissertation on the language of commands and requests used by teachers in a local primary school.[3] This study reveals a form of role-playing characterized in part by an apparently complex yet not random set of teacher-requirements, finding expression in (to some extent) correspondingly patterned formal selections. Similarly, the necessity to allow dimensions of situational relevance to emerge from observed language behaviour as data has been further underlined for the writer by a tentative functional analysis of (so far) two three-year-old children in a natural play situation lasting one hour, recorded and observed unseen by Mrs J. Y. Tough of the Institute of Education, Leeds. After much discussion, the transcribed material received further subsequent annotation in terms which indicated whether these infants were describing or (alternatively) manipulating objects, addressee, or self in the immediately tangible situation or in reported or imagined situations; operating with comparisons of one sort or another, with dependence relations, with relations of compatibility and incompatibility; expressing certainty or uncertainty; anticipating or recalling; clarifying; and all of this (and of course more) addressed to self, another participant or an object. Whether one calls such factors semantic, or educational, or psychological or anything else, they seem nevertheless to have the character of minimal situational themes, each one quite difficult enough to pin down and relate to formal features without seeking more abstract categories. A final example is provided by the persuasive notion held by one investigator in the United States that the school pupil's maturity of mind (and place in society?) is well predicted by the extensiveness of his means for expressing tentativeness. It is absurd to protest that these things cannot be 'objectively' observed and therefore should remain outside linguistics. The study of language *should* be concerned with the grass roots of social linguistic behaviour, forming and perpetuating what Firth called our 'linguistic human nature'.

Subject-matter appropriate to the second language learner can similarly be very much more specialized than one might expect. Here are two accounts of the Mongolian marriage ceremony, which may be compared with each other, or with the reader's experience, in any terms, including linguistic not least, one might wish to choose.

> The marriage ceremony nowadays differs from those of pre-Revolutionary times. It has become simplified ... It is the job of the parents to prepare for the wedding day. They may erect a new yurt in the countryside, and also divide some head of cattle, horses and sheep for the newly married couple. According to our tradition there should be three kinds of men's contest at the ceremony—horse-

racing, wrestling and archery. The parents provide the prizes. The eldest parent will give the couple our ceremonial long blue silk scarf, which is a symbol of happiness and friendship and eternity. Inside the scarf there should be a silver cup full of milk, and the couple drink from the milk wishing their marriage to be just as friendly and nice. Then the elder ones wish them a long and prosperous life.

The second passage:

Recently we have seen a new marriage custom. This is where on the eve of the marriage the local collective prepare for the wedding collectively, with their organization or enterprise. In the capital and provincial centres there is some sort of registry office, where they can be registered and have their party. The people who work with the couple give them presents; mostly they prefer to present them with a radio set or camera or other cultural goods, but sometimes they give them a present in cash, and give the money to the bank and the cheque to the couple for their future life. Then they're given a month's leave to rest in the rest-homes, and this is paid for by the State. This custom has a future.

Restricted subject-matter means restricted language. Lexical restriction, most in evidence in the preceding examples, can be matched by grammatical restriction, as in the following description of the finer points of the Mongolian race-horse.

. . . The head of the horse should be not too big, not too small, just medium-sized. The shape of the nose should be like the nose of the sheep. The legs should be long and narrow, and the hooves well-shaped and round, not broken. The tail should be fairly thin. The head, the top of the shoulder-bone, and the backbone should be in one horizontal line. The chest should be a little bit higher and bigger than the bottom, which should be narrowed. The nostrils have to be broad, to allow the horse to take deep breaths. The teeth should be well arranged, and have sharp ridges along the top. The eyes should be brown, and the ears should be long and have a sharp point, like a deer's ear.

In this passage, one notes the frequent resort to *should*-expressions, the use of not-this-but-that, similarity, 'in order to' and the like. Once the speaker has launched himself upon this topic (an understandably favourite one in Mongolia: 'the man who has no horse is no man'), he will very probably be led sooner or later to exercise himself quite rigorously in certain parts of the grammar; the teacher, in turn, is enabled to further the process, thus initiated, of attaining more acceptable and more diversified means of formal expression for the corresponding situational features.

Each item in a list of favourite 'centres of interest', to a greater or lesser extent, will naturally control formal selection. The adult Mongolian learner of English might draw up some such list as the following: agriculture (especially animal husbandry, land cultivation and dairy farming): national customs; national legends; travel inside and outside the country, including transport by ox, camel and horse; sightseeing; sport, especially national wrestling, horse-racing and archery; Mongolian cooking; theatre, ballet, drama, cinema; at home, including the yurt in the countryside; Mongolian literature and history; research into locally relevant scientific and technological problems; wild life and hunting; clothes, especially the national dress; jobs and hobbies; and so on. What might a *given* group of learners wish to say about such matters? What they do say can be recorded on the spot and selectively analysed in the search for apparently stable form-situation correlations. These may very well be of particular interest wherever English is used extensively not only as a 'window on the world' but also as a means of enabling outsiders to look in.

Learning situations invite the use of a scale of realism: there are 'real' situations outside the classroom, simulated inside the classroom, and 'unreal' inside the classroom, for example. The analysis of related language behaviour is as feasible, and necessary, in the case of the last two as in the first. Moreover, the language of aspects of 'real' situations is not *always* best observed outside the classroom. Much of what would be readily acknowledged as useful in the forms of language is hard to catch even in the largest naturalistic observation net; for example, compared with the labour of brute observation, the lexical information provided even by simple speeded word-list responses to given centres of interest may be very considerable. From another point of view, the classroom is the logical place for eliciting many forms of self-expression, including the learner's expression of his knowledge of and feeling for his own country. Avowedly simulated and 'unreal' classroom situations deserve, but do not get, form-situation analysis. The experienced teacher knows that many classroom situations do not markedly reflect what goes on in the outside world, yet may motivate his classes to produce fairly specific ranges of formal usage in a spontaneous manner. For example, the relatively tight, yet not rigid, control over responses which can be exercised by requiring a class to contribute to a map of the home town on the blackboard, explaining it as it progresses, answering and asking questions, giving directions, and so forth, is well known. Again, the teacher who acts as the shopkeeper (the customers his pupils) presumably knows quite a lot about the formal restrictions he thereby invites. There are many such situations, which can of course be forced in varying degrees in the direction of overtly formal procedures (as when a 'travel agency' setting is made, not entirely unnaturally, to provide intensive practice in if-clauses of various sorts). Games too sometimes possess great powers of restriction on choice of language. Here is a game with almost infallible motivational appeal and some rather specific formal consequences: the class members are each told to choose any one professional job; they are then told that they are all stranded together on a desert island which has room for four only; one by one they have to argue why their particular job makes them indispensable. 'Twenty Questions' too could have been invented as a language-teaching technique. The formal potentialities of pictures, singly and in combination, with or without directions or text, are well understood—in principle. There seems every reason why learners' responses to pictures should be analysed, both in the L1 and L2, under particular forms of control from the teacher as well as more spontaneously.

Procedures which have appreciable power of command over formal selection (more, or less, 'real' situations) may be referred to as *situational teaching units*. Even if one leaves aside their motivational advantages (which, incidentally, can indeed be lost through mishandling or over-use), they can achieve formal ends which cannot—at face value—so readily stem from purely formal procedures. The reason for making this assertion is that they succeed in bringing together in one place formal features which, although normally found in very different parts of the grammarian's description, belong together for certain practical purposes. Skill in handling such formal complexes cannot be assumed to follow automatically from exposure to the separated parts of the language, however logically ordered. Situational teaching not only motivates. It also makes formal sense. This being the case, descriptive linguistics, if it aims to have relevance for language teaching, should include in its purview the analysis of situational classroom procedures.

But formal procedures are by no means less important, if only because it is still in all probability premature to envisage a situationally taught syllabus which succeeds in teaching the various patterns (or rules) of the language in a rational progression, at the same time reinforcing much of the old while introducing a little of the new at each stage. So many of the forms of language do *not* seem to be easily elicited in any particular density through the exclusive use of situational techniques—even when these are shifted somewhat in the direction of formal procedures through the deliberate highlighting of required formal features.

Both situational and formal procedures can be characterized by the degrees of restriction which they place upon formal choice. Here are six formal procedures, scaled from most restrictive to least (or most 'open-ended'). Each is concerned with one or the other of two rather broad areas of English grammar.

In the first procedure, material for which is exemplified in a fragmentary fashion below, one presents (on the blackboard for example) what might for convenience be referred to as a 'multiple pattern', indicating in tabular form some examples of the ranges of choice available at particular places. Italics indicate relatively open lexical choice, while double arrows allow reversal of direction. The learner is enabled to pick his way through the successions of steps, thereby forming acceptable sentences. It is interesting to question, incidentally, to what extent the set of six multiple patterns has taken shape in the first place on (admittedly rather skeletal) situational grounds.

TIME NOW: 3 p.m.

1 RELATIVE TIMES: 4 p.m. ‖ 4 p.m. or before.

I	shall *start reading*	when	he	*goes*
	shall *begin*	as soon as		has *gone*
		the moment		
	←‖→	immediately		
		after		(*goes*)
	←‖→			has *gone*
	shall be *looking* ...	while		(*reads*)
	←‖→			is *reading*
The *sun*	will be *setting*	as	we	*leave Ulan Bator*

TIME NOW: 3 p.m.

2 RELATIVE TIMES: 2 p.m. ‖ 2 p.m. or before.

I	*stopped reading*	when	the *telephone*	*rang*
	looked up	as soon as		had *rung*
		the moment		
	←‖→	immediately		
	←‖→	after		(*rang*)
				had *rung*
	was looking ...	while		was *ringing*
	←‖→			
The *sun*	*was setting*	as	we	*left Ulan Bator*

84 JOHN PRIDE

TIME NOW: 3 p.m.

3 RELATIVE TIMES: before (or up to) 4 p.m. | 4 p.m. |
---|---|---
I | will be *busy/at home* | until | you *return*
 | will *wait here* | |
 | will be *sitting here* | |
 | will be *busy/at home* | when |
 | will have *finished* | by the time |
 | will have been *reading* for *two hours* ←→ | before |
 | will (still) be *sitting here* ←→ | when (by the time?) |

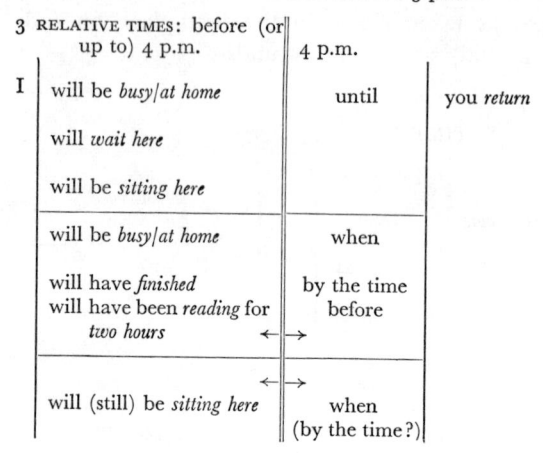

TIME NOW: 3 p.m.

4 RELATIVE TIMES: before (or up to) 2 p.m. | 2 p.m. |
---|---|---
I | was *busy/at home* | until | you *returned*
 | *waited here* | |
 | was *waiting here* | |
 | was *busy/at home* | when |
 | had *finished* | by the time |
 | had been *reading* for *two hours* ←→ | before |
 | was (still) *sitting here* ←→ | when |

In the above, set 1 should be compared with set 2, and 3 with 4. Two others (at least) remain:

  4 p.m. onwards/4 p.m.

('I shall wait for you/be waiting for you from the moment/from the time/from when you leave ...')

2 p.m. onwards/2 p.m.

('I've waited/been waiting ... you left,' etc.)

Whereas the procedure just outlined requires the learner to step from one of a set of *given* possible choices ('shall start reading' or 'shall begin,' for example) to one of the next set in succession, the second (more open) procedure is to allow him to add choices of his own at the relatively open places (italics). He is now involved in lexico-grammatical (and situational) constraints: compatibilities and incompatibilities in lexical company within specified grammatical patterns (also purely lexical constraints, occasionally, no doubt).

Slightly less restricted is the procedure in which examples of a particular pattern are presented to the class, and the item(s) operating at the same specific place in each example of the pattern underlined, thus 'I *expect* he'll be late', 'He *said* he *hoped* you could come', etc. The requirement put before the class is to devise similarly patterned sentences, using in each case the item(s) stipulated by the teacher: 'think', 'believe', etc. This procedure is nearly the most restrictive of several which will exercise the operation of 'complementation verbs' (several hundred in English) in a very large range of contrasting patterns. For example (our fourth procedure) the teacher may report the preceding technique, without however providing acceptable items. Then again, fifth examples of several such patterns might be given, the task then being to place a one-word ('think', 'believe', etc.) into as many of these as possible. In all these procedures, both teacher and class are liable to be faced with problems of grammatical 'sameness' and 'difference' the significance of which—for learning purposes—should be weighed not only with linguistic but also pedagogical discrimination. The sixth and last procedure, which serves as a 'most open-ended' outlet for the three preceding, illustrates the last point more clearly. It is very simple in principle. The class is given the beginning part of a sentence (or rather the same beginning of many acceptable sentences), or perhaps one lexical item only, and required to complete as many *different* sentences as possible.

'Difference', of course, may be grammatical, but may also be lexical, semantic, etc. The teacher has naturally to be clear about what he wants, what he says he wants, and what he gets. The learner is tested for his powers of resourcefulness—which will tend to be grammatical in the main. The writer at one time tested fifty ten-year-old Edinburgh schoolchildren on thirty-five such sentence-beginnings, chosen so as to invite as grammatically wide a range of continuations as possible, over a period of some weeks, allowing ten minutes per item for the writing out of sentences. Twenty-five thousand response tokens resulted; these were scored, and each pupil ranked, for each item, according to how much grammatical variation was displayed. Some individuals (not always those with the highest intelligence scores) displayed an interesting blend of formal *and* situational inventiveness—a finding later substantiated in work with Swedish and Mongolian learners.

Learning is more likely when there is much variation in approach along with a bias towards allowing freedom in response within clearly understood restrictions. Both requirements are facilitated by returning frequently to essentially the same learning problems, now situationally, now formally, and in general allowing greater freedom in response each time, proceeding as it were cyclically, as Bruner puts it, like a spiral staircase. Perhaps there is an overlaid requirement too that the advanced learner should be working largely situationally in any case. Grading might with reason be said to concern not only the sequencing of material to be taught but also the utilization of different techniques for *developing different responses* to given material: one should not be content, that is, merely to teach material. Responses to any effective situational procedure seem worthy of descriptive linguistic analysis. It is also suggested that responses to the more open-ended formal procedures that do exist could also be profitably analysed—in the first place for testing purposes perhaps. To stand any chance of success, however, work of this sort has to be done on the spot, in the classroom, and with clearly specified, probably local, ends in view.

NOTES

1 And semantic, too, for that matter, if one takes a neo-Firthian view of situation: See John Lyons, 'Firth's Theory of Meaning' in *In Memory of J. R. Firth*, Longmans, 1966.
2 See J. B. Carroll, *Foreign Language in Primary Education*, U.N.E.S.C.O. Institute for Education, Hamburg, 1963, Ch. XX.
3 By Miss E. Rudd, 1965.

6
Linguistics and the Teaching of Literature

ALEX RODGER

> 'There's glory for you!' 'I don't know what you mean by "glory",' said Alice. 'I meant, "there's a nice knock-down argument for you!"' 'But "glory" doesn't mean "a nice knock-down argument",' Alice objected. 'When *I* use a word,' Humpty Dumpty said in a rather scornful tone, 'it means just what I choose it to mean,—neither more nor less.'
> LEWIS CARROLL, *Through the Looking-Glass*, Chapter 6

What is the use of linguistics in the literature class? Will it help to improve the reading habits and comprehension of our students, and if so, how? Can a concern with such matters as phonology and syntax really help assist in refining the sensitivity of their responses to poetry and sharpening their powers of interpretation? Will it not, rather, threaten or even destroy immediacy of contact between the student and the text? And will the use of linguistic techniques improve our own teaching or merely hamper it with technicalities?

My two contributions to this volume try to suggest some of the answers to such questions, by argument and by demonstration respectively. In the circumstances both are bound to be incomplete. Nevertheless both are necessary. Theoretical expositions of the subject are too complex and too abstract to allow more than fragmentary illustration, while most of the linguistic textual analyses hitherto published tend to take interpretation of the text for granted, and so beg a number of crucial and controversial questions. This paper therefore attempts a partial survey of the main issues involved, while the second offers an exemplificatory, if equally partial, analysis of a text.

All the issues raised in my opening paragraph centre on literary meaning, its interpretation, and the aims of the teacher of literature. Now, I assume it as axiomatic that our task is not to hand over pre-digested meanings but to teach our students how to read and interpret for themselves. It is not (or should not be) our business to indoctrinate them with an academically hallmarked and guaranteed set of received opinions on certain authors and their works. When they leave us, they should not be critical parrots who have been taught what to think and feel about a number of pre-valued prescribed books, but reasonably skilled and sensitive readers able to think, feel and judge for themselves, with fidelity to the textual facts, in response to any work of literature they may choose to read. In other words, our primary duty is not so much the teaching of *knowledge about* literature as the imparting of skill in the recognition and comprehension of literary modes of meaning. Extrinsic facts about the lives and opinions of authors, about sources and influences, about genres, conventions, fashions, schools and movements are a secondary matter. Literary history has its value and its uses, but its massive critical and evaluative generalizations are justifiable (or otherwise) only in terms of individual texts, which in their turn can only be truly known through the basic activity of literary study—the reading, and interpretation of the works themselves.

Obviously, the more remote in time the text, the greater the reader's need for a sufficient knowledge of the historical facts, linguistic and cultural, necessary to his full understanding and enjoyment of it. Nevertheless if literary value as such is claimed for the work, that value must be an intrinsic one. A work is neither better nor worse for being 'historical' nor for embodying the ruling ideas of its age. The poorest and most inept works of an epoch often exhibit these as much as, if not more than, the greatest. We may, if we wish, read the imaginative literature of the past for the light it throws on the culture of the past; but if we do, we read not as students of literature but as social or cultural historians, in which case the work itself has for us a merely instrumental, rather than an intrinsic literary value. Again, as literary readers, we may have to reconstruct laboriously some part of an author's social or intellectual background before we can fully understand and enjoy his works for their own sake. We should not, however, make the mistake of valuing the works in direct ratio to the amount of effort it has cost us to master their background of reference and allusion. On the contrary, our scholarly labours are themselves only justifiable in terms of the intrinsic literary value of the works themselves. If we set out to absorb Vico's cyclical theories of history or Swedenborg's symbolic metaphysics in order to construe some of the later works of Yeats, it is because the poems themselves are worth the effort.

All the extrinsic aspects of the study of literature, then, depend upon the precondition of an intelligent and sensitive reading, comprehension, and enjoyment of individual works. As teachers, however, we are concerned not only with the 'private' art of reading, but with more public matters of literary culture in general—with literary *criticism* in the widest sense of the word. This activity has recently been concisely summarized as the attempt '... to define the meaning and value of literary artefacts by relating subjective response to objective text, always pursuing exhaustiveness of explication and unanimity of judgment, but conscious that these goals are unattainable.'[1] Now if some degree of unanimity of judgment can be assumed as a feasible aim of criticism, it follows that the meaning and value it seeks to define are to some extent *public*. They must represent a consensus of verifiable opinion among competent readers about textual *facts* and their implications. The value thus cannot be any purely subjective value. We can and frequently do value artefacts of various kinds for quite subjective and adventitious reasons. The most meretricious of popular songs may acquire subjective value for us because passage of time has made it powerfully evocative of some highly valued phase of our personal past, but few of us would care to assert its musical quality or defend the literary value of its lyric on those grounds. The value the critic seeks to define must therefore have some objective basis that can be agreed upon. Again, the same is true for 'meaning'. If a work 'means' utterly different things to different people, they are unlikely to assign the same value to it.

So if criticism is not simply the assertion of subjective evaluations founded on subjective interpretations of meaning, the critic must have some objective evidence on which to base both. The critical quest is thus one for a meaning which reconciles the greatest number of 'subjective responses' with the greatest possible number of demonstrable textual data; and here 'objective text' must have primacy over 'subjective response'. The latter must work within the limits imposed by the former, which are limits set by or derived from *the normal communicative function of language itself.*

This is a crucial point. The language of literary texts is not a wholly different medium from that used in all other (non-literary) forms of linguistic communication. Unlike the painter or sculptor, the writer takes over a medium already meaningfully structured and systematized. As the most complex and subtle mode of human communication, language already has its own built-in rules, conventions and norms. These the writer may exploit and arrange in unusual ways that extend or even partly transcend the normal communicative resources of the language. But the meaning of his work depends upon the norms of that language, even where it most deviates from or violates them. The facts of objective text are thus *linguistic* facts. Everything else 'in' a work is inference from these. For in life itself, concrete situations are 'given', and we respond to these linguistically, adjusting to, controlling, changing, or even opting out of them by means of language. When we read literature the position is a different one. What is given is language, from which we as readers must infer the implied context of situation, whether the writer directly addresses us in his role as poet, or creates some fictional or dramatic world by means of language from which we infer personages, actions, settings, etc. The psychological and moral impact of a literary work is thus a product of our ability to relate our most highly developed awareness of the workings of language to our knowledge, of, and insight into, those aspects of life relevant to the work. We arrive at a valid interpretation of it only when we have achieved a high degree of reconciliation between the two, i.e. between our sense of worldly or situational probability and the linguistic facts of the text as a whole.

It cannot be sufficiently emphasized that in this relationship the text is primary. What is disturbing about much that passes for critical interpretation or explication, even of the 'close analysis' kind, is its tendency to bend the facts of 'objective text' to fit the vagaries of subjective response, or to base interpretation on too few of the former. Too many critics remind us in these ways of the Humpty-Dumpty of our epigraph. Not all are as haughty or as wilful as he about meaning, but many seem to assume that when the poet uses a word—or indeed any unit of meaning right up to the whole text—it means just what *the critic* chooses it to mean according to his own ingenuity, or erudition, or both. The root of the difficulty here is the nature of our knowledge of language. Our response to any ordinary non-literary utterance in our own tongue may involve all sorts of intuitively-acquired awareness of the structural and social norms of English. Each of us has some such accrued linguistic background that enables him both to recognize and to respond immediately to the familiar features of a new utterance, and to assess and come to terms with the less familiar. We are continually obliged to exercise this faculty of assessing the linguistically 'odd' in terms of the known by such mundane utterances as the headlines in popular daily newspapers. It is one thing, however, to be able to respond to and understand language in this instinctive and comparative manner, and another to be able to account explicitly for our responses in terms of the language itself. Just because the bulk of our language-awareness is *intuitive* rather than *explicit*, we find it difficult to describe the ways in which language has meaning for us.

The same is even truer about our responses to literary texts. From the creative writer's point of view, literature might be said to be the most carefully considered use of language, even when that consideration is not of a fully conscious kind. For the reader, the result might be described as the unusually effective use of language to create unique meanings. But because our responses to most everyday non-literary language are in the nature of attention to the 'message' rather than to the form, we tend to forget too easily that the form of literary language draws attention to itself, and that there may well be nothing there in the nature of a 'message' that is in any sense separable from the precise form of the whole text. In poetry in particular, the poet not only exploits the normal patterns of the language in unusual ways that give them additional and unique meaning within the context of his poem. He also creates new kinds of meaning by deliberate and significant linguistic unorthodoxy, by deviation from or even downright violation of the familiar and predictable patterns. He may further reinforce these new kinds of meaning with other additional patterns contrived from the accidents of language —rhyme, alliteration, assonance, puns, ambiguities and the like. The relations between his rhyme-scheme, metrical pattern and stanzaic arrangement, on the one hand, and his grammatical and lexical patterns on the other add yet another kind of meaning to the whole. What we think of as the meaning of a poem is thus a network of interrelated meanings in sound, rhythm, morphology, syntax, vocabulary, etc., and not a matter of some detachable 'message' or paraphrasable content.

All this is no doubt familiar enough, in one way, to most of us. Critics of the 'practical criticism' or 'close analysis' schools have been telling us for years that there are different kinds of meaning in the language of literature, especially in the language of poetry. We have been taught to seek out 'sense, feeling, tone and intention' as complementary aspects of literary meaning. But these are present in ordinary non-literary utterance as well, as Dr Richards himself points out.[2] And when it comes to relating them to the linguistic facts of any given text, we are still at a disadvantage; for if we cannot offer any explicit account of how and why the patterns of ordinary everyday spoken and written usage affect us as they do, we can hardly expect to be able to explain clearly the impact upon us of the unusually effective organization of that same language. I am not denying the experienced reader's ability to grasp and interpret the meaning of a text intuitively. Indeed it would be surprising if any of us formed our first or even second impressions of a text in any other way, since this is, as we have seen, the way we understand *any* new utterance. So as skilled intuitive readers we may be able to 'follow' the poem and to grasp as a unity the complex of meanings.

But difficulties arise when we have to demonstrate the *validity* of our response to the text. When, as critics or teachers, we attempt to define the meaning and value of the work, not for ourselves alone but for other competent readers, our inability to describe explicitly the linguistic facts of the text puts us in an awkward and even invidious position. We have to assume that the intuitions of others are, *or should be*, identical with our own. In the struggle to equate subjective response with objective text, the latter remains an unknown term to be given value according to the private intuitions of each reader. Our criteria for the establishment of public meaning remain almost entirely subjective and impressionistic. We are reduced to describing our intuitions themselves, rather than the linguistic facts that give rise to them. And since the lay terms in which most of us try to describe our own psychological processes are commonly no more precise and explicit than those we use for the description of the workings of language, we tend to end up describing our subjective impressions, intuitions and emotions in language which is itself largely impressionistic, intuitive and emotive.

My contention, then, is that as long as our grasp of a text's meaning *remains* purely intuitive, just so long does that meaning remain as private to ourselves as the most imperceptive of misconstructions or the most wilful of Humpty-Dumptyisms. As teachers of literature, we must be able to do rather more than assert the superiority of our own intuitions over those of our students, however tactfully. If we are very good at this, we may impress and even convince the naturally gifted student, and some of our intuitive accuracy may rub off on him—though he too will end up in the subjective-impressionistic dilemma. For most, however, our insights will remain a mystery because we can only transmit their content and not our way of arriving at them. The self-doubters will never read with confidence, and the cynics are unlikely ever to read seriously again when they escape our clutches. To meet the exigencies of academic life, both will turn to critical mediators—out of laziness, disillusion or despair—rather than to the texts themselves. We may infect the born intuitionist with our own enthusiasms, but we shall have taught no one how to relate subjective responses to objective text in a way that ensures the greatest degree of unanimity about the meaning of the whole.

The weakness of 'practical criticism' is its inevitable concentration, given the categories of meaning it employs, on *referential* meaning (i.e. sense, the 'things said') and *emotive* meaning (i.e. the affective attitudes both expressed in the language and evoked by it). Since poetry characteristically tends to subordinate the referential to the emotive function, to make statements 'for the sake of their effects upon feelings, not for their own sake',[3] it is perhaps not surprising that we tend to describe poetic effects emotively. Yet these two linguistic functions are far from being the only ones relevant to literary meaning in the fullest sense. They represent, in fact, only two aspects of a single mode of meaning, the *contextual* mode, in that they can be roughly equated with (*a*) the subject of discourse, and (*b*) the feelings the poet wishes to express about that subject together with those he wishes to evoke in his readers, both by his use of expressive-evocative language and by his tone or attitude to them as his addressees.

An exclusive concern with *referential* meaning leads to our treating the language of the text as if it were transparent. We take the dangerous short-cut from bare comprehension of the language to premature evaluation of the work as a 'criticism of life'. This sort of approach afflicts criticism of the novel and the drama more than that of poetry, but is dangerously inappropriate in all critical discussion since it ignores those very aspects of meaning that distinguish a literary text in form and function from non-literary discourse on the same topics. Over-concentration on *emotive* meaning does not completely by-pass the linguistic form of the text, but is over-selective in its criteria of meaning and insufficiently exhaustive in explication. By focusing too narrowly upon the more strikingly effective words and phrases of a text, we risk basing our interpretation on these 'magnetic peculiarities of language'[4] alone, and of greatly exaggerating their contribution to the whole at the expense of other aspects of its meaning.

Much critical discussion is an uneasy fusion of these two ways of dealing with the language of texts. Explication of this kind may well overlook the contribution to total meaning made by less obvious but more pervasive modes of meaning such as phonology, syntax, and the relations between these and the other modes of meaning.

In poetry especially, the extra depths and densities of meaning that arise from the patterning of normal and unusual linguistic features alike may constitute a major part of the poem's total meaning. Failure to grasp these additional modes of meaning, and to take account of them in our interpretation of the whole text, may mislead us into dilution, distortion, misconstruction or even complete incomprehension of its significance. A seeming absence of portentous themes or ideas, for example, does not necessarily make a poem trivial and worthless, any more than radical linguistic unorthodoxy necessarily makes another poem incomprehensible and inexplicable. Conversely, the banal and inept expression of the most potentially profound of notions and sentiments is not a poem at all, any more than the startlingly unusual use of language that proves, on closer inspection, to say little or nothing.

As readers, as critics, and above all as teachers, we need a way of describing linguistic causes rather than psychological effects. The strength of descriptive linguistics as an aid to literary explication is that it is based not on the peculiarities of any given text but on the structural and social norms of usage from which those peculiarities are meaningful divergences. Linguistics is concerned with making explicit and analytical that intuitive background of operational skill in our own tongue that enables us to understand it at all. If many of us are unable to relate subjective response to objective text in any other than subjective terms, it is because our own training in the language disastrously divorced grammar from language as it occurs in normal social usage, and insulated literature from both.

A prescriptive grammar, unrelated to the ascertainable norms of syntax and vocabulary to be found in the wide range of English language-varieties, is irrelevant to the understanding and appreciation of literature. To re-equip ourselves with a descriptive grammar that can account for these norms, as well as for literary exploitation of and divergence from them, is not so formidable a task as it might seem. It is largely a matter of making conscious and systematic what we already know in a pre-conscious and *ad hoc* way. The effort is doubly rewarding; we are not only released from the circular definitions of literary subjectivism, but begin to pay to literary texts the kind and degree of attention that their complex of modes of meaning demands if we are to understand them and enjoy them fully. At the same time, it helps to save our students from the worst misconceptions about literature that can arise from a pre-linguistic attitude to meaning in language of any kind. For meaning, in this sense, is no Platonic abstraction detachable from the precise form of the text, but 'the whole complex of [communicative] functions which a linguistic form may have'.[5] These functions or modes of meaning—phonetic and phonological, morphological, syntactical and lexical—all contribute to the meaning of any utterance as a complete 'locution' in a given context of situation. Descriptive linguistics enables us temporarily to isolate these different aspects of meaning so that the contribution of each, plus its relation to the others, may be assessed.

Here we must be prepared to stop clinging possessively to our intuitive first impressions. Analysis does mean a temporary detachment from immediacy of response to the direct impact of the whole; but then, so does any thorough kind of explication. What we lose in immediacy we gain in depth of insight. We don't have to throw away our first impressions, but we must be prepared to modify them, perhaps radically, in the light of what analysis reveals. Further, we must not mistake analysis itself for interpretation. Some latter-day linguistic analysts remind us less of Humpty-Dumpty than of Alice, whose prim rationalism they push to the point of denying that literary 'glory' exists. If the sin of Literary Humpty-Dumpty is the cooking of impressive but insubstantial *soufflés* with himself as the main ingredient, that of Linguistic Alice is the breaking of literary eggs without the making of sustaining interpretative omelettes. Perhaps the best any of us can do is to offer the humbler dish—scrambled egg. Just how scrambled will depend both on the nature of the text and the sophistication of our students. Explication should be as exhaustive as possible without being exhausting. But an explication based on the linguistic facts of objective text will prove a more satisfying dish than the *omelette surprise* of impressionistic guesswork, and one much more conducive to unanimity of critical judgment.

NOTES

1 David Lodge, *Language of Fiction* (London, 1966), p. 65
2 See I. A. Richards, *Practical Criticism* (1929), pp. 180–8; and D. Thomson, *Reading and Discrimination* (1934), p. 12.
3 I. A. Richards, *op. cit.*, p. 186.
4 See J. McH. Sinclair, 'Taking A Poem to Pieces', in *Essays on Language and Style* (1966), ed. Roger Fowler, p. 68.
5 J. R. Firth, *Papers in Linguistics 1934–1951* (1957; reprinted 1964), p. 33. The whole of this paper, 'The Techniques of Semantics', is relevant to the topic of literary stylistics, as are several other papers in the volume, especially 'Modes of Meaning', pp. 190–215.

7
The Teaching of Reading

JULIAN DAKIN

Section I A Theory of Reading

1 RESULTS OF RESEARCH

In the past, research into reading has concentrated on what seemed most readily measurable. Research which took the child as the centre of attention studied his eye-movements or his ability to recognize words. Research which concentrated on the classroom, rather than on the individual child, sought to establish which teaching methods and materials obtained the best results. Yet despite the considerable volume of research, results are still surprisingly inconclusive. On a large scale no single method of teaching reading has proved more effective than any other. This is the conclusion of both Gray,[1] who conducted a UNESCO survey, and of Russell and Fea,[2] who reviewed the evidence for *The Handbook of Research on Teaching*. Not only is no single method more successful than any other, but all methods fail with a rather alarming proportion of children. Morris found in 1958 that 10 per cent of English primary school children could not read by the age of eight. Of that 10 per cent, only 12½ per cent achieved a reading age of twelve by the time they left secondary school. Even the effort and enthusiasm put into the i.t.a. experiments have not greatly reduced this margin of failure.

2 THE VARIABLES

Failure is, as Morris's[3] results suggest, of two kinds. There are children who do not learn to read at all. And there are those who do learn, but still fail to achieve the normal standards of their age groups, and whose reading in some cases seems to deteriorate rather than improve as they move through and out of the secondary school. There are, of course, teachers, schools, and even whole areas, that obtain very good results. What makes for success and what causes failure? A very long list of variables could be drawn up. In this paper we will consider only three, the children, the teacher and the materials.

Each can be considered independently of the others. All children have their individual abilities and weaknesses; they develop at their own rate and it seems likely that the way in which they learn changes in the course of their development. The teacher has his own weaknesses and abilities too, and he has the more or less permanent problem of having too many children to teach and too little time to teach them in. The materials have their own structure, their own plan of development, and their own weaknesses, which both teacher and children must overcome. But although all three can be discussed independently, they are also united in a three-cornered relationship, a kind of eternal triangle, each side of which constitutes a different dimension of method:

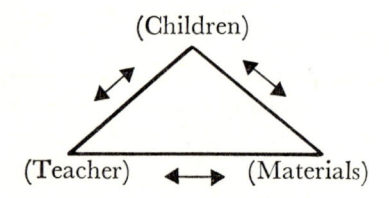

(Children)

(Teacher) ←→ (Materials)

Fig. 1. An eternal triangle?

The brackets round *Teacher*, *Children* and *Materials* are reminders that each has its own identity and its own kind and rate of development. The two-way arrows suggest the different kinds of relationship that are set up in the classroom. The teacher has his own methods of teaching the materials and his own methods towards the children. The children evolve their own methods of learning in response both to the teacher and to the materials. Finally the materials were written by authors who have particular kinds of teacher and particular kinds of children in mind. In this sense they embody their own methods too. The arrows impose both a direction in the way in which learning will take place, and limitations on what will be learnt. Success or failure depends on what is learnt, not on what the teacher and the materials set out to teach. The job of the teacher and the materials is to promote in the children successful techniques of learning.

3 THE CHILDREN

Success in reading partly depends on home background and I.Q. Failure to read does not seem to correlate with any single factor, but rather with a cumulation of handicaps such as poor vision, poor hearing or left-handedness. These factors are of course outside the teacher's control. What he can control is the pace and method of instruction to suit the children he has to teach. It is worth remembering that each child is an individual and that he has to learn for himself. Research, in the past, has concentrated on four important respects in which children differ from each other:

1 *Reading readiness.* Some children start reading much younger than others. Russell and Fea report that preparatory training in the nursery school generally promotes reading readiness.
2 *Pace of learning.*
3 *Strategy of learning.* Russell and Fea and many other authors suggest that different children learn in different ways.
4 *Eye-movements.* When a child, or an adult, is reading:
    (a) His eyes move along the page in a series of jerks, with a momentary fixation between each move. Reading takes place during the fixations.
    (b) The exact point fixated may be on any part of a word or in the spaces between words.
    (c) The eyes often move back (regress) along a line as well as forwards.
    (d) The number and length of fixations and regressions depend on the individual and on the nature of the reading material.
    (e) There is now good evidence that, as a child grows older, the number and length of his fixations and regressions is reduced. This reduction matches a corresponding rise in comprehension rate.

(*f*) Although there are erratic patterns of eye-movements which characterize poor readers, Vernon[4] found that good readers do not all seem to read in the same way.

What these four points suggest is that any method of teaching must be flexible enough to cater for different rates of progress, and diversified enough to allow for individual differences in children's techniques of learning.

4 QUESTIONS AND ANSWERS

Eye-movements are, of course, the only direct indication of what is going on when a child is reading. They suggest several interesting questions:

1. Do the eyes fixate at linguistically random intervals along the line, or do they fixate on or before certain kinds of words?
2. What causes regressions?
3. What goes on while the eyes are fixating?

Curiously enough, there are no established answers to these questions. Indeed much research has concentrated simply on counting and timing fixations and regressions, without posing any questions about the psychological processes that must relate to eye-movements. The emphasis on measurability in the work on eye-movements and on word-recognition has obscured our lack of understanding about what it is a child is doing when he is reading connected prose. After all, he cannot simply be moving his eyes along the page. He must in some way be processing the symbols that he sees. If we want to improve our teaching techniques, it seems at least hopeful to try first to improve our understanding of how the child processes written language. This is merely a way of saying that if we want to teach reading, we must first develop our notions of what reading is.

5 ENDS AND MEANS

Although we are here primarily interested in how a child learns to read, it seems simplest to approach the problem from the end rather than from the beginning. In other words, if we could describe what an adult is doing when he is reading, we would then have a clearer idea of the behaviour towards which the child is being guided. We should also be able to gain a closer understanding of the child's reading processes by comparing them to those of adults, and in particular by examining the kinds of mistakes that children make. The child's reading must, of course, also be related to his general linguistic and cognitive development. Only when this double comparison has been made, will we be able to see what kinds of problems reading poses for the child. Even a brief examination of adult reading would suggest that the child has to master not a single skill but a process involving complex interactions between at least three different kinds of skill: recognition, structuring and interpretation.

6 RECOGNITION

There is certainly some sense in which we recognize words and letter patterns on the page, but not in any simple way. It is quite easy to demonstrate, for instance, that adults do not read letter by letter. Words which are deliberately misspelt, such as

'paaaage'
'sincc'

can be flashed on a screen and will be read as 'passage' and 'since'.

It is also easy to demonstrate that adults do not always read word by word. Words like 'the' and 'and' can be repeated on a page without the reader noticing or even being able to discover the the mistake immediately when asked to do so. (If you read the last sentence again, you will notice that the word *the* has been slipped in twice—at the end of one line and the beginning of the next).

Adults and children also show tendencies, when reading aloud, to re-order or modify the words in a sentence. For instance, 'So off went Chicken Licken' might be read as 'So off Chicken Licken went'.

All this suggests that the processes involved in mature reading are only remotely governed by *recognition* of letters and words on the page. Of course we can devote our whole attention to recognition, as when we are looking for a particular word or letter in the dictionary. Many children pass through a stage during which they appear to be recognizing only individual words. They read each word of a sentence as if it stood in isolation and may not be attaching any meaning to what they read.

7 STRUCTURING

Recognition of words or letters does not then seem to be the only skill involved in reading. The words in a sentence have to be grouped together and seen as having a grammatical structure. Direct evidence of the process of *structuring* can be found in the way children read aloud. At a certain stage they do not pronounce each word in isolation, but as part of a phrase, or of a whole sentence. They select a particular intonation pattern at the beginning of the sentence and follow it through to the end. But they can only do this successfully if they are anticipating what is coming next, if they are predicting from the first few words of the sentence what kind of sentence it is going to be. Sometimes these predictions are wrong and a child will make a false grouping of words or find he has chosen the wrong intonation. He may then rather unhappily change his intonation half-way through but more often than not he will quickly read the whole sentence again with a different intonation. If the child is indeed structuring what he reads and predicting what will happen next this would explain why he does not need to read letter by letter or word by word. He is anticipating what is coming next and the actual words on the page are snatched at only as evidence to confirm predictions and to create new ones. We can now venture to explain why 'So off went Chicken Licken' was consistently read by one child as 'So off Chicken Licken went'. The child was structuring the sentence rightly as a stylistic re-ordering of 'So Chicken Licken went off' but he had forgotten or ignored exactly which type of re-ordering he was dealing with.

We can now take another look at eye-fixations. As can be seen in Fig. 2 below:

1 Except at the beginning of sentences, the fixations do not often fall on grammatical words like 'of', 'the', 'at', 'him', 'and', etc. Almost invariably they fall on content words, e.g. 'gorgeously', 'recently', 'assassin', etc.
2 Of the two regressions in the passage, one falls on a grammatically ambiguous phrase: 'Although there . . .'.

The gorgeously costumed imperial plenipotentiary suffered excruciating anguish at the recollection of his personal thoughtlessness and carelessness. There lay before him the recently appointed ambassador but now ruthlessly murdered by an hireling assassin. Although there undoubtedly existed several indications of his personal innocence, what people of intelligence would hesitate to proclaim the startling circumstantial evidence preponderously conclusive.

Fig. 2.[5] Fixation points of the eyes whilst reading. Early measurements by Professor W. F. Dearborne (reproduced with his very kind permission). The dots show sharp fixation points; the arrows indicate by their length and direction possible small movements of the eyes whilst fixated. Modern measurements show that such tremors are in fact negligibly small.

It is as if the skilled reader were looking primarily for lexical information with which to confirm his predictions of structure and to promote new predictions. Where his predictions go wrong he is forced to regress and have a second look at grammatical items. These are very uncertain hypotheses, but they are at least hypotheses. Any theory of reading must at some point attempt to tackle the confusing and conflicting evidence of eye-movements.

8 INTERPRETATION

We can read a page silently, without understanding what we are reading. If we are reading aloud we can make the material sound perfectly meaningful to a listener, although we may not be paying any attention to its meaning. This suggests that in addition to the processes of recognition and structuring, there is a third process of *interpretation*, which may or may not be operative at the same time as the other two. The relations between the three skills are very complex. There are several reasons why we might suppose structuring to be prior to interpretation:

1. We cannot interpret sentences which we cannot structure, e.g. 'This is the rat the cat the dog the cow tossed chased killed'; 'and where George had had had had had had had'.
2. The converse is not true. We can structure sentences we cannot interpret, e.g. 'The mome raths outgrabe'.
3. We could not interpret ambiguous sentences like: 'She didn't like his playing cards' or 'The detective looked hard' if we had not structured them one way or the other first.

9 CONTEXT

On the other hand, if structuring is always a necessary preliminary to interpretation, we might expect that we would, on purely structural grounds, produce two analyses and two interpretations for ambiguous sentences like the ones quoted above. If we do, we appear to be totally unaware of it. We have to think quite hard before we become aware of ambiguities, even when we are told to look for them and the sentences are out of context. When we are reading such sentences in context: 'She didn't like his drinking so much and his playing cards', we are so unlikely to notice the ambiguity that it seems at least reasonable to suppose our interpretation of previous bits of text is influencing our perception of structure. It seems that we make predictions about both structure and interpretation, and just as our predictions of structure influence what we recognize on the page, so our predictions of interpretation influence how we structure it.

10 THE NEED FOR A THEORY OF READING

We have studied a tentative theory of reading for two reasons:

1. Before we can study how children learn to read we must be able to *describe* what they have to learn to do;
2. We must also be able to *explain* how they do what we can observe them doing.

The theory outlined above leaves open the question of how to describe the different kinds of skill. It suggests merely that each might best be described in its own terms, and without any necessary preconceptions that the analysis of the reading skills will be done in exactly the same way as the analysis of spoken skills. Any interesting descriptions of these skills will need to be tested both by experiment with human beings and in experiments with machines designed to simulate human behaviour. There are already programmes written which simulate the recognition of handwriting. The Edinburgh English Language Research Project[6] is developing a programme designed to simulate the structuring of written material. No programme yet exists, however, which can simulate interpretation, or the complex inter-relationships between the three skills.

11 THE EYE-VOICE SPAN

The eye-voice span is one further example of the complexity of behaviour that has to be accounted for. When a skilled reader is reading aloud, his eyes are fixing on words anything up to half a line ahead of where his voice has got to. At the same time as silently reading ahead of what he is reading aloud, he is also listening to himself and occasionally making corrections of what he said half a line or more back. No explanation of how he manages all this at once will be attempted here.

Section II *Theories of Learning*

1 THEORIES OF LEARNING

So far we have discussed only a theory of reading. We have not tackled the related question of how children learn to read. In a sense this is a subsidiary question, and a general theory of reading should provide a viewpoint from which we can look at accounts of the learning process. Very surprisingly there are few published descriptions of how or what children learn. There are plenty of descriptions of what the teacher did and what materials were presented to the children but little about what mistakes the children made and how these can be explained, or of what generalizations and learning strategies the children seemed to be developing. There are only the bleak indications of before-and-after test scores. Since, on a large scale, no single approach has ever produced better results than any other, the different theories of learning can only be assessed in the light of what little we do know about how children read.

2 THE METAMORPHOSIS THEORY AND THE EVOLUTIONARY APPROACH

There are two extreme views of how children learn to read, both of which can be reduced to arguments about psychological priorities among the different levels of skill. At one end of the scale, the child is regarded as an organism rather like a tadpole or a caterpillar. He is considered to pass through quite different stages in his progress towards reading, each of which must be mastered before the next can be approached. This approach can flippantly be called the metamorphosis theory. Thus Fries[7] considers that the child must first learn to recognize and distinguish between the letters of the alphabet as purely visual symbols, with no declared relationship to language. Next he must master the rules of single syllable spelling patterns. Only when he knows all the basic spelling patterns of the language, is he ready to venture into reading whole sentences. Some phonic theories would substitute for Fries's visual discrimination stage, a process involving not only recognizing the different letters but sounding them as well. At the other end of the scale is what might equally lightly be called the evolutionary approach. The child is considered not as a tadpole, but as some eo-form of primate, with very much the same equipment as an adult human, but in a primitive state of development. The teacher's job is to help him evolve towards adult behaviour, in essentially a straight line. Thus even the earliest reading material presented is in the form of sentences, but sentences within the child's experience. The notion of reading as a form of language (i.e. communication) is there from the beginning, and the child's ability to read is to keep pace with his developing control over language.

3 LINGUISTIC AND SITUATIONAL GRADING

One further major distinction in approach must be noted. In any reading course some items are presented before others. The items presented together may resemble each other *linguistically* (i.e. they may contain similar arrangements of letters or structures) or they may be related to each other by *situation* (i.e. they contain sets of words or sentences which are used in the same situation). While linguistic grading usually goes with the metamorphosis theory, and situational grading with the evolutionary approach, this is not always the case. There are mixtures, or inter-breedings, of all four approaches. The Gayway books, for example, very cleverly conceal their phonic material in stories, while Lefevre[8] starts from whole sentences, like a good evolutionist, but has each sentence resemble the next in grammatical structure, without any necessary relationship to the child's experience or any linking story line.

4 PROS AND CONS

Each of the approaches outlined above makes certain assumptions about how a child learns to read. The strict metamorphosis theory assumes that the first skill to be learnt is that of recognition, which is regarded variously as logically or psychologically prior to the skills of structuring and interpretation. The strict evolutionary theory regards interpretation as being psychologically co-extensive with structuring and recognition. (These assumptions are discussed in more detail below.)

The theory behind *linguistic grading* seems to be that:

1 The child already knows how to use and interpret language in its spoken form.
2 He therefore needs only to learn the formal devices by which speech is represented on the page.
3 These can most readily be learnt when the child's attention is specifically drawn to the formal properties of written language, its letter shapes, spelling patterns and structural cues.
4 The formal properties of written language should further be presented in a graduated way, moving from smaller to larger, since the child's learning strategy is essentially synthetic. He proceeds from the parts to the whole.

The theory behind *situational grading*, on the other hand, seems to be that:

1 Written language is not just recorded speech. As Vygotsky[9] has pointed out, writing is a different kind of language with different structure and different functions.

2 The child cannot, therefore, be expected to transfer his existing habits of structuring and interpretation from speech to writing. He has to learn new habits at all levels.
3 In his speech the child is more aware of meaning than of form.
4 The most effective bridge between speech and writing must, therefore, lie in meaning and in displaying the relationships between the two kinds of language and familiar situations.
5 From understanding pieces of written language, the child can then be led to forming generalizations about the structure of written language. His learning strategy is essentially analytic, from the whole to its parts.

5 EXPLANATION AND DESCRIPTION

There are two different kinds of argument going on here. On the one hand there is an argument about *explanation*. Can we explain the child's development better if we consider him as being more like a caterpillar or more like a lower primate? On the other hand there is an argument about *description*, the argument between the linguistic grading approach and the situational grading approach. Since these two approaches give diametrically opposed descriptions of what the child does, it should be possible to devise experiments which would discriminate between them. We are now, at least, in a position to consider different methods of teaching reading and to decide, firstly, to which skills they award priority, and secondly, what descriptive or explanatory arguments they use to justify the priority they have awarded to particular skills.

6 THE ALPHABETIC METHOD

The last serious proponent of this approach was Bloomfield.[10] The child was to be taught to name the different letters of the alphabet and then to read individual words.

/siː ei tiː/ = /kat/
/diː ou dʒiː/ = /dog/   etc.

The grading of words might be linguistic (i.e. lists of words all starting with the same letter) or loosely situational (i.e. familiar words chosen independently of initial letter). Bloomfield himself wanted to combine the naming of letters with phonic grading. The interesting thing about the alphabetic method is that it worked—many people were taught to read in this way. Since it seems absurd to suggest that naming letters helps us to read words (in any literal sense), it must be that learning was taking place independently of the method. This suggests a very necessary caution in assessing the results of other methods. It may be that the child's strategy of learning is totally or partially independent of the methods by which he is being taught. We cannot therefore attribute the children's success to the method of instruction unless it achieves results that other methods do not achieve and that are consistent with the theory of learning that underlies it. The converse is not necessarily true. If a method leads to failure, we cannot blame the children. It is the method that has failed to promote, or has perhaps actively inhibited, learning strategies that would otherwise have led to success.

7 FIRST PRINCIPLE

We are now in a position to state a first principle. A method is not necessarily right if it succeeds, but it is certainly wrong if it fails.

This principle needs several qualifications:

1 It may not be the method (i.e. the materials) that are failing but the teacher. Other teachers might be able to use the same materials more successfully. The role of the teacher is discussed more fully below. But already we have an interesting question. Is there any ideal set of materials that is teacher-proof, or should different kinds of materials be designed to fit the capabilities of different kinds of teachers?

2 The failures a method produces may only be temporary, i.e. they are predictable stages on the road to ultimate success. This argument is seldom used formally, but it suggests an interesting question. Is there a natural acquisition process for reading similar to the process that has been suggested for the child's acquisition of spoken language? Are the materials designed to follow this process? If they are, they should predict the mistakes a child will make at different stages.

3 The failures a method produces may be explained in a more general sense. The method is only suited to certain kinds of children, and others will learn badly by it or not at all. This is quite a reasonable argument in that it suggests different children learn in different ways. It is none the less dishonest unless the method predicts in advance which children will learn from it and which will not. It is of no use to the teacher to be told that only those children will learn from a method who do in fact learn from it.

8 THE PHONIC METHOD

The notion behind this approach is that the letters of the alphabet —in isolation and in certain combinations—can be sounded in regular ways. The basic unit is the grapheme, a term which corresponds very closely to the phoneme in speech. Syllables consist of graphemes and have a three-place structure.

Initial grapheme	*Medial grapheme*	*Final grapheme*
c +	a +	t
d +	o +	g
th +	a +	n
c +	a +	tch[11]

The child is taught the sound values of different letters. He may be explicitly taught to sound the letters:

$$/K/ + /a/ + /t/ \quad /Kat/$$

or he may be expected to induce the sound values from selected examples, and to generalize these values to new words:

```
cat   car   come   etc.
fat   far   etc.
mat   etc.
```

Stott[12] follows the inductive approach. The children are first taught to recognize the initial letters of words, then initial consonant and vowel combinations, then final letters and final combinations.

9 ARGUMENTS ABOUT PHONICS

The proponents of a strict phonic approach (as outlined above) argue that:

1. It is possible to describe English spelling on phonic lines. While this is true, it is quite irrelevant. We can also describe English spelling on quite different lines. (Fries's description is discussed below). The question is whether teaching phonics is the best way of teaching reading. Russell and Fea quote opinions that strict phonic work is too difficult for some young children.
2. We read phonically in any case, by constructing wholes out of parts. If we take this to mean we read letter by letter or grapheme by grapheme, this is simply not true. Adults and children can certainly be made to read this way, but they can also recognize whole words and whole sentences. In any case it is difficult to see how a child gets from what is in terms of phonics a three syllable word /kə-a-tə/ to the single syllable 'cat'.
3. Only by the acquisition of some kind of *phonic sense* will a child be able to work out the pronunciation of words he has not met before. This is true but it does not follow from this either that we need to pronounce what we read or that the acquisition of this phonic sense must precede all other skills.

We can see that the arguments for an initial phonic approach rest entirely on the merits of the metamorphosis theory and of linguistic grading. While the prior teaching of phonics does not exclude the subsequent teaching of other skills, the phonic theory in itself does not suggest any ways in which these skills could be taught. It makes heavy demands on the child's powers of abstraction, and risks purely mechanical reading at the syllable level only. It is a common experience that many children do read mechanically, without attention to meaning, and that it is very difficult to cure them of this fault. We must not blame *them*, but the method by which they were taught, which initially hid from them any notion that what they were reading was meaningful language. At its worst, the phonic method can only be said to teach children how to pronounce written language, not how to interpret it.

10 THE WHOLE-WORD METHOD

The whole-word method starts from the observation that we do not read letter by letter, and deduces from this that we must therefore read word by word. What we recognize is either word shapes, or spelling patterns. The advocates of word-shape note that some children have no difficulty in recognizing 'aeroplane' and 'cat', while often confusing 'was' and 'saw' or 'it' and 'is'. Children must therefore be taught to recognize each word as a whole with its distinctive characteristics of length, height and depth, and sequence of letters. Fries and Bloomfield take up the spelling pattern as the perceptual unit. They argue that there are a finite number of spelling patterns of which most of the words in the language are composed. Written words do not consist of a linear sequence of letters, in the same way that spoken words consist of a temporal sequence of phonemes. There are distinctive arrangements of letters that correspond to the phonemes. Thus the two final letters of 'all', and the arrangement of consonant and vowel letters in 'late', indicate particular phonemic vowel qualities. Fries emphasizes not only the consistent correspondence between spelling patterns and pronunciation, but also the consistent contrasts between spelling patterns. He draws up long lists of words which contrast with each other in only one respect:

man	mane	mean
dan	dane	dean
can	cane	
etc.		

He wants the child to study these lists and to learn the patterns by contrasting them with each other. He does not seem concerned that most of the words in his lists will be unknown to the child. On the contrary he makes the most interesting claim that any child who can talk can learn to read by use of these lists within a year.

Fries's spelling pattern approach is obviously based on linguistic grading. The word-shape approach more often leads to situational grading, and a child is taught to recognize familiar words which do not necessarily resemble each other in shape or spelling. Neither approach can meet any of the objections that were raised in the discussion of phonics.

11 THE WHOLE-SENTENCE METHOD

The whole-sentence method is based on two arguments:

1 Sentences are not just an accumulation of words but a structuring of elements. Thus 'John saw Mary' does not mean the same as 'Mary saw John' although the words in each sentence are identical. Nor is the structuring a simple matter of sequence. In the two sentences:

> 'John is eager to please'
> 'John is easy to please'

the sequence of noun-verb-adjective, etc. is the same, but in the first sentence John did the pleasing, while in the second somebody else did.

2 Language is a process of communication. We do not communicate in isolated words or sounds, but in sentences. Since the child can already understand spoken sentences, the object of teaching him to read is to get him to search for the meaning in written sentences.

Nobody would dispute either of these arguments, but neither in itself proves the value of the whole-sentence approach from the beginning. The real question is how can we help the child to make the jump from speech to reading. Lefevre concentrates on the first argument and suggests that the jump can most easily be made at the level of structuring. In writing there are not the same direct indications of structuring that rhythm and intonation give to speech. The child should therefore hear sentences being read aloud and have his attention drawn to the way in which the words on the page are structured. Moreover this must be done in a systematic way, if the connection is to be easily made. Lefevre therefore proposes that the child should be taught to read lists of sentences that resemble each other structurally. He wants to give the children a conscious knowledge of structural patterns, i.e. a knowledge of grammar through which they can describe the structure of sentences. Lefevre is thus merely taking a different starting point from that of the phonic approach. His arguments still rest on the merits of linguistic grading.

Most whole-sentence advocates, however, follow the other line of argument, and advocate situational grading. They argue that the child has little conscious awareness of sound or structure, but is interested in describing his experiences, and can readily grasp that writing is just another method of communicating. Lamoreaux and Lee[13] get the child to dictate to the teacher orally. The children then practise reading the sentences they have composed, and whose meaning is already known to them.

The whole-sentence method does not of course exclude the subsequent use of phonics or word recognition. It merely argues that the child's early generalizations about sound and structure are unconscious, and that his prime motivation for making such generalizations is awareness of similarities and differences of meaning. The chief argument against this approach is that some children are very slow to make such generalizations on their own, and are reduced to a virtual standstill by their inability to handle words they have not met before, or to remember words which the teacher thinks he has taught.

12 THE CLASS READER

The materials we have discussed so far have all been designed to teach reading in a certain way. Before we attempt any general conclusions about them, it might be useful to study another kind of material widely used by teachers: the class reader.

There are a large number of reading courses on the market. Most have accompanying pre-reading and supplementary materials which allow the teacher to teach phonics or word and sentence recognition. The reading books are graded in the sense that only a certain number of new vocabulary items are presented in each book, and each item is frequently repeated. The grading may incline either towards phonics or towards situations. They are also graded structurally, although in a far less conscious way. Early books tend to consist of sentences either in the imperative mood, or in the simple present tense. The children are supposed to work through the books at their own pace, with the teacher or a group leader listening to their reading as often as possible. Some children go through the books very quickly. Others get stuck early on in the series and have to be given alternative material. What is the function of these reading books? We might define the function of a book as either:

1 To give us pleasure. The interest of the material should create a desire to go on reading.

2 To give information. Here the material does not have to create an interest in us. We may be assumed to be reading it precisely because we are already interested in the subject.

There are many books for children which can serve either or both functions. In the later stages most reading courses develop in these directions and include interesting story material, or useful information. But it is a sad characteristic of most of these courses that in the early stages, when the children are still grappling with the elementary problems of recognition, structuring and interpretation, neither function is fulfilled. The material is dull and conveys virtually no information except through pictures. The children who like the books like them because the pictures are good, or because they can see that they are getting on fast in comparison with other children in the class. The children who are not getting on so fast are hindered because:

1 As Vernon and Inglis[14] pointed out, many of the vocabulary items are unknown. This is not so true of a series like the *Key Words Scheme*[15] which has based its vocabulary on studies of primary school children's spoken vocabulary.
2 The structures may also be unknown or unnecessarily artificial. The simple present is often used where either the present continuous or the past tense should be used, and we can find such oddities as: '... a big train pulls out of the station. They look as it is going by'; 'I, Meg the Hen, live in the little tin house'; 'See the boat'.

Since the structural grading in these courses is more or less unconscious, there is no guarantee that the structures in the books correspond in any way to the child's control of structure in his speech. Such studies as the Nuffield Child Language Surveys in Edinburgh and Leeds may eventually provide a sounder basis on which to base structural grading.
3 The situations may also be unfamiliar, or of no concern, to the child. Various writers have commented on the extent to which these materials assume acquaintance with farm life, exotic animals, expensive toys, and the intimate details of middle-class home life. Once more, the Nuffield Child Language Surveys in Edinburgh and Leeds[16] may provide useful information about children's interests.

In short, unless the children have been very carefully prepared for each stage in the reading course, the materials can act more as *tests* of reading ability than as practice material. In particular, it is up to the teacher to prevent the children from developing purely mechanical habits which the dullness and repetitiveness of the text would otherwise serve to promote.

Section III Conclusions and Inconclusions

1 CONCLUSIONS

The discussion of the various approaches to the teaching of reading reveals that each approach is:

1. Fairly explicit about what the child *ought* to do (and what the teacher ought to do).
2. Highly inexplicit about what the child actually does do. In particular there is no explanation of *how* the child makes the generalizations which each approach assumes he will make.
3. Quite unable to meet any of the requirements of the principle discussed in Section II:7.

Both Gray and Russell and Fea presume, from the inconclusiveness of research evidence, that the teacher would be well advised to adopt a mixture of all methods. While this may be honest advice, it does not explain why mixtures of methods are more successful than their individual ingredients, nor why in principle they should be more successful. We still need detailed studies of what actually happens when individual children are faced with different kinds of materials.

2 THE TEACHER

Morris concluded that the cause of most failures lies with the teacher. Schools which have the same kinds of children and use the same materials get widely different results. Morris draws up an interesting scale against which to assess teaching, and shows that in nearly every case where the results are bad, the teaching is also bad. Her conclusions place a heavy responsibility on the trainers of teachers. But they do not suggest an answer to the question we raised earlier. Should all teachers be trained to do the same things as well as they can, or should they be encouraged to do different things according to their abilities? What things should they be trained to do, and what materials should they use? We are moving round in a circle rather than drawing interesting conclusions from the triangle of variables. Research and theory in the past have concentrated on looking at the child from the angle of the materials and the teacher. But the child is precisely the variable we know least about. How does he approach the teacher and the materials? How does he learn?

NOTES

1 L. S. Gray, *The Teaching of Reading and Writing*, UNESCO Monograph on Fundamental Education X, 1956.
2 N. L. Gage, ed., *Handbook of Research on Teaching*, Rand, McNally and Co., 1963. (N.B. All the references in the text of this paper are to articles by D. H. Russell and H. F. Fea.)
3 J. Morris, *Reading in the Primary School*, National Federation for Educational Research, 1959.
4 M. D. Vernon, *The Experimental Study of Reading*, Cambridge University Press, 1931.
5 Fig. 2 is taken from C. Cherry, *On Human Communication*, M.I.T. and John Wiley, N.Y., p. 287.
6 J. P. Thorne, H. M. Dewar, H. Whitefield and P. Bratley, 'A Model for the Perception of Syntactic Structure', *Proceedings of Journée Electronique*, University of Toulouse, 1966; and J. Dakin and P. Bratley, 'A Limited Dictionary for Syntactic Analysis', in *Machine Intelligence Workshop 2*, Oliver and Boyd, 1967.
7 C. C. Fries, *Linguistics and Reading*, Holt, Rinehart and Winston, 1963.
8 C. A. Lefevre, *Linguistics and the Teaching of Reading*, McGraw-Hill, 1962.
9 L. S. Vygotsky, *Thought and Language*, M.I.T., 1962.
10 L. Bloomfield and C. L. Barnhart, *Let's Read: A Linguistic Approach*, Detroit, 1961.
11 The written symbols 'th' and 'tch', though they consist of

two and three letters respectively, represent single sounds and are accordingly treated as single graphemes by this approach. But see A. McIntosh and M. A. K. Halliday, *Patterns of Language*, Longmans, 1966, pp. 98 ff.

12 D. H. Stott, *Programmed Reading Kit*, Holmes, 1964.
13 Lamoreaux and Lee, *Learning to Read through Experience*, Appleton-Century Crofts, 1953.
14 P. E. Vernon and W. B. Inglis in *Studies in Reading*, Vol. I, Scottish Council for Research in Education, University of London Press, 1948.
15 J. McNally and W. Murray, *Key Words to Literacy*, Schoolmaster Publishing Co., 1962.
16 R. J. Handscombe, *The First Thousand Clauses*, Nuffield Foreign Languages Teaching Materials Project, Occasional Paper 11.

ACKNOWLEDGMENTS

I would like to thank Miss Margaret Donaldson, Department of Psychology, Edinburgh, Miss J. Reid, Department of Education, Edinburgh, Mrs Ruth Clark, Nuffield Child Language Project, Edinburgh, and, of course, the editors of this book, for very valuable criticisms of an earlier version of this paper. I would also like to acknowledge my debt to Mr David Bradley, British Council, India, whose experiments with school children in Gorbals Primary School, Glasgow, helped to clarify the theory of reading proposed in this paper.

8

The Teaching of Writing

HUGH FRASER

Every child has language as his birthright. That is to say, every normal child acquires in the course of time the spoken language of the society into which he has been born. There are one or two points we can make about the nature of this process.

1. While parents and others may assist the child by teaching him names for things, correcting his pronunciation, expanding his utterances into more fully grammatical forms, etc., the learning situation becomes increasingly active and informal. The child early on starts to generalize from his language experience and with a fair measure of success predicts and produces structures he has not been taught.
2. By the time the average child has reached the age of five he has acquired a considerable vocabulary—5,000 to 6,000 words is a common estimate—and a fairly extensive command of the grammar of his language. He is still making occasional mistakes, and some of the more complex structures are still beyond his control, but if one is to judge by results, i.e. his degree of success in understanding others and in making himself understood, he has already come a long way.
3. There are strong arguments for the proposition that we can account for what happens only by accepting that children have a predisposition to language learning that in all normal circumstances will lead them inevitably to acquire the language of their environment.

We might briefly, then, describe the average child's acquisition of the spoken language as active, informal, effective and inevitable.

What has been said so far refers only to the spoken language—the language of *sound*. Spoken language soon becomes an integral part of the child's behaviour, an increasingly spontaneous activity which only occasionally requires a conscious attention and calculation in its interpretation or production. In a natural, if not entirely effortless way, the child acquires the ability to interpret and produce the sort of sound patterns that enable him to communicate with other members of his society.

Sooner or later, however, the child born into a literate society has to learn to cope with the written language, which is language in an entirely different guise, and here the child finds himself in a situation of a much more demanding kind. He now has to master language in a new and puzzling form, as patterns not of sounds but of *shapes* which are individually designed and collectively organized into larger units. Their design and the manner of their organization are matters of conventional agreement, and vary from society to society. They may be black shapes on white paper, or chalk marks on a blackboard, or indeed any appropriate shapes on a contrasting background; but however they are produced, the relation between these patterns of shapes and language as the child knows it is a purely conventional one. (It is also true, of course, but not strictly relevant here, that the sounds and patterns of sounds of any spoken language themselves stand in conventional relationships to 'reality'.) There is no *a priori* reason therefore why in our society the marks *cat* in that order should have any meaning for the child. Nor, initially, can we expect the sequence *mother* to have significance for even the most affectionate of children. These and other sequences will have meaning for the child only when he has been taught something of the conventions with which our society has chosen to operate. The meaning the marks have is not a *necessary* meaning, but an *agreed* one, a conventional one, and until the child has been made privy to our agreements, the written language has no meaning for him.

Again, just as spoken language has a sequence in time, written language has direction in space. In our language community it is conventional to begin at the left and work horizontally across to the right. In Arabic writing the direction is from right to left. (In

1929 the Turks changed from Arabic to Roman script and so reversed the direction of their writing.) The tradition in China has been to employ for their ideograms a *vertical* sequence that begins on the right, though they are now being encouraged to simplify their ideograms and work towards an alphabet. Boustrophedon writing, writing that goes alternately from right to left and left to right, was a feature of some ancient languages.

The point here is that even the direction in which we string together our conventionally agreed symbols is itself a matter of convention that may vary from one culture to another.

In its earliest stage learning to write involves the mastering of relatively low-level skills; learning to hold the pencil or crayon effectively, and imitating carefully the model letters, words and sentences presented by the teacher. This stage is completed successfully by the normal child. It is when children have to pass from the imitative to the creative aspect of writing that the real troubles begin. Here they are being faced with a task that demands an integration of much more complex skills. They have not only to think out clearly what they intend to write—and this is difficult enough for many of them—but, in addition, to organize these thoughts on paper, to manipulate language in what is a comparatively unfamiliar form, and—the crucial test—to do this in such a way as to make themselves understood by the reader.

This is the most difficult achievement that we demand of children. The whole business of translating from 'inner speech' to writing is one of extreme complexity, and it is not surprising that so many of our pupils experience difficulties, in some cases temporary, in others permanent.

At this point we might have a closer look at the differences between the spoken and the written language. These can be considered under four main headings.

I PRODUCTION

Here the differences are most obvious. Speech is produced by the vocal organs and apprehended by the sense of hearing. Writing results from a physical act of a different kind and is apprehended (Braille excepted) by the sense of sight.

2 ACQUISITION

Whereas speech, as has been said, is acquired more or less inevitably by the average learner merely through exposure in a normal human environment, the ability to write seems to depend to a much greater extent upon formal instruction. The majority of the world's population, while proficient enough in speech, cannot write, simply because they have not been taught. (Motivation, too, is a factor to be considered. In many societies situations in which writing is essential for purposes of communication do not exist, and incentive to learn is therefore weak.)

We might say briefly that in the nature of things speech is acquired; writing has to be taught.

3 FUNCTIONING

In speaking we are able to convey meaning not only by the words we choose and the way in which they are organized, but also by intonation. We are further assisted by being able to resort to physical movements like pointing, shrugging our shoulders, and indeed a whole range of facial or bodily gesture. The listener in fact derives meaning not only from the language we use but also from the physical behaviour that accompanies it. (Irony, for instance, may be betrayed not by the language or even the intonation, but by the look on the speaker's face.)

Moreover, because of the presence of our addressee we are able to get valuable feedback that enables us to modify our language as we go along. A look of puzzlement warns us of the necessity to rephrase what we have just said, a look of disbelief may cause us to emphasize a point or present other evidence that will help to confirm our assertion. We can chop and change, in short, as often as is necessary to ensure that we are being understood.

In writing we are at a comparative disadvantage. We cannot convey meaning by intonation or gesture, and we are deprived of the feedback that would give us a second chance to make ourselves clear. Removed as we are from our reader in space (and, often, time) we have none of the advantages that derive from being in a shared situation. While some compensation is afforded by the availability of devices of punctuation, italicizing, underlining, etc., it remains true that in writing we have to try to make ourselves understood with fewer aids at our disposal.

4 STRUCTURE

Language has meaning, but not all meaning is conveyed through language. As we have seen, in a normal speech situation (here we must exclude radio talks, taping and any other situation where the speaker and listener are not visible to one another) we are able to supply or reinforce meaning by various forms of non-language behaviour. The language therefore does not have to bear the full load.

Secondly, in all but rather formal speech situations we are liable to interrupt ourselves or be interrupted, abandon sentences in mid-stream as a new thought or a more effective structuring occurs to us, search openly for the word we want—'The—er—you know what I mean—the—mm—it was on the tip of my tongue a moment ago . . .'—and so on.

Speech, therefore, *need* not be, and frequently *cannot* be, as fully organized, as grammatically 'regular', as the written language generally is.

Conversely, since in writing we are subject to neither interruption nor feedback, and since the reader's only evidence for our meaning will be in the silent language on the paper, we have both the opportunity to present our language in a more carefully considered fashion, and, more importantly, the need to do so if we are not to throw an unfair, perhaps impossible, burden of interpretation upon the reader.

Special cases apart, then, the written language will be more deliberately structured than speech, and will conform more closely to what we might think of as the grammatical rules of the language. It is also likely to display a greater complexity of structure and sophistication of vocabulary than would normally be appropriate in a speech situation.

Since we are largely dealing with unobservables, any account of what is taking place when we write will be of a strictly unscientific kind. With this reservation in mind it could be said that when preparing to write something that is in any sense original we seem to begin with relatively vague, not fully verbalized notions of what we intend to put on paper. In endeavouring to give a complete linguistic shape to our thoughts we engage in an inner debate in which we draw upon our language resources, selecting and rejecting, arranging and rearranging, testing and judging both words and groupings of words until we are satisfied that we have arrived at the language that will best convey our meaning or intention to the reader. And, of course, when we go over what we have actually written we may be dissatisfied for one reason or another, and make various alterations designed to improve what we have produced.

What seems beyond doubt is that the language resource referred to varies from one individual to another. To explain why this should be so we might perhaps think in terms of two basic factors:

(*a*) our individual *aptitudes* for language learning, and
(*b*) our individual backgrounds of language *experience* (or *opportunities* for learning).

It seems reasonable to assume that no two individuals have precisely the same aptitude for language (or other) learning; and certainly no two individuals can be said to have backgrounds of language experience that offered them identical opportunities for learning. The resource, then, that any one person can bring to a language situation is unique, and will depend on the aptitude he began with and the opportunities for learning he has had.

As teachers we are particularly concerned with the fact that many of our pupils have resources which, even allowing for maturational factors, we can only describe as markedly limited. It may be that these pupils are deficient in aptitude, that they lack that ability to make the most of their language experience that characterizes our brightest children, or that they have come from environments that have not provided them with adequate language experience, i.e. where the language they have encountered and on which they have modelled their own has been of an unduly restricted kind. (In most such cases it would be true to say that they are deficient in both aptitude *and* experience.) But whatever the reasons, many of our children are at a disadvantage because of the poverty of their language resources, and maturational processes alone do not appear to resolve their difficulties. Where writing is concerned, therefore, they are effectively handicapped before they even put pen to paper.

There is probably some ambiguity about this term 'language resource'. For present purposes it is to be interpreted as meaning:

(*a*) resource in terms of vocabulary;
(*b*) resource in terms of the ability to organize language units into (a variety of) acceptable grammatical structures.

(We can simplify subsequent discussion by referring to these as vocabulary resource and organizational resource respectively.)

There is a third 'resource', which, though not so strictly a language one, is linked with these—and that is the ability to choose with some sensitivity the particular words, phrases or sentence forms most apt in a given situation. It should be noted however that this resource presumes the existence of the other two, and cannot function without them: in other words, we cannot choose unless our language resources are extensive enough to offer us the opportunity of choice.

In the past we have perhaps tended to concentrate on extending children's vocabulary resources, but there are good grounds for supposing that deficiencies in organizational resource are *at least* as responsible for their difficulties with language. In writing, especially, the inability to produce 'well-formed' sentences, and to subordinate and co-ordinate freely and effectively, is a crippling one which no amount of vocabulary teaching *per se* will overcome, and represents a far more fundamental problem for both learner and teacher.

In addition to these basic problems of language resource, we have to take account of the observable fact that many learners have difficulties in those areas of language convention that apply specifically to the written language, i.e. spelling and punctuation. At one end of the scale the errors may not be so serious or so numerous as to make interpretation too difficult for the reader:

> Unfortuneatly the afternoon was very wet and Tom could not go to the picnic he soon forgot his disapointment

> when a nock came to the door it was uncle Fred he was a small plump man very funy to look at ...
>
> (Boy A, 12 yrs., I.Q. 102)

In the bottom streams of a Comprehensive (or Secondary Modern) school, however, examples like the following are not unusual.

> Last sumer in cevlinog parc I so a alsation dog was wander adowt parc. After a we will is ran by me. I sat suday wot is was they tod me. That it was ruing adowt the parc for tow weset. They tod me that it eat rats. And exdud trid to cast her dut node did when they trid to cash her grow and smapt.
>
> Wum day they was a complad the dog. Utill the rangers can dut they were not sup. Utill they calld the plest they sjerst to pot dow a pet of met with a durg in the mit then they put it dow. The dog eat the met and fate it went uncoscious. And they tock the dog away and they adow the pust. And they pust were tanc to hormes. And the alsatian was tran for pelles dog.
>
> (Girl B, 14 Yrs, I.Q. 73)

The spelling in this second example is fairly typical of that often found in the work of backward children.[1] If the essay is atypical it is because the girl shows some awareness, however imperfect, of the notion of punctuation. Lastly:

> My favourite television programme is Bewitched one day she went to see her new house and her mother just waved her hand and there was trees and flowers all over the garden then they went into the house and she wobeld her nose and it was all furnished but she had married a human and she promised that she would not use her witchcraft again and she would by all her furniture and plant all the plants by seeds.
>
> (Boy C, 12 yrs, I.Q. 90)

In these few representative samples one is struck immediately by the errors in spelling and punctuation—the overt evidence of a failure to master the conventions of the written language. But in a very real sense our greatest concern in such work is *not* with these obvious and visible errors; we are concerned not so much with what the child has done badly, but with what he seems unable to do at all. Even after we tidy up such texts by correcting the spelling and tinkering about with the punctuation we are left with material that suggests a general poverty of language resource, and is most marked by a repetitiousness of sentence structures. The inability to spell and punctuate with reasonable accuracy is something we have to deal with, certainly, but is not the most serious of such children's problems. Their troubles go much deeper.

What seems to emerge from a study of these (and a very large number of similar texts) is that there are certain clearly definable deficiencies in the written work of many of our children.

(*a*) There is a general lack of resource which is most obvious where the organization of their language is concerned. Subordination is largely absent, and co-ordination tends to be clumsy or repetitive, or both.

(*b*) This inadequacy of resource is usually accompanied by poor spelling and faulty punctuation.

Questions that naturally arise at this point are—How extensive is the problem? How many children are involved? Can we say that the problem is confined to those in schools or classes of a particular kind—say, Secondary Modern schools, or classes of a low level of attainment in Comprehensive schools? The answer is that all the evidence shows that the problem is much more widespread. Examining bodies, employers, Colleges of Education, even Universities (who are getting our *best* pupils) complain regularly that many of those coming to them from Senior Secondary schools are unable to write with clarity, let alone a pleasing style. It is conceivable that these people are setting unrealistic standards, but it seems much more probable that where writing is concerned there is a considerable degree of underachievement even on the part of many of our brightest children.

Within school itself we have children who fail in Science and Maths and History and other subjects, *not* because of the difficulties inherent in the subjects themselves, but because they seem unable to meet the language demands the subjects make upon them. The most charitably inclined teacher of, say, Science, has often the greatest difficulty in deciding from a pupil's written work whether or not he has grasped a concept or fully understood an experiment. How for instance does one mark the following answers? (The questions are from a Third Year Test Paper, and there are 2 marks at stake in each.)

1. Describe the energy transformations involved when you bounce a rubber ball on the ground.

   Answer A. It goes from kinetic energy to Potential as it bounces up again. And then changes to potential and so on.

   Answer B. Chemical of the body—kinetic to throw the ball down then gravitational to bring it to earth then kinetic to push it up again.

2. (A diagram shows an aerofoil section, i.e. a cut-across view of an aeroplane's wing.) Explain how the wing gets its lift.

   Answer A. The wing get its lift because by Bernoullis' effect it says Fast Flow Pressure law. When the air goes over the top of the wing it has to go faster in order to keep the same speed ∴ causing low pressure above the wing.

   Answer B. The top of the wing there is a slow moving air. At the bottom the air is moving fast. Bernoulli states that if there is a fast flow the pressure will be low. Therefore the Pressure under the wing is least and air pressure pushes the wing up.

Teachers in other subjects face similar problems. They often find it quite impossible to decide whether the pupil *knows*—in some sense or other—what he is trying to say, and wonder if they are unfairly penalizing him for the inadequacy of his English rather than his ignorance of their own special subjects.

It is often said that *all* teachers are teachers of English, and there is some truth in this, but there can be little doubt that the fundamental responsibility for teaching the English language remains in the English classroom. Other teachers have their parts to play in introducing pupils both to the technical terms involved in their subjects and to such specialized forms of language as may be appropriate in each field, but it is surely the English teacher's responsibility to see that his pupils have a basic competence in language on which his colleagues can build for their own requirements.

In deciding on a method of approach to our problem we must be clear about two things. Firstly, there is no evidence to show that hallowed procedures like analysis and parsing, which have so long been a feature of grammar teaching, in any way assist the learner to *produce* better English. The results of a number of research studies conducted over the past seventy years suggest that those children who are not trained in analytic procedures do at least as well in their productive work as those who are.

Secondly, it should not be assumed that the fault lay in the grammar(s) used, and that therefore all we have to do is to replace the old grammar with one that is more modern or scientific. It is one thing to provide a more consistent and comprehensive description of the language, which is what modern grammarians are trying do do—it is another thing to provide a description which makes easy sense to the sort of children we have in mind and which has as its aim an improvement in productive resource, not analytic power. It is this latter type of description that the situation seems to demand.

Such a description, bearing in mind the needs and the limitations of the learner, will of necessity be both simple and selective, and will concentrate on those areas where the learner is weakest, i.e. on the organization of language into an adequate variety of sentence structures. It will be intended, in short, as a valid but comprehensible description of the commonest and most useful sentence types in English, one which will assist the child to master these for his own purposes.

A description of this kind is sketched briefly in the following pages, together with some indication of the teaching method with which it has been integrated. Both the description and the method were evolved *in a classroom* to meet the needs of Secondary school children of limited attainment.

It became clear that the children concerned benefited from this approach, and as a result there were requests from other teachers for classroom material of this kind which they might use. Material was therefore prepared in booklet form late in 1964, and with the assistance of certain Colleges of Education and Education Authorities was duplicated on a large scale for trial in different parts of the country.

Although the material was designed in the first instance as a remedial programme for children in Scottish Junior Secondary schools (in the age range 11–15 years and with I.Qs ranging from 70 to around 100), its use has been extended to other types of pupil. Comprehensive schools and Senior Secondary schools with classes of a low level of attainment have been using the materials, and Primary school teachers have also been employing it, many of them having argued that there was no need to wait for a remedial situation to develop before giving children the systematic training involved.

Many of them argue further that where writing is concerned we have remedial problems on our hands within the Primary school itself, and that the logical solution is to tackle the problem there. If this is accepted, it raises two questions, i.e. where in the Primary school should we start? And should the whole class work through the scheme, or should we exclude those whose writing suggests that they will progress satisfactorily without such training? Although most of the Primary schools which have been using the material have concentrated on Primary VI and VII and have brought even the bright pupil within the scope of the scheme with apparent success, it will be some time yet before any reasonably definitive answers can emerge.

One thing which has become clear is that the children enjoy the work involved, and develop a greater confidence and pleasure in their writing. To quote from a report (Ball, 1966) on Primary children who had worked through part of the scheme:

> If any firm conclusion can be drawn at this stage it is that, apart from their work with those sentence patterns which already formed, in a limited way, part of their spoken or written English habits, the children gained considerable

confidence in their ability to write stories interestingly. That this maturing ease of written style should be detectable in the free written work of the top group is perhaps not remarkable. One would expect such development month by month as they grow up. What is, I think, significant is that similar assurance was becoming apparent in the writing of those groups within the class of very average or even less than average natural ability in written English. We found children turning to story writing in periods of free choice of activity who had previously preferred almost any other form of self-expression. What they wrote was not miraculously good, but it was sensible and fairly fluent and sometimes surprisingly imaginative. The good was very good and displayed qualities of maturity which seemed to derive at least in part from the work with sentence patterns. An interesting indication at this level was that children in the two top groups became unexpectedly self-critical of monotony in their writing and seemed able to do something about it.[2]

It is not possible to give here more than a quite inadequate outline of the material referred to; the interested reader will find fuller information in the published version,[3] the contents of which are very briefly discussed below.

In the first section the pupil is presented with a list of simple sentences consisting of a subject and a verb (with or without a direct object).

Examples   The car stopped.
John scored a goal.
The window was open.

He is shown that such sentences consist in some basic way of a subject and one verb, and agrees readily to the proposal to call sentences of this kind S1 sentences (S for subject and 1 for one verb). This shorthand is most valuable for purposes of classroom communication, and is indeed the basis for all subsequent description.

The pupil then transcribes the sentences supplied, and is

encouraged to complete each sentence with a substantial full stop. If in fact he completes this simple task without error or omission he gets full marks—possibly for the first time in his school career.

In the oral work that follows, pupils are asked to supply sentences which conform to the S1 pattern, and when the teacher is satisfied each pupil goes on to set down in his workbook a number of S1 sentences of his own creation. Here again there is every opportunity for scoring highly, and this principle of making success readily attainable is adhered to throughout. At no stage is the pupil asked to attempt anything unfairly difficult.

Briefly, then, what we are doing in the first section is getting the children used to two things:

1 The idea of using symbols to describe particular types of sentence pattern.
2 The habit of stopping at the end of a sentence.

(There is an insistence on the latter point *not* for reasons of pedantry or fussiness but because, as every teacher knows, unless the child can develop the notion of the sentence as the unit of writing he will not progress.)

Marking can be done swiftly, and, since scores will be high, will itself constitute an important motivation. The child accepts as fair and proper that he should be penalized for mistranscriptions and for omitting full stops, and the teacher will find that because the pupil realizes he has the chance to score highly he will be particularly careful. He should not normally be penalized for misspelling a word of his own choosing; it is important that he should feel free to try a word he is not quite sure of.

In the second section we are concerned with adjuncts (adverbs, adverbial phrases and prepositional phrases) and their use in S1 sentences.

Examples The lion roared *angrily*.
Uncle Bill visits us *now and again*.
I saw them *in the distance*.

The sequence is, as before, transcription, oral work, then the composing of suitable sentences. (A considerable list of common adjuncts is supplied.) The child experiments with adjuncts at different places in the structure of the sentence and uses his own 'ear' (with almost unfailing success) to determine where a given adjunct is usually most happily placed. S1 sentences containing more than one adjunct are also introduced in this section.

Examples   Columbus sailed *to America in 1492*.
             Next winter they are going *to Switzerland for a fortnight*.

Section 3 concerns itself with the subordinate adverbial clause, which the pupil learns to refer to as a C clause and uses in conjunction with the S1 sentence to produce S1C sentence patterns.

Examples   S1   They left the beach.
             S1C They left the beach when it started to rain.
             S1   George caught up on him.
             S1C George caught up on him before they reached the tape.

A list of the thirty-six commonest Subordinating Conjunctions (i.e. C-words) is supplied.

After the usual practice in handling this form the pupil is led to see that S1C pattern sentences can almost always be changed into CS1 patterns without significant change in meaning, and he goes on to practise the conversions, as well as composing CS1 sentences of his own.

The Adjectival clause is introduced in section 4 and is for obvious reasons labelled the W clause. We deal first with SW1 pattern sentences.

Examples   S1   The guide was very experienced.
             SW1 The guide who was leading them was very experienced.
             S1   The sailor gave a loud cry.
             SW1 The sailor who was first to see land gave a loud cry.

Subsequently the pupil has practice with the S1W pattern.

Examples   S1W They managed to get a room which overlooked the beach.
             S1W I know a man who owns a yacht.

The only Relative pronouns (Who-words) studied in this section are 'who', 'which' and 'that'. Others are dealt with in a later section.

In section 5 the pupil practises the use of sentences of the S2 pattern (subject and two verbs), and in section 6 has practice in the handling of the present participle, which is naturally enough labelled as 'Ing'.

Examples   Ing S1   Seeing their mother, they ran up to her.
              Ing S1   Snatching the purse, the thief ran off.

Section 7 deals with the linking of sentences, a theme which is treated more extensively in a later section, and section 8 deals with simple examples of the Noun clause (N).

Examples   S1N   We promised that we would be there.
              S1N   Billy Bunter grumbled that there wasn't enough cake.

Section 9 provides a graded introduction to Direct Speech which is based on the work done by children in the previous section on the Noun clause.

The rest of the book, which extends to 15 sections in all, considers in greater detail some of the resources of language organization that have already been treated. The W clause, the N clause, and sentence linking are all taken a stage further, and there are sections which show how easily quite complex sentence structures can be produced using only the simple elements with which the child is now thoroughly familiar.

What the material is doing, really, is giving the child an understanding and a control of the basic features of English sentence structure. We use terms like W clause and C clause because they facilitate communication, but in fact the child is getting a grounding not in a new and interesting and comprehensible way of talking *about* language, but in the *use* of language, and in particular he is gaining through guided practice that mastery of the organizational resources of the language which he so badly needs.

A brief word or two now about motivation before we go on. Despite the attitude adopted by some modern theorists, there seems no reason to believe that we have to search far for ways of encouraging children to write. They don't have to be excited, or anxious to give expression to their 'deeply felt emotions'. They are in fact willing enough to write, or indeed to do anything else we ask of them, *provided they have a reasonable chance of success in what they are doing*. It is children who *know* (whatever the teacher says) that they don't write well—or sing well, for that matter—who are apt to give us only a grudging and limited performance when asked; and we can't really blame them, for we behave the same way ourselves. It is this *consciousness* of inadequacy, not the absence of motivation, contrived or otherwise, that is at the root of their reluctance to do more than a minimum. The answer is to concentrate with these children not on increasing their motivation (though this is always desirable) but on increasing their resource, and hence their confidence.

As was said earlier, aptitude varies, and we must accept that there will be pupils who, even with the most favourable opportunities for learning, will be unable to master some of the more complex structures of language. Because of this, the material has been so arranged that even if such children reach their limits about half-way through the book they will nevertheless have covered the basic and indispensable elements of sentence structure, and will, in all but extreme cases, have achieved at least some new resource and confidence in their writing. We talk sometimes of the 'slow' learner, but this is an oversimplification: in most cases children of this kind not only learn more slowly than others but are incapable in the long run of learning as much. So although maturation is a factor that must be taken into account, we ought not to talk as if it and motivation were the only factors.

While the material is designed to assist the child to develop organizational resource, there has also been an attempt to grade the vocabulary content, and as the child works through from the earliest stages, where both structure and vocabulary are at their simplest, he is gradually led on to language which is more sophisticated in terms of both.

As far as punctuation and spelling are concerned, marked improvements are reported by teachers who have been using the material. The improvement in punctuation (which is merely the surface indication that the child has developed the notion of 'sentence') is not surprising, because of the attention devoted to it, especially in the early stages; improvement in spelling is perhaps less to be expected, but is nevertheless a feature, and seems to be accounted for by the fact that the work involves a fair amount of transcription, so that the child is consistently given the opportunity of seeing and writing words in their correct forms.

Two final points. The material is not intended to be used in a narrow prescriptive way: the child must not be given the impression that he may use in his written work only those resources which are detailed in the book. As was said earlier, the description employed is both simple and selective, and sets out to represent in a clear and understandable way only the most useful sentence structures of English. Children who are capable of adding to these in their writing should be given every encouragement to do so.

And, lastly, the scheme does not pretend to cover all that is involved in the teaching of writing. It is concerned only with assisting children to acquire those basic resources they will need whatever the purpose of their writing may be.

NOTES

1 If we make some adjustments in essay B we have: Last summer in Kelvingrove park I saw a Alsatian dog was wander about (the) park. After a wee while it ran by me. I asked somebody what it was they told me. That it was running about the park for two weeks. They told me that it ate rats. And everybody tried to catch her but nobody did when they tried to catch her (she) growled and snapped.

One day there was a complaint (about) the dog. Until (=when, *or* and so) the rangers came there were now pups. Until they called the police they suggested to put down a piece of meat with a drug in the middle then they put it down. The dog ate the meat and after(wards) it went unconscious. And they took the dog away and they adopted the pups. And the pups were taken to homes. And the Alsatian was trained for (a) police dog.

Two points that might be made are: (*a*) the story was sketched orally by the teacher, and the word 'unconscious' supplied. (*b*) With one odd exception, on every occasion where the letter 'b' was indicated the girl has written a 'd'.

2 The excerpt is from an interim report on an experimental use of the material: Jessie C. Ball, *Sentence Patterns and Primary IV*, Moray House College of Education, Edinburgh.

3 Hugh Fraser; *Control and Create* (Introductory Book), Longmans, 1967.

9
The Teaching of Meaning

S. PIT CORDER

If you were to walk into a room full of English-speaking people, just stand there and utter the sounds /wud/ and nothing more, the people, if they heard you, would probably stop talking, look up and prepare to listen, evidently expecting you to say or do something else. If you didn't, they would be rather puzzled and some might uncharitably begin to wonder whether you were feeling all right. For your hearers, what you had said would have been meaningless.

Now imagine that you were to walk into a room full of foreigners who knew no English, go up to an object, examine it carefully, scratch it with your finger nail and utter the sounds /wud/?, they would probably accept your behaviour as reasonable, since it is the sort of behaviour they are familiar with. It would have been accepted as meaningful, although, of course, they would not have known what the meaning of your utterance was.

Now let us suppose you were to walk into a room full of English-speakers and perform the same actions. They would not be particularly surprised, and would probably respond by saying something like: 'Yes, that's right', or 'Oh, is it?' or 'No, it isn't'. Not only would they have accepted your behaviour as meaningful, they would also have been able to interpret its meaning, they would have understood your remark, they would have known what you meant.

We can now set about interpreting these three episodes. In the first, your behaviour was regarded as meaningless because your listeners were unable to perceive any relationship between your utterance (a word in their language), what you did, or what they were doing, or any thing, person or event in the situation. Your utterance was an isolated act, it was 'out of context'. In the second episode, on the other hand, your listeners were able to perceive a relationship between your act of examining and scratching an object and your uttering of a 'word' or 'sentence'. There was a relationship between them which they recognized as in some way familiar. The act was in this sense meaningful. But, of course, what they did not know was the convention of the relationship between the utterance and the features of the situation. They did not know what the meaning of your utterance was, because they did not know the 'rules' or conventions of the language. In the third episode, not only did your English-speaking audience recognize your behaviour as meaningful, they also knew what the meaning of your utterance was because they knew the conventions of the relationship between your utterance and the features of the situation. They knew the meaning-rules of the language.

Meaning has to do with relationships, not any random, *ad hoc* relationships, but conventional relationships, or rule-governed relationships. That is, meaning is systematic; it is a matter of systems of relationships. Our ability to understand meaning involves a knowedge of the conventions of these relationships. These are both things we have to learn. Relationships exist for us only when we see them; we only understand their meaning when we recognize their systematic nature.

To realize that an utterance is meaningful is not the same therefore as knowing what its meaning is.

Now let us consider these episodes again. Was your utterance predictable in any episode? In the first case, what you did, or subsequently failed to do, was so unpredictable that it amazed your listeners. In the second and third cases your action was certainly not easily predictable but it was, equally certainly, not wholly improbable, since your listeners showed no surprise. It was an action of the sort that your listeners accepted in the circumstances as possible or even as reasonable.

Whether something has meaning or not has to do with its predictability. It is not by chance that people often say of 'conventional' polite phrases like 'thank you', 'after you', or 'don't mention it' and so on, that they have little or no meaning. Think of the case of being introduced to someone for the first time. What choice of language does one conventionally have in these circumstances? Actually, none at all. Conventionally there is only one thing you can say if you are a speaker of Standard English, and that is /haudjudu:/; this is a situation in which we have no choice. We are forced by society to behave in a wholly predictable fashion. You could, of course, maintain that you might refrain from speaking, but this would be regarded as highly unconventional, and when discussing language we have to do with what is conventional. Difficult cases make bad law.

Now, since our language behaviour in that situation is wholly predictable, it tells our listeners nothing new, nothing that they did not know already. It communicates nothing to them; it is without meaning or significance. It is not difficult to think of other situations of this sort in which we utter language forms which are wholly predictable in the circumstances. When the bride says 'I will' she has no choice. And it tells us nothing. After all, if she has allowed herself to get as far as the altar she can scarcely say 'I won't!' It would be more than unconventional!

We can enunciate a principle: if any utterance or part of an utterance is wholly predictable in a certain situation, then that utterance has no meaning. The corollary is that the less predictable an utterance or part of an utterance is in a certain situation, the more meaning it has. Put more precisely, the amount of meaning a bit of language has is a function of the number of alternatives possible (available to the speaker) in that situation. The conclusion of the argument is that if an utterance is wholly unpredictable it might mean anything or everything and is therefore useless for communication. This was the case in our first episode. We are still talking about being meaningful or having meaning; we are not yet talking about what meaning an utterance has.

Let us now relate the notion of amount of meaning to the case of a child learning his mother-tongue. It is a matter of common observation that when a child is beginning to acquire the use of a word, he frequently misapplies it, that is, he is liable to use it in situations which are, to an adult at least, inappropriate. They are, of course, not inappropriate to the child. This can only mean that the child's conventions of language use at that moment in his development are not those of the adult. It does *not* mean that the child does not have any conventions, that his behaviour is unsystematic.

Consider the common case of a child who, having heard the word 'doggie' in a certain situation, applies it to all small four-footed animals: dogs, cats, rabbits, etc. We might be tempted to say that the child was making the word 'mean too much'. In terms of the adult's language system it would be more exact to say that the word 'meant too little'. The child has, apparently, no choice available in the circumstances. It is doggie or nothing. Now, from the point of view of the teacher it is immaterial how much meaning a term may have in a child's language. The child must become an adult, and use adult language. For the teacher, the child's doggie has too little meaning. It is the teacher's job to give it more meaning. He does this, quite obviously, by increasing the number of alternatives available to the child in 'small animal' situations.

There is something else we can learn from this example. When someone uses a term or a bit of language,* the amount of meaning it has for him may not be the same as it has for his hearer. This is something we tend to overlook. The amount of meaning a bit of language has can never be assumed to be the same for both hearer and listener, since the number of alternatives available to each one, i.e. the choice, in the circumstances, is likely to be different. Amongst adults of similar education and background this may be a matter of little importance as far as communication is concerned, since similar education and background imply a similar range of alternatives. But when dealing with children it is something we need constantly to bear in mind. They have fewer alternatives all round than the adult. Teaching children language involves providing them with more alternatives for every situa-

* I am deliberately using expressions like: term, bit of language, item of language, throughout this article because I wish to avoid using the expression 'word'. To do this might give the impression that the only meaningful part of language was the lexical item.

tion, giving them more choices. Put another way, it means making all their language mean more.

If a child's development, experience and knowledge could simply be arrested while he went on learning more of his language, then he would develop an enviable degree of meaningfulness of language use. But such a notion is, of course, absurd. A child's knowledge and experience are growing all the time, so is his knowledge of language. The child's attempt to make his language mean more is constantly being frustrated by his increasing knowledge of the world and understanding of it. He is always meeting new situations. We never seem to be able to give him enough alternatives. Indeed our own teaching contributes to this state of affairs, because it is we, the teachers, who are busy creating the demand for more alternatives. We are both creating the demand and attempting to satisfy it simultaneously.

I have been speaking so far about the notion of *having meaning* or *significance*, and of the notion of *amount of meaning*. I have not yet dealt with the problem of what meaning a bit of language has. The expressions 'in the circumstances' or 'in a certain situation' have been used frequently and it is evident that an item of language only has meaning when it occurs in a context of some sort. We saw this from the episodes with which we began this article. This context may be a situational context; that is, the situation in which it occurs: the people, things and events of the outside world which are present and are relevant for accounting for that bit of language. Relevant here means recognized by speaker and hearer alike as entering into a complex of relationships with each other and with the language used. When we were talking about the expression /haudjuduː/ we described the situation in which that bit of language was predictable as one in which a person was being introduced to another for the first time. That was its situational context. We saw that it had no meaning in that situational context because it was wholly predictable. In another situational context, of course, that same item might well be meaningful. But if we take a leave-taking situational context instead, the choice available to a speaker of standard English is wider. He may say: 'good-bye', 'so long', 'be seeing you' 'till next week', etc. By virtue of the choice available, none of these items is wholly predictable in that situation and each therefore has more meaning in the context.

The items just listed all stand in a relationship of substitutability to each other in the same context, but as we have seen they also bear a relation to the situation itself. It is a combination of the relations they bear to each other and the relations they bear to the situation itself that differentiates them, that determines what meaning they have.

Now it is a naïve but widespread belief that meaning in language is simply a question of a one-to-one relationship between an item of language—usually thought of as a word—and an observable entity or quality of the objective world. For this relationship to hold it is necessary to assume that the meaning of a language item is a permanent inherent unchanging feature of that item. Now we do not need to deny that such relationships may exist and can be demonstrated on occasions. A relationship of this sort is a *referential* relationship. But obviously such a relationship can be shown to exist only for a part of any language since there must be large numbers of language items for which no referent exists in the objective world. It is certainly true of most grammatical items within language. What is the objective referent of gender, number, tense, person, subject, object, etc.?

Since this is so obviously the case, some people have argued that where there is no objective feature in the world for an item to refer to, then such bits of language must refer to an idea or a concept which the speaker and hearer share in common. Unfortunately this is not a useful notion, for two reasons. Firstly, because, even if it were true, it could not be proved; the principal evidence we have that anyone possesses a concept is that they can talk about it! We know that a concept exists because we have a word for it. The proof is therefore circular and we cannot thereby get any further in our discussion of meaning. Secondly, even if it were provable that some bits of language refer to ideas or concepts, it would surely also be true of those items which can be shown to have reference to observables as well. Presumably we have a concept *apple* as well as a concept *love*. To say that *love* refers only to a concept whilst *apple* refers both to a concept and to an object in the outside world does not help us in any way to talk about the meaning of *love*.

This is not to be taken to imply that we need deny the usefulness of the notion of concepts, only that in a discussion of the nature of meaning it can play little part.

Items of language, even when they are complete utterances, occur most frequently in the environment of other items of language. They bear relations to the items which surround them in addition to those relations of substitutability which they bear to those items which can occur in the same context or environment. The possibility of an item occurring is obviously determined by its linguistic environment, just as the possibility of a whole utterance occurring, such as 'How do you do?' or 'Good-bye', is determined by situational context. 'Good-bye' cannot occur in a greeting situation any more than 'How do you do?' can occur in a leave-taking situation.

Given a sentence like: *My car is —————— than yours*, we would have no difficulty in specifying exactly which part of speech *must* occur in that environment. What we cannot be so exact about is *which* word will occur. In other words, the class of word is wholly predictable and therefore adds nothing to the meaning, while the actual dictionary item is highly unpredictable from the environment and therefore carries a lot of meaning. Nevertheless, we should have no difficulty in compiling a long list of comparative adjectives which could not occur in this environment: *steeper, bitterer, richer, tastier.* . . . Now, suppose you and I had an argument about the relative merits of our cars and, to settle it, arranged to have a race, and suppose I won, this situational context would increase considerably the probability of one word occurring in that environment rather than another. We could rule out *slenderer, loftier, harder, cheaper*; we could probably rule out *more beautiful, smarter*, and we should predict, *faster* or *more powerful* with *quicker, speedier* and *swifter* as poor runners-up.

Discussions of meaning in language tend to concentrate on the vocabulary element of the language. This is so for two reasons: firstly, the relationship of reference which we have spoken about is one into which only the vocabulary elements enter, and, as we have seen, these relationships are the ones which are thought of by many as the only meaning relationships. But secondly, because in the learning of the meaning of our mother-tongue the learning of that part of the meaning of our language which is conveyed by the grammar is completed, for the most part, by the child in his first five years of life, and is already handled by him with some confidence by the time he reaches the age of formal education in the primary school. And yet, as we have just seen from our example of: *My car is ------ than yours*, we cannot separate the choice of vocabulary from its lexical environment and its membership of a grammatical word-class. It is not accidental that there are a number of words which none of us have ever bothered to look up in a dictionary, or asked our pupils to look up: *would, can, before, when, and, although, so, you, some, most, but, all*. The reason is not that they have no meaning, since evidently any one of these can be substituted for another member of the same word-class in the same environment, but because they are fairly predictable from the linguistic environment. The child has learnt to do this before he ever comes to school. Note again, however, that he does not always use them in a way an adult does, That is, he doesn't always know what meaning they have in adult language. Witness such typical utterances of a child as this '*It's called a bicycle because you ride it*', or '*All the big ones won't fit in with the little ones*'.

The meaning of an item of language, then, is determined (*a*) by the relation of substitutability it enters into with other items of the same grammatical class, (*b*) by the relations it enters into with other items in the linguistic environment in which it occurs (we can call these its *collocation* relationships) and (*c*) by the relations it bears to the features of the situational context in which it occurs, a special case of which is its referential relationship.

Let us now consider another example. Here is a hypothetical conversation:

> TOM: Dad, what is salsify?
> DAD: It's a vegetable.

What has Tom learnt? He has begun to acquire a new vocabulary item. What meaning has it for him at this point? Notice, Tom's father defined salsify. A definition is a simple, copulative sentence in which the terms on each side of the equation bear a certain relation to each other, usually of identity or inclusion. When we can invert the sentence without change of meaning, e.g. *Mr Jones is the Mayor of Casterbridge/The Mayor of Casterbridge is Mr Jones*, we have a case of identity. When we cannot invert them: *A rose is a flower/A flower is a rose*, we have a case of inclusion. These are two sorts of the relationship which we have called substitutability. They are known technically as synonymy and hyponymy. Dad's definition of salsify was a case of an inclusive relationship.

Tom now knows that he can replace the word *vegetable* in a sentence like: *The family ate vegetables with their meat*, by the new word *salsify* in addition to the words he already knows, like *peas, cauliflower, carrots* and *beans*. He has learnt some, but by no means all, of the meaning of *salsify* which is determined by substitutability. He has also learnt some of its collocation relations—evidently, since he can use it in a sentence in the environment of other grammatical and lexical items: *family, eat, meat*, and still produce acceptable English. But, again, he has not learnt all its possible collocation relationships. For example, he does not know the attributive collocations of *salsify*. He will not be able to say: *Salsify is long and white*; he will not be able to speak of '*Eating salsify with a fork*' nor '*The gardener dug up some salsify*'.

His father has taught Tom one small part of the intra-linguistic meaning of *salsify*. What he has not done at all yet is to teach him its application to a situational context, i.e. its extra-linguistic meaning. Tom will not know in what situations it is appropriate to utter *salsify*. He cannot, yet, on the appropriate occasion say '*Look, Dad, the people at the next table are eating salsify*'. He has not yet learnt to identify the object in the world outside to which the term *salsify* is applied, that is, its referent. (The author of this article has also not yet learnt all the applications of the word *salsify* in situational contexts.) For Tom to learn this, his father would have to show him an example of salsify, point to the plant, to the root, before and after cooking, and say: '*Look, Tom, that is salsify*'. When Tom's father has done that, Tom will have learnt a great deal more of the meaning of *salsify*. But just making the acquaintance of the plant and vegetable won't tell him all its meanings.

He must handle it, grow it, eat it, even cook it, to learn the full applicability of the term. His knowledge of the meaning of *salsify* depends upon his knowledge of the nature and uses of salsify as plant and vegetable.

We can now see that there are stages in the learning of meaning, and we can also see that most of us never do learn the whole meaning of the lexical items we have 'acquired'. Indeed, in a strict sense, we never will learn the meaning of all the items we use regularly. It is true that we sometimes use terms of which we do not know the applicability. This would seem the case for a lot of the scientific vocabulary used by the layman.

From what has been said it will be clear that we can accept the linguist's dictum that a word in isolation, i.e. without a linguistic environment and not uttered in a situational context, has no meaning. Bits of language and whole utterances only have meaning when they are in a conventional relationship to each other and to the world outside. How, then, can we talk about learning the meaning of a single item like *salsify*? We can only do so if we look at language as a self-contained system in which terms have a potentiality of occurrence, i.e. a place in the system. We can then talk about an item having a potential meaning. By this I mean that in the language as a system, words, for instance, have the potentiality of occurring in certain limited and specifiable environments and in certain limited and specifiable situational contexts. When we talk about the meaning of a word we are, in fact, specifying the conventional relations this word enters into in the system. Only a part of this potential meaning is realized when somebody actually speaks or writes the word on a particular occasion.

The teaching of meaning, then, is the teaching of the potential meaning of the items of language in question, and, as we have seen, it isn't something which can be done on one occasion by one statement once and for all. The learning of meaning is nothing more nor less than the learning of the systems of language. By the time a child comes to school this remains very largely a question of the lexical systems of the language.

When Tom's father said '*Salsify is a vegetable*', he was not teaching Tom the whole meaning of the term *salsify*; he was giving a meaning or part of the potential meaning of the word. We saw that a lot more teaching was needed before Tom had a working knowledge of the meaning of *salsify*. By working knowledge I mean the ability to use the word correctly in a number of its commoner linguistic environments and apply it appropriately in a number of common situations. Our aim in teaching is to give the pupil a working knowledge adequate for his needs, since we, ourselves, have no more than this at any time. A complete knowledge of the potential meaning of language items is assumed to be unattainable. No individual can ever have a knowledge of the whole potential meaning of anything in his language; he can only know the whole meaning of the items he has himself met in their various environments and contexts. We are all constantly meeting 'familiar' words used in ways which are new to us. We are all learning more of the potential meaning of our language. Let us remember that we are also creators of our language in this sense. We also innovate; we also use words in environments and situations in which we have never heard them, or, for all we know, others have never used them. Our innovations, however, are not random but principled. We stretch the conventional system but we break it at our peril.

We have identified three meaning relationships: *applicability* (including reference), *substitutability* and *collocability*. Let us now see what procedures we use when we undertake to teach meaning. Each of these meaning relations is taught by different techniques. To teach a working knowledge of a bit of language, we will have to employ more than one technique, but some items will lend themselves more readily to one rather than another.

There are some teachers who identify the teaching of meaning exclusively with the use of the dictionary. This is very often regarded as the repository of the word-meanings of a language. We can start, therefore, with the dictionary to see what aspects of meaning it handles, and what techniques it uses. Here is an entry from the *C.O.D.*:

> Squab (ŏb) a. adv., and n. short and fat, squat, whence squabby a.; (adv.) with heavy fall, as *come down s. on the floor*; (n.) short fat person, young, esp. unfledged pigeon, stuffed

cushion, ottoman; *s.-chick*, unfledged bird; *s. pie*, pigeon pie, pie of mutton, onions and apples.

Leaving aside the information about pronunciation (ŏb), the first thing a dictionary does is to assign the word to a grammatical word-class (a. adv. and n.). This tells us part of its grammatical meaning. Thus, for example, we are told that *horse* is a noun, that *man*, *house* and *murder* are nouns and transitive verbs. Now, we 'know' from our descriptive knowledge of the grammar of our language that nouns may function as subjects and objects of verbs. This information would then enable us to produce such sentences as: *The man murdered the man, The man housed the horse, The men manned the house*, which are correct English; but it would not prevent us from producing: **The house murdered the horse*, **the man murdered the house* or **the horses manned the house*, **the horse murdered the man*, etc. Evidently the grammatical information in the dictionary does not tell us all we need to know about meaning! But it does give us some of the grammatical knowledge we *must* have before we can learn the lexical meaning of words, namely the word-class membership of the word, since the intra-linguistic meaning relations depend upon this. However, from a practical point of view the shortcomings of the grammatical information in a dictionary are no great matter, since we have noted that by the time a child comes to school he has largely mastered the grammatical systems of the language, even though he has no descriptive knowledge of it. What, therefore, the child must be able to do on meeting a new word is assign it to its grammatical class. He must do this before he can begin to learn its lexical meaning. Given a word in isolation, a child cannot confidently assign it to its class. If a word is formed with a derivational or inflexional suffix, such as *-ly*, *-tion*, *-er*, *-ic*, *-ance*, *-'s*, *-ing*, he will normally make a fairly good assignment, but many new words he meets have no such structural grammatical clues. Give a child a word like *bithulic*, *salter*, *grievance* or *dastard*, and he will do quite well, but offer him *squab*, *inane*, *dank* or *chagrin* and he will have nothing to help him. In such cases he may, as we know, make assignments on the irrelevant criteria of superficial similarity to words whose grammatical class membership he already knows, e.g. *squab/swab*, *chagrin/grin*, *dank/thank*. Again, this should be no problem, since we do not (or should not) expect children to assign unknown words to their grammatical classes unaided. Only very old-fashioned teachers give lists of isolated words for children to work on. And, of course, given an environment, the child's performative knowledge of grammar will enable him to make a fairly confident assignment of a word to its primary class. It will not, however, always enable him to assign it to a sub-class. We can take *salsify* again as our example. From his father's definition Tom could not be sure whether *salsify* belonged grammatically with the 'vegetable' words like *parsley*, *sage* and *rhubarb*, which normally function as mass nouns, i.e. *some parsley*, *some sage*, *some rhubarb*, *some salsify*, or like *carrot*, *potato*, *radish* which function both as countable nouns and mass nouns, i.e. *three carrots*, *four potatoes*, *six radishes*, but not *three salsifies. The dictionary will not necessarily help him either.

The cardinal rule, then, for teaching the meaning of a new word is that it shall be presented in a linguistic environment which will enable the learner to make a reasonably confident assignment of it to a word-class. All this is fairly obvious, but not always done in practice.

A dictionary, however, gives more information about a word than its grammatical class membership. Dictionaries give us information about the intra-linguistic relations between words, the meaning relations of substitution and collocation. Let us take each in turn. Traditionally speaking they give *synonyms* and *definitions*. Both of these show substitution relationships. We have already spoken about definition of identity and inclusion. In technical terms, these are equivalent to the relations of synonymy and hyponymy. Thus a statement like: *Aslant means obliquely*, or *The man next door is our grocer*, are statements of synonymy. We do not need to enter here the discussion in which linguists and philosophers are engaged as to whether there are any true synonyms in a language. The position adopted here will be that no two words or expressions are synonymous in *all* their potential environments or contexts, but that in any given environment or situational context two terms may be in a relation of synonymy. Dictionaries offer a number of terms which in one environment or context or another are synonyms of the head word. The giving of a synonym therefore teaches something of the meaning relationship of substitutability.

The relationship of inclusion (or hyponymy) is illustrated in the dictionary by the sort of statement Tom's father made when he said '*Salsify is a vegetable*'. The term on the left of the equation is a member of the class named on the right. Most definitions in the dictionary are of this sort: e.g. *asp: small, venomous, hooded serpent of Egypt and Libya*. These are not synonyms. There are no environments in which one is substitutable for the other without change of meaning. However many more attributes may be piled on to the right-hand term, the relation is still one of hyponymy.

Another type of definition relationship given in the dictionary is that of antonymy, definition by opposite. This is also a substitution relationship. Thus we may find: *bachelor: unmarried man; light: not dark; rare: unusual*. Only relatively few words enter into antonymous relations with other words.

There is, however, one very important meaning relationship of substitutability which the dictionary does not state. This I shall call exclusion. This also is a relationship into which only certain classes of words enter. Consider this exchange:

A. I see Mary's wearing a blue dress again.
B. Yes, but I think she looks much nicer in a −−−−−− one.

The only word which can occur in this environment is a colour adjective. The one colour adjective it cannot be is blue. Colour adjectives, temperature adjectives, kinship terms, military ranks belong to sets of words which bear to each other a relationship of exclusion. This means that the use of one in an environment specifically excludes the possibility of all the other members of the set, thus, when A said: '*I see Mary's wearing a blue dress again*', he was saying by implication '*I see Mary's wearing a not-red, not-yellow, not-green, not-orange, not. . . . dress again*'. The use of the term *blue* does not, of course, necessarily exclude any number of other adjectives with which *blue* does not stand in this relationship. Thus while Mary's dress cannot be both *blue* and *red* at the same time, except in the obvious sense that her dress is of two colours, it can be *blue, old, long, unfashionable, ragged,* etc. simultaneously. *Blue* does not stand in an exclusion relationship with any of these, nor does any one of these stand in that relation with any other, since they can all occur simultaneously in the same environment, *a . . . dress.*

Young children when learning their language sometimes fail to recognize this exclusion relationship and will utter sentences like these '*He's my friend; he's my Daddy*', or '*We didn't go for a holiday, we went for a week*'.

I have spoken about this particular meaning relationship at some length since it is the most important intra-linguistic meaning relationship which the dictionary does not handle. We can now pass on to the way that the dictionary deals with collocation relationships.

It does this by citation. This means the giving of a linguistic environment for a word which shows some of the other words with which it conventionally collocates. For example: *Ram: v.t. rammed his clothes into a bag, his hat down on his head, had the list rammed into me by repetition, r. the argument home.* Now it is evident that no dictionary can cite all the collocation relationships into which a word enters. It chooses therefore the less common examples rather than the more common. Thus, for a learner meeting a word for the first time, what it tells him is not usually what he wants to know at that moment. Furthermore, it is the less common words which will be looked up in a dictionary and in these cases dictionaries usually give few, if any, citations. For *squab*, for example, we found in the *C.O.D.* only *come down squab on the floor*, for *inane* and *dank* we found none.

A dictionary then, can handle, up to a point, most of the intra-linguistic meaning relationships of a word, the relationships of substitutability and collocability. It does this by definition and citation. A teacher is, of course, able to do this himself verbally equally well. He may not be able to state all the synonyms of a word off-the-cuff (nor of course does the dictionary), but he can handle the statements of hyponymy, e.g. *apple: round firm fleshy fruit of a rosaceous tree*, as well as the dictionary. Furthermore he is much better able, from his knowledge of his own pupils, to couch his definitions in terms which they already know. The jibe that a dictionary defines easy words in terms of difficult words and difficult words in ... is not without foundation.

As far as giving meaning by citation is concerned, the teacher can again do vastly better than the dictionary, since he can, in a few moments and with a few well-chosen sentences, present collocations for a word in much greater variety and quantity than can the dictionary; and for the learner at least he can pick out the most useful collocations rather than the more *recherché* ones, with which the beginner is not concerned.

For the extra-linguistic meaning relations of applicability and reference the dictionary normally does nothing. It is true that there are illustrated dictionaries which attempt to set up reference relations for some few words, but, because of restrictions on space, this is usually done only for rather rare words. The dictionary then normally presents only what we have called the intra-linguistic meaning relations of substitutability and collocability. It is the teacher who must supply the all-important applications of words.

The procedure of showing the application of a word I shall call contextualization. Let us take the simplest application relationship, that of reference, as an example. The teacher can point to an object or action or the picture of an object or action while saying, for example: *this is an urn* or *that is a dodo* or *the man is bowling*. Or he can draw the learner's attention to a quality of an object, its colour, texture, shape, dimension, taste, smell, etc., e.g. *This liquid smells acrid* or *that stuff is friable*. He can do this for any attribute of an object or material which is perceived by the senses. This process of creating a relationship between a word and a single feature of the objective world I shall call ostention. It plays, as we know, an important part in the teaching of second languages. It also plays an important part in the teaching of the mother tongue, but, ironically, it is a technique more used by teachers of science or geography, e.g. *This is a test-tube, That is a peninsula, The liquid is effervescing*, than by the English teacher!

The teaching of application relationships, other than those of reference, is done in two ways. These I shall call description and demonstration. The first is done through language, by giving a description of the situations in which a term is applicable. This technique is best shown by an example. A teacher who wanted to teach the applicability of the expression 'so long', might say something like this: *We have two young people who know each other pretty well. They have been talking together; one has to go away now, but he expects to see the other again fairly soon. His last words on leaving the other will probably be 'so long'.* Or in a lighter vein, taken from an article by Elizabeth Caylay in Punch:

> Our seventh daughter is learning football. Yes, I DID say football. Her boy-friend likes the game, but 'Boys play so rough'. So my little daughter has persuaded her classmates to provide both team and opposition, and on a Saturday afternoon twelve little girls—and one gangling youth—kick a muddy leather ball across a muddy field. That, to me, is True Love!

Demonstration as a technique of teaching meaning is shown more clearly in the teaching of foreign languages, where it is more and more beginning to take over this function from translation. It means presenting a real or simulated scene in which the speaker and hearer play a part and in which the unknown word or expression occurs in the dialogue. The learner is then able to perceive the relationship of applicability for himself. He is able to 'understand' the meaning of the word by direct observation of how it is applied. This is in fact the way we learn the applicability meaning relations of the overwhelming mass of items in our mother tongue. As we have now come to expect, we do not learn the whole applicability of a word in one demonstration or one description. It is only by the observation of hundreds of instances of the occurrence of an item in different situational contexts that we obtain a working knowledge of its applicability. Furthermore, we are all well aware that we frequently make wrong deductions, we 'misread' the situation and hence are liable to 'misapply' the word in the future until we are corrected or, more likely, correct ourselves from further observation.

This introduces our final point in the discussion of the teaching of meaning. Not only must the teacher provide the pupil with the opportunity to learn the conventional meaning relations, both intra-linguistic and extra-linguistic, he must also correct misuses occurring from faulty observation or overgeneralization by the pupil. Faulty observation has already been dealt with. Overgeneralization can best be shown by reference to our previous example of 'doggie'. The child having learned that he may apply *doggie* to a situation in which a dog is present, then assumes that he may apply it to a situation of which any small four-footed animal is a feature. Or at a later stage, a child having learned that 'tax' is what his father is paying when he receives a 'bill' from the government, speaks about his father paying 'tax' when he receives a bill from his lawyer. We are all familiar with this sort of error; it is the basis of many of the 'cute child' stories. It is also one which we sometimes commit ourselves.

We can now sum up. No item of language has meaning in isolation. Meaning is a set of complex relationships which exist between language and the situation in which it occurs. These have been called application relationships, a particular case of which is the referential relationship. But language items also stand in various relationships to the other items of language with which they co-occur in utterances. These we have called collocatio relationships. They also stand in a number of different types of relationship with other items of language by which they could be replaced in a given linguistic environment. These we have called substitution relationships. In teaching meaning we are concerned with getting the learner to perceive these relationships. For each type of relationship there is a technique of teaching. The extra-linguistic relationship of applicability is taught by contextualization, the showing of the relationship between the language item and the relevant features of the situational context, either by demonstration or by description of the situation, or, in the case of the referential relationship, by ostention. The intra-linguistic relationship of collocation is taught by citation, the presentation of an item in a linguistic environment. The substitution relationships of an item are taught by definition. This is true of all the different types of substitution relationship except that of exclusion (*blue* is *not-red*, *not-yellow*, *not-green*, etc.).

When we teach a language we are concerned with meaning all the time. What we seek to achieve in our pupils is a working knowledge of the potential meaning of the items of the language, their place in the systems of relationship in the language. We cannot teach all of the potential meaning on a single occasion, since we can only show a limited number of the meaning relationships into which an item may enter. In any case, to learn the whole potential meaning of even a small part of our own language may be beyond the capacities even of the teacher. The teaching of meaning is a task in which all teachers engage; it is a task we should undertake in a spirit of patience and humility.

ACKNOWLEDGMENT

For the theoretical aspects of his contribution the author wishes to acknowledge his indebtedness to the work of Professor John Lyons, particularly as outlined in his 'Structural Semantics', (P.P.S., Blackwell, 1964).

10

The Teaching of Grammar

W. R. O'DONNELL

Since 'The Teaching of Grammar' is clearly a part of what we call 'The Teaching of English', it will probably be helpful if we preface our discussion of the former by a brief consideration of just exactly what is meant by the latter. In fact, two things seem to be meant: the teaching of English language and the teaching of English literature, and we would do well to distinguish these two things, at least in our minds.

Traditionally, of course, the two are dealt with by the same teacher, and as a result they are not infrequently looked upon as being merely different aspects of the same thing. Occasionally, indeed, an even less realistic view is taken and it is held that the English teacher's main concern is with literature, language being considered only to the extent that it is felt to be useful in the study of literature.

We may readily grant that literature is language at its most sophisticated. Nor would anyone wish to deny the importance of the study of literature as a humanizing discipline. But language has other important, and perhaps more important, uses; so that, for example, there is really no obvious reason why the study of language should be more closely linked to the study of literature than to, say, the study of science. The one is just as dependent upon the proper use and understanding of language as the other. And the teaching of language is justified by all its uses, not merely that use which is of particular concern to the teacher of English.

Certainly literature, no less than science, is more than just language. Both have an important language component, as do most human activities, but they each have a content which makes them important subjects in their own right. It is not being suggested here, therefore, that literature is of minor importance. It is unfortunately necessary to stress this, because any attempt to insist upon the importance of language is invariably interpreted as an attempt to devalue literature in some way. Literature must, of course, continue to be accorded an important place in 'The Teaching of English'.

Moreover, literature and language will no doubt continue to be dealt with by the same teacher, under the general heading of 'English', and there is really no objection to this. It is not being suggested that they be separated, only that they be distinguished from one another. Both will be better taught if the teacher is quite clear that they are not the same thing; so that he is clear, for example, that the aims of language teaching are not absolutely determined by the requirements of literature teaching. But the point of insisting upon the distinction here is to call attention to the fact that though grammar may have a contribution to make in both language and literature teaching it will be a different contribution in each case. Accordingly, our reasons for teaching grammar, the grammar we teach and the way we teach it, even what we mean by the term 'grammar', will all very much depend upon whether we are thinking in terms of literature or of language.

In discussing the teaching of English language, of course, it is necessary to make yet another important distinction: between teaching *about* language and teaching the *use* of language. Most of the dissatisfaction with the traditional teaching of grammar derives in fact from a failure to recognize this distinction. For though the majority of teachers have looked upon it as teaching the *use* of language, and have accordingly expected an improvement in their pupil's language performance, school grammar has really been teaching *about* language. And the dissatisfaction has been consequent upon the realization that it has not produced the hoped-for result.

It is tempting to conclude that the school grammar has failed because it has been the wrong grammar, and that better results might be obtained with a new 'linguistic' grammar. But the real explanation for the failure is simply that human beings learn to use language by using it, not by talking about it. It is true that part of the process must in some sense be the handling of a grammar, in that human beings learn to interpret (and produce) a theoretically infinite number of new sentences; an ability which can be explained only by postulating an internalized grammar of some kind, whether this be in the form of a series of abstract patterns or, as seems more likely, a set of abstract rules which make possible the realization of acceptable patterns. But we have to distinguish this (internalized) grammar which the human being can use, but not necessarily talk about, from any other kind of grammar which he can talk about, but not necessarily use. And it appears to be the case that the (internalized) grammar is not acquired as a result of exposure to the other kind. Instead it seems to be necessary to have experience of the language itself, from which the grammar is built up by a process of abstraction. In acquiring grammar for use, that is to say, the human mind operates most efficiently on language—not by studying language about language.

If this appears to claim too much for natural processes it should be reflected upon that any human infant, no matter what his parentage, will learn the language of the community in which he is brought up, whether that language be English, Chinese, Eskimo or whatever. It follows that although human infants are not born with innate knowledge of any particular language it must be that they are endowed from birth with the capacity to learn a natural language; otherwise they would be unable to learn any language at all. We are not, of course, able to describe this mental equipment at present, but evidently the conditions it requires for its operation include experience of the language to be learned.

Now, it would be quite unrealistic to hope to alter the nature of the learner in order to adapt it to what is to be learned. Furthermore, if human beings are predisposed by nature to learn in a particular way it would be perverse not to take advantage of the fact. The teaching of grammar, therefore, at least in so far as it is directed towards an improvement in the use of language, will involve exposing the learner to material in a form which best suits his learning abilities; that is, it will involve giving him experience of real language from which the grammar may be abstracted, rather than presenting him with a body of rules to be memorized.

In the natural (i.e. pre-school) language-*learning* situation, the material from which the grammar has to be abstracted occurs unsystematically, and besides may contain a fairly high proportion of language which is deviant by reason of its structural incompleteness. If language *teaching* is to improve on this it must do so by increasing the proportion of non-deviant language and arranging for a more systematic experience.

This is where the linguist may be able to help, by providing a means of specifying 'deviance' and making possible an organized sequence in the presentation of material. This, as a matter of fact, is the proper function of the linguist's 'grammar' in this particular area of language teaching. Naturally the sequence suggested by a grammar will not necessarily be the best possible. Determining the best possible sequence is a matter for some long-term research; by educational psychologists rather than linguists. Nevertheless, by providing clearly defined stages, grammatically sequenced material will at least avoid the probable waste inherent in completely random experience.

Assuming, then, a reliable descriptive grammar which would make possible the required selection and staging, a convenient way of arranging for the necessary language experience in the early primary school is provided by children's rhymes. Children learn them readily and enjoy doing it. It is not improbable, in fact, that such rhymes already play a part in the language learning process, in that normal children will (though not at any conscious level) treat any rhymes they learn as opportunities to build up their internal knowledge of grammar. It is suggested, however, that rhymes might be made to play an even more effective part, were teachers aware of the possibilities they offer and prepared to take some advantage of these.

This suggestion should not be understood to imply that children's rhymes in the early primary school are to be justified only by direct reference to their usefulness in the learning of grammar. There must never be any doubt that the primary justification for rhymes is the pleasure they give, and once they cease to give pleasure their usefulness in the learning of grammar is at an end.

Nor should it be taken as implying that only rhymes can be used for the purpose of assisting children to internalize a grammar. But rhymes are an obvious and convenient place to begin, and, moreover, they do give an opportunity for the interested teacher to test the argument offered here. And, no matter how persuasive an argument, no practising teacher should ever be convinced until he has tried out what it leads to—in the classroom.

Teachers who possess the necessary grammatical knowledge will probably prefer to collect and arrange their own material. Many, however, will feel unable to undertake this task for themselves, either because of lack of specialized knowledge or because of shortage of time, and any who do will find it useful to consult *Songs and Rhymes*,[1] where they will find a collection of suitable material, classified according to (among other things) grammatical structure. This material will enable them to make their own experiments and come to their own conclusions.

Children's rhymes will clearly be appropriate only in the very early Primary school, however, and the question arises as to how it might be possible to continue to exercise some guidance over the child's experience of language.

One possibility is poetry, which would be the natural development of the use of rhymes and songs. It may, it is true, be objected that we have more important reasons for teaching poetry in the Primary school, and it would be difficult to dispute this view. On the other hand, it need not be assumed that these reasons would prevent an attempt to present poetry in stages influenced by grammatical considerations. In other words, given that a number of poems are equally attractive (from the point of view of enjoyment, for instance) it is difficult to see why one should not select those which may be in addition helpful to the children's internalization of grammar. In any case, it would seem to be desirable to avoid too many grammatical difficulties too early, since poetry can hardly be expected to work its magic if it is inaccessible by reason of its complexity. There would seem to be no compelling reason, therefore, why poetry should not take over where rhymes leave off and help to teach grammar as well as doing all the other things it is supposed to do anyway. Grammar is not *the* reason for teaching poetry (so that one would not exclude poems which had no obvious grammatical contribution), but it could be *another* reason. It goes almost without saying that the children should never at any time be made aware of this other reason.

Unfortunately, no published material is yet available which would make classroom experiment possible; so that any teacher who would like to see what he can do in this way with poetry would have to devise his own material meantime. But there is an alternative, and in some ways more attractive, possibility in graded reading. Most teachers are intuitively convinced that reading is a very important factor in improving the use of language and hence encourage their pupils to read as much as possible. Grading, however, ensures that pupils are never confronted with language with which it is beyond their ability to deal. Each child is allowed to read at his own level at his own pace, and he competes only with himself. He enjoys reading because what he is asked to read is just difficult enough to offer a challenge. He is able, with a little effort, to cope successfully and he is motivated, not only by the pleasure he discovers in reading but also by his success, to improve gradually but steadily. And all the time he is reading, he is being exposed to structures which he can handle; sometimes with an effort. He is thus able to continue with the process of abstracting the grammar and build upon the foundations laid down in his early primary schooling.

It is not recommended that children ever be asked explicitly to 'learn the grammar' of a piece of reading material (or, for that matter, a rhyme or poem). The mental equipment of the child does not operate in this way. What should happen is that the child should be presented with reading material which is just within his competence *and which is also intrinsically interesting or pleasurable to him.* But the experience of real language thus arranged means that learning goes on without his being aware of it. Indeed, it is impossible for the normal healthy child not to learn. The point of exercising some control over the circumstances surrounding his learning is simply to ensure that he learns the grammar we want him to learn—as painlessly as possible. Children will learn *some* grammar from their reading if it is not too difficult for them: careful grading will make certain that they learn Standard English grammar.

Unfortunately, the availability of graded word lists, and the absence of any corresponding list of structures, has meant that the emphasis in the grading of reading material has tended to be lexical (according to vocabulary) rather than grammatical, and for the purpose of teaching grammar grammatical grading is clearly to be preferred. However, the S.R.A. Reading Laboratories, which provide the most useful material so far available, operate in such a way that the effect of the emphasis on vocabulary is to a considerable extent overcome. Each child begins with a diagnostic test which enables the teacher to place him with regard to his reading ability. Thereafter, as the child improves at one level he is introduced at the next level to material deemed to be slightly more difficult, but never at any time required to deal with material with which, by a little effort, he cannot score highly in the comprehension test which accompanies each passage. Though the grading is lexical, therefore, the reading material is always within the limits of the child's grammatical understanding as well, and though the material is not ideal it is considerably better than unsystematic exposure, and in fact very satisfactory results have been obtained with it.

To sum up thus far; it has been suggested:

1 that teaching the use of language must be distinguished from teaching about language,
2 that teaching the use of language comes first,
3 that learning the use of language involves (among other things) acquiring an (internalized) grammar,
4 that the child naturally learns such a grammar as a result of experience of real language in use,
5 that teaching can improve upon the natural situation by providing for a guided experience of language,
6 that, in the early Primary school, children's rhymes may be used as one means of providing such experience,
7 that the process begun with rhymes may be continued by means of graded reading.

It has been pointed out that, whatever the arguments put forward, most teachers will very properly wish to reserve judgment until they have tested the suggestions arising out of them for themselves—in the classroom. It was to make this possible that reference was made to actual material. But a word of caution is perhaps necessary concerning the results to be expected from the use of this material. We are discussing only grammar. If the material is used properly it might be expected to improve the learner's (internalized) grammar, and hence his language performance. But this is only part of the language-learning process. The point is that we must not be thought to be suggesting that children's rhymes, for instance, will solve all the teacher's problems. They will not. What they will do is help with one particular problem; and other problems must be dealt with in other ways.

If sufficient practice is arranged the (internalized) grammar learned in the way suggested here should be available to the child in his speech and he should be able without difficulty to turn his competence (his internalized knowledge) to good account in producing acceptable English. The question arises, however: what kind of practice is necessary and how is it to be arranged?

One obvious way of providing practice, of course, is by means of the 'speech and drama' type of activity which is becoming so popular in schools, and this kind of activity will certainly help. However, it is open to question whether 'speech and drama' would *by itself* provide adequate practice of the right kind. There is often, after all, something artificial about it, and it is desirable that at least some practice be given in more realistic situations.

Now, realism in speech situations means using language to co-operate with others in order to achieve some common aim. What is required for realistic practice, in other words, is the kind of situation in which language plays an essential but unobtrusive part; where language itself is not the end but a necessary means to some other end. And this kind of situation is, of course, very easy to arrange in the classroom.

For example, teacher and pupils might undertake to write a play together. To the pupils the object of the exercise is the creation of their own play, but to the teacher it is the creation of opportunities for discussion and conversation—about the kind of story to be tackled, the limitations of the classroom as a stage, the appropriate dialogue in given situations, and so on. It is naturally a long-term project extending over several weeks, at the end of which a play emerges in which the pupils take part, perhaps before an audience of pupils from other classes. But during the course of the project the class has really been learning to use language by using it for a purpose, under the teacher's guidance. And with this kind of practice, *in addition to speech and drama*, the child learns not only to produce the right noises but also to produce them effectively.

An important point for us as teachers is that once the grammar has been learned, only adequate practice is necessary to produce acceptable performance—in speech. The same is not true of writing. Writing is a quite distinct activity from speech and is not to be thought of simply as a means of recording speech. Furthermore, since it involves the use of a tool of some kind, such as a pen, writing must be regarded as in some sense more artificial than speech, for, though none of the so-called 'vocal organs' has speech as its primary function, nevertheless speech only uses the equipment provided by nature. In addition, it must be remembered that the need to write is a sophisticated need— most of the world's population manages without writing, as we do ourselves for much of the time—whereas speech is essential to ensure the satisfaction of even our most elementary needs; so that the child has stronger reasons for learning to speak than he has for learning to write. And, finally, opportunities for practice are considerably less frequent where writing is concerned. It need be no cause for surprise, therefore, that writing is not learned but must be taught.

For a few, the most intelligent, it is necessary to teach little more than the appropriate motor-perceptive skills. They themselves seem able to take it from there. But for the majority this is not sufficient. The problem is: what does the teacher do about it? Does he give opportunities for practice and hope to teach by correction? Or does he do what many teachers are now being asked to do and give opportunities for practice without correction, in the hope that all will be well eventually? Or does he instead look for some means of making the grammar already internalized by the child available to him in the new medium?

The plain fact is that correction all too often fails to bring about the desired improvement. In any case, though the opportunity to make mistakes is probably a necessary part of learning, it is clearly not true that children learn only from mistakes, and, accordingly, teaching only or mainly by means of correction is negative teaching.

Nor are teachers who eschew correction noticeably more successful. It is true that younger children write more readily if they are not over-corrected, and believers in this method claim that the result is more 'interesting' language. But it often happens that children become critical of themselves, despite the encouraging noises made by the teacher, and dry up; not because they have nothing to write, but because they have not acquired the skill which would enable them to write it. And, in any case, is 'interesting' writing good enough? Or, to put it another way: is the alternative to negative teaching no teaching at all?

Clearly it is not. For we might instead set ourselves the task of teaching in such a way that our children are given more opportunities to succeed. We might, that is, try positive teaching. It is not after all the correction itself which disturbs the child so much as the underlying failure that the correction implies. It is no service to our pupils, therefore, merely to give up correction. The only honest way to deal with the problem is to increase the opportunities for success, after which the question of correction no longer looms so large.

The answer is graded writing. The child begins by writing simple structures and masters the production of these before going on to ever more complex ones. And all the time he is succeeding, not failing. The grading is, of course, grammatical; so that what the child is really doing is learning to call upon and employ his (internalized) grammar in the unfamiliar, and perhaps unnatural, medium of writing.

Some teachers will of course shudder at the thought of teaching writing in what might appear to be a rather formal way, and some theorists will offer all kinds of objections. But the children enjoy it; their production improves both in quality and quantity. In other words: it works.

Moreover, it is not being suggested that this is the only writing children should do. We are here concerned with grammar, and graded writing is suggested as part of the process of teaching grammar. It is accepted that other things have to be taught about writing which cannot be dealt with in the same way, and that other kinds of writing activity will be necessary which we shall not have space enough to discuss here.

Teachers who are interested in pursuing the possibilities of this approach are referred to *Control and Create*.[2] The material in this book was originally devised for a remedial situation with backward children in the secondary school, but it has also been used, suitably modified, with all kinds of children in the Primary school, where it has proved very successful.

Teaching an internalized grammar by means of rhymes and songs, and teaching how this grammar is to be used in speech and writing are all part (and only part) of teaching the use of language. This would seem to be the proper aim for the teacher of English throughout most of the Primary school years: to teach the use of language. It is not suggested, and this is repeated for the sake of emphasis, that the use of English is only a question of (*a*) internalizing a grammar and (*b*) employing that grammar in speech and writing. But these are evidently very important factors. Though it will therefore never be enough for the teacher to teach the grammar, the teaching of grammar (in the senses we have used here) must not be overlooked if the child is ever to learn to use his language effectively.

However, if the use of language is effectively taught throughout the Primary school it will eventually be possible to give some attention to teaching *about* language. Or, to put it another way, good language teaching in the Primary school will ensure that the child eventually has enough control over his language to make it worth talking about. Two questions then arise:

1 Ought we to teach about language in school?
2 What part does grammar play in teaching about language?

The short answer to the first of these questions is surely that it would be irresponsible not to teach something about so important a phenomenon as language: for language is extremely important, both to the individual and to mankind in general. To the individual because it enters in some form into almost all his other activity, and not as a refinement but as an essential component; so that, for example, whatever subjects he studies at school he must study through the medium of language. To mankind in general because language makes an essential contribution to whatever progress mankind manages to achieve; when man lands on the moon, for example, it will be as great a triumph for language as it is for science. Consequently, no education which pretends to be more than mere training can possibly justify the exclusion of language as an object of study.

The primary aim of teaching about language is, of course, to increase knowledge and understanding of the nature and function of language; as an end in itself. It is not necessarily, that is to say, part of teaching the use of language. In considering the second question, therefore, we are not concerned with grammar for use but with grammar for insight; with a series of illuminating statements concerning one aspect of language activity. And the answer to this question is simply that these statements will be examined and discussed, together with other statements concerned with other aspects of language, in order to provide maximum understanding of the phenomenon we call language.

'Maximum understanding' clearly rules out the traditional school grammar; because it is prescriptive; because it is concerned with what 'ought to be' rather than what 'is'. Which is not to say that prescription is absolutely wrong in all circumstances, only that it is inappropriate where the intention is to provide insight. What is necessary in that case is a descriptive grammar; a grammar that concerns itself with what 'is'. There are, however, two quite distinct possibilities.

The first is an abstract classificatory grammar which will make possible the processing and description of particular samples of real language (text). This kind of grammar makes statements concerning language at two levels of abstraction. At the higher level, statements are made about the kinds of (grammatical) patterning found in language considered as an abstraction from all its particular occurrences (i.e. all natural languages). That is to say, it attempts to state in the form of a theory precisely what is universal in grammar, at the level of abstraction appropriate to such generalization. At the lower level, descriptive statements are made about the kinds of patterning found in particular languages; each particular description being regarded as an example of the theory. Thus, for example, it is stated in the theory that the grammatical patterning in language (i.e. all languages) involves what are called 'units': in the description of English in particular the units may conveniently be specified as sentence, clause, group, word and morpheme. In other words, units are a universal feature of grammar, but the kinds of units and their number may vary from language to language.

The theory may be viewed as an abstract construct which makes possible the description of particular languages: the descriptions in turn being regarded as abstract descriptive constructs which make possible the processing of particular texts in the language for which a given description is provided. Thus in a given English text one would seek, for example, exemplars of sentence, clause, etc.

On the face of it, it would seem an attractive possibility to begin the subject of grammar in school with the description of English grammar, continuing thereafter to a consideration of the theory of which it is an exemplar, thus providing the desired insight into language through the particular language with which the pupils are most familiar. It is, however, open to doubt whether such a procedure would ensure the 'maximum' understanding for which teaching about language should aim.

For one thing, the theory as it stands is framed from observation of language which has actually occurred, and so it is designed to account (*a*) only and (*b*) completely for what has occurred in any given text. It therefore, on the one hand, provides only limited insight into what has not occurred, and paradoxically enough this may be more important than what has, and, on the other hand, it lacks any theoretical criterion of deviance and so fails to provide any insight whatsoever into the notion of grammaticality. Moreover, it fails to raise other very important questions, such as how language is learned or how it is used. Though a classificatory grammar such as we have been discussing may therefore be a useful analytical tool, it ought not to be employed to provide insight if a better grammar for this purpose can be found.

The alternative to classificatory grammar is what might be called explanatory grammar, since it sets out not so much to describe actual samples of real language as to explain the conditions which make possible their production. Thus a really insightful attempt to teach about language might reasonably begin by considering a circumstance which is a matter of common observation; namely that human beings learn, on the one hand, to produce an indefinitely large number of acceptable sentences which have never been heard before and, on the other hand, to interpret an indefinitely large number of sentences which have never been uttered before. The reader may well ask himself, for example, what it is that enables him to understand this present sentence, which he has almost certainly never encountered in his entire life.

Part at least of the explanation is that the speaker/hearer must have certain internalized knowledge available to him. The meaningfulness of an utterance, that is, cannot be accounted for completely as a property of what is actually said or written, but must depend in part upon knowledge possessed by the user. An utterance in Chinese, for example, would be meaningless to most Britishers despite the fact that it would be correctly interpreted by very young Chinese.

Equally clearly one component of the necessary internalized knowledge is a grammar of some kind which the speaker/hearer may make use of, either productively or receptively, as the need arises. What we mean by an explanatory grammar is a grammar which characterizes this knowledge.

It is not merely a question of providing a catalogue of available information, but also of specifying its organization. Some insight may be gained into this from observation of the circumstances in which the information is acquired and used. For example, as has already been pointed out, one of the circumstances surrounding its acquisition is a limited exposure to real language. It should be added that the exposure will be quite different in every case, for only by the wildest of coincidences would two human beings be exposed to exactly the same set of utterances in the same order, at the same stage of development, and so on. Since all educated speakers of, say, English nevertheless acquire more or less the same (internalized) grammar, it follows that the process might better be described as one of abstraction of a limited number of elements, together with a system of rules for their combination, rather than as a process of anything like direct imitation. The purpose of an explanatory grammar, therefore, will be to specify the elements and make explicit the rules.

Possibly a word of explanation will be helpful concerning what is meant by 'rules' in this connection. Thus, it is a matter of common knowledge that birds are able to build nests, and one might be led by observation of nest-building behaviour to conclude that they followed a system of rules in order to do so. Indeed, were one so disposed one might set out to write out these rules; perhaps in the form of a knitting pattern. But this would not mean that birds had either read or had explained the rules which were written down, only that there was an observable 'regularity' about this behaviour. In the same way, when we speak of grammar 'rules' here we must not be understood to be even suggesting that human beings have either read or had explained to them a list of sentence-building rules, or even that they are conscious of following rules. Our rules are to be interpreted as an explicit statement of the observable regularities in their language behaviour. Human beings 'know' these rules in the sense that their behaviour conforms to them, but precisely what psychological form this knowledge takes is something about which we can do no more at present than speculate.

A word of caution is also necessary with regard to the term 'generative' which is often used to describe the kind of grammar we have been discussing. 'Generate' in this context does not mean 'produce', and the grammar is not to be thought of as generating sentences in the same way as power-stations generate electricity. What it means is 'accept' or 'enumerate'. That is to say, sentences may be grammatical or ungrammatical according to whether or not the explanatory grammar accepts them. 'Grammatical' is thus fundamentally a matter of what we may conveniently call intuition, which the explanatory grammar attempts to externalize. We 'know' as native speakers whether or not a sentence is grammatical. Our explanatory grammar seeks to account for this knowledge.

If all this is borne in mind there will be small likelihood of the grammar being improperly used. It will not be used, for example, in the hope of improving the use of language, though some American teachers have in fact claimed that it may be used successfully for that purpose. Its proper employment is to provide insight into the nature of grammar, and hence language, by bringing the user into the centre of the picture. Language, after all, does not just happen; it is produced and interpreted by human beings.

It is for the teacher of English to decide whether insight into language is a legitimate teaching aim. If it is, then an explanatory grammar is part (but only part) of the answer. But this kind of thing is probably inappropriate before IVth or Vth form—and teachers who wish to confine their attention to teaching the use of language would be well advised to look elsewhere for assistance.

Elementary published versions of the kind of grammar discussed, based on the work of the American linguist Noam Chomsky,[3] are at present available only from America. They are, however, easily obtainable; the simplest being *English Syntax*.[4]

Teaching the use of language and teaching about language do not exhaust the responsibilities of the teacher of English. Since it is part of his job to teach literature we must ask whether or not grammar has a contribution here.

That it has is made clear elsewhere in this volume. This in fact, is where the classificatory grammar may have an application (though an explanatory grammar can also be used to aid the teaching of literature). One of the devices employed in the teaching of literature, after all, is the device of comparison—comparison of a given literary text with some other text, either literary or non-literary—and certainly comparison implies a precise account in the same terms of the things compared. Classificatory grammar would seem to make this possible.

The choice of texts to compare is not, of course, something which can be decided by the grammar, but is a matter for the intuition of the individual teacher. Nor can the grammar itself suggest any kind of value judgment on a particular text. All it can do is make possible a comparison in fairly precise terms from which a deeper understanding of the text may be expected to result. Judgment is a matter thereafter for the individual.

As yet, unfortunately, only a very limited amount of work has been done in this particular area and consequently it is not at present possible to refer teachers to published material which they might try out in the classroom. However, the paper on 'Linguistic Form and Literary Meaning' (A. Rodger) demonstrates the application of classificatory grammar to in the study of poetry and interested teachers are referred to that paper for a treatment which may help them in preparing material of their own.[5]

To sum up: it has been the purpose of this paper to consider 'the teaching of grammar' in relation to 'the teaching of English' as a whole, rather than as a thing apart. It has attempted to make the point that what we mean by 'the teaching of grammar' will very much depend upon what we are teaching grammar for; that the first question to ask is not 'Which grammar shall we teach?' but 'Why teach grammar?' Possible answers have been suggested to both these questions, as well as to several others. We cannot hope to convince everyone that these are the right answers, but it would be a considerable advance if we could persuade the majority of teachers of English that the questions asked were the right questions. The trouble with most of our 'new grammars' has been that they provided answers to which nobody had any questions. We shall not begin to get somewhere with the teaching of English until we get the questions right; and in the right order.

NOTES

1 J. Dakin, *Songs and Rhymes*, Longmans, 1967.
2 H. Fraser, *Control and Create*, Longmans, 1967.
3 N. Chomsky, *Aspects of the Theory of Syntax*, M.I.T. Press, 1965.
4 P. Roberts, *English Syntax* (Teachers' Edition), Harcourt, Brace and World, 1964.
5 And see also A. McIntosh and M. A. K. Halliday, *Patterns of Language*, Longmans, 1966. R. Fowler ed., *Essays on Style and Language*, Routledge & Kegan Paul, 1966.

11

Linguistic Form and Literary Meaning

A STYLISTIC ANALYSIS[1] OF AN EARLY ENGLISH LYRIC

ALEX RODGER

THE TEXT[2]

Modern Printed Version

    The maidens came
    When I was in my mother's bower;
    I had all that I would.
        The bailey beareth the bell away;
5   The lily, the rose, the rose I lay.

    The silver is white, red is the gold;
    The robes they lay in fold.
        The bailey beareth the bell away;
        The lily, the rose, the rose I lay.

10 And through the glass window shines the sun.
    How should I love, and I so young?
        The bailey beareth the bell away;
        The lily, the rose, the rose I lay.

MS Harley 7578

> The maydens came
> When I was in my mothers bower
> I hade all yt I wolde
> the bayly berith the bell away
> 5 the lylle the rose the rose I lay
> the sylver is whit red is the golde
> the robes thay lay in fold
> the baylly berith the bell away
> the lily the rose the rose I lay
> 10 and through the glasse wyndow
> shines the sone
> How shuld I love & I so young
> the bayly berith the bell away
> (the lily etc.)

The problem posed by this short but striking lyric is obviously one of overall interpretation. What is it about, and what does it all mean? Does it in fact mean anything very definite at all, or is it no more than a vaguely emotive lilt-and-jingle, meant to please the ear of singer and listener alike? And supposing it is thus more expressive than communicative, what mood or sentiment does it express—joy or grief, anger or love, hope or despair, rebellion or resignation, or some blend of several of these? Groups of readers with whom I have discussed it have offered a remarkable range of purely intuitive interpretations. Some have seen it as a gay description of preparations for a village festival, others as a funeral dirge or as the anguished refusal of youth in springtime to mourn the death of a parent, others still as the imagined utterances of a dead child. Many have come nearer the mark without being able to say how or why, and quite a number (not all of them young or inexperienced readers) have resented and resisted the idea that such a lyric might be closely questioned for its precise meaning, preferring their private speculations to the notion of some public significance in the language.

Clearly the extrinsic approach can be of little help here. We cannot hunt down the meaning of this poem in the life of the author, for it is anonymous. We can say little or nothing about it in terms of the prevalent genres and conventions of its period, for it closely resembles none of the other lyrics among which it was first printed in a modern edition. We know that it dates from the very late fifteenth or very early sixteenth century, and that it was set to music. Beyond that we know nothing but the text itself. Its earliest modern editors placed it in the class of 'light and amorous ditties', offering no further comment on it.[3] But can we in fact call it either 'light' or 'amorous' with any assurance? We can hardly say what it *is*, in this sense, until we know what it *means*; and a major part of my purpose here is to suggest that an acceptable answer to the question 'What does it mean?' depends upon the answers to the prior, but much less frequently posed question: '*How* does it mean?' For the difficulties of this poem seem to me to arise much less from historical changes in language and social customs than from its own peculiar mode of communication. Since it is more than four hundred years old, we must obviously interpret it in the light of any relevant knowledge we may have about life at that time. But the real keys to its significance lie, I suggest, in the relations between its metrical and its linguistic form; and this is probably much more the case with the lyric poetry of any period than many of us imagine.

In an 'explication' almost as oblique and elliptic as the text itself, the American poet and critic Archibald MacLeish has described the poem as having '... the folk song's weatherworn senselessness in sense'.[4] Like many impressionistic judgments, this one is convincing only for a moment. It suggests an intelligible whole made up of unintelligible parts, a dubious proposition in itself. In any case, the separable parts that make up the poem are by no means unintelligible, or 'senseless'. Their component words, readily identifiable as 'parts of speech', form units which are grammatically intelligible, i.e. sequences whose familiar patterns or structures enable us to assign to them such abstract grammatical functions as 'dependent clause', 'subject', 'predicator', etc. Meaning is inevitably present because structure is present. This would not be so were the text composed of lines like these:

LINGUISTIC FORM AND LITERARY MEANING 179

> Was mother's came
> I bower the my in maidens I;
> Would had I that when all.

This is non-sense because it is patently a non-sentence. Thus 'given' formal meanings, with which we must come to terms, already invest the grammatical units that make up our text. That this is so becomes even clearer when we realize that, by a slightly different use of the intuitions whereby we grasp those meanings, we might unscramble the pseudo-text above only to arrive at something very different from what the poet wrote, e.g.

> When my mother's maidens came,
> Was I in the bower?
> I would I had all that!

Even if we equate 'senselessness' with some sort of semantic incongruity or absurdity *within* the grammatically intelligible units, Mr MacLeish's description does not fit the poem. We do not find the components combining to form utterances suggestive of wildly improbable situations, such as 'The window layeth my love in fold', or 'And through my glass mother shines the bell'. Even these are not intrinsically senseless, but could be perfectly acceptable within a given context. The first might well be the heroine's cry of dismay, uttered at a moment of farcical crisis, in some analogue of *The Miller's Tale*. Given an initial capital at *Mother*, the second might be a profoundly moving utterance in the context of a religious poem involving a legendary glass statue of the Virgin, through which its sculptor, now a kneeling penitent, can see the local cathedral bell. Such ostensibly improbable utterances are not intrinsically senseless, but have potential meaning. In our poem, the relations between grammar and vocabulary are not startling in this way. The lexicon for each clause fills out the structure in a readily acceptable way. We may worry about the situational significance of *the bailey* and his actions, but there seems nothing surrealistically improbable about his carrying a bell. What puzzles us is why he is mentioned at all—what his connection is with everything and everybody else mentioned in the text.

If the 'parts' are neither non-grammatical nor situationally absurd, can the whole poem be said to be 'senseless'? If it were, it would hardly hold our attention at all; and the whole is clearly meant to be meaningful. We are aware of some latent significance in it which is greater than the sum of the mere parts, yet tends to elude us. Mr MacLeish's impressionistic description of the poem is therefore no more accurate when reversed. What we have here is not 'sense in senselessness' either, but a text in which the parts, intelligible in themselves, comprise a whole that is neither incoherent nor utterly devoid of significance, but *enigmatic*. The ostensibly naïve simplicity of the parts clashes with the effect of an elusive yet resonant import in the whole.

The moment we stop guessing intuitively at the significance of the whole and begin to examine the relations among the parts, we raise a host of questions—too many, indeed, to be systematically listed here. Most of them arise from our need to infer from the given language what is going on in the 'inner world' of the poem, i.e. in its implied context of situation. It is clear that we must postulate such an inner situation, distinguishing it from the outer or 'performance' situation involving the poet as 'sayer' and ourselves as his addressees; for the *I* of the poem does not seem identifiable with the poet. We must therefore ask ourselves:

1 Who are the participants in the inner situation?
2 Among these, who addresses whom?
3 What is the field or subject-matter of the utterances?
4 What is the social purpose, role or function of the discourse in that inner situation?
5 Does the language imply a situation involving formal or informal social relations among the participants?
6 In what mode, i.e. under what physical conditions of communication, are the utterances made?

All these are linguistic questions demanding linguistic answers,[5] for we have nothing but the language of the text from which to infer the answers, except our knowledge of how language works in given situations, and of anything relevant to the subject-matter of the poem. But since the nature of this subject-matter is the very thing that is most obscure about the text, we shall have to proceed from the linguistic end first.

There are other questions, too, of a more obviously linguistic nature. Is there, for example, only one change of tense in the poem, namely at line 4? Is the whole text from there on in the so-called 'simple present', or does it revert at lines 5, 7, 9 and 13 to the 'simple past' of lines 1–3? And what are the grammatical (and therefore *contextual*) implications of our acceptance of either of these readings? Even if we decide in favour of the simple present for the whole of lines 4–13, we still have another decision to make: are all occurrences of that tense describing *habitual* actions or unique happenings at the moment of utterance? Or are some of them the former, and some the latter?

Many other questions of a mixed kind must be answered before we can truly say we understand the poem. Whose, for example, are *the robes* mentioned in line 7—the bailey's, the mother's or the maidens' robes? And what sort of *bower* is intended—a garden arbour, or a boudoir? Is line 6 a reference to specific objects, or a generalization about precious metals? If the former, then what are the objects? If the latter, why is the speaker so emphatic in the statement of the obvious? And why is *the sun* dragged in in an equally 'obvious' yet apparently irrelevant statement at line 10? Finally, what about the repeated lines, the 'refrain'? Are they dramatically vital to the meaning of the whole poem, or are they simply the conventional choric intrusion characteristic of folk song, signifying little or nothing?

A line-by-line scrutiny of the text raises all these points and many more. None of these questions is idle, perverse or merely pedantic. All arise from a proper concern with the local and total meanings conveyed by just these words in this precise order. Yet the whole text is only thirteen lines long, and only nine of these lines embody new (i.e. non-repeated) matter. The questions cannot be answered in simple linear sequence, for they are of different kinds and involve different modes of meaning. Of our numbered *contextual* questions, for example, we are really only in a position to answer one. It seems fairly certain that the whole text represents the language of a single participant. Though others are mentioned, there is nothing in grammar or syntax, or in the modern punctuation, to indicate a change of speaker. The pronoun *I* occurs nine times (if we include its possessive form, *my*) in the text, and while these occurrences are heavily clustered near the beginning in lines 2, 3 and 5, and near the end in lines 11 and 13, the single occurrence in stanza II (line 9) seems a reasonable ground on which to assume that the whole text is uttered by the same participant. For the moment we shall call this person *P*— a doubly useful symbol in this instance, since it stands both for the linguistic notions of 'Participant' and 'Performer' (not all participants need be vocal) as well as for the more literary concepts of 'Protagonist' and the poet's 'Persona'—his mask, or temporary identity. It is also a label suitably vague as to sex, for we have no direct grammatical evidence of the sex of *P*, who is either the son or daughter of the mother whose house or garden seems to be the setting for the situation. We know from line 11 that *P* is self-avowedly young, but we don't know how young. We also know from the same line that *P* is involved in a situation to which *love* is relevant, but don't know whether the reference is to erotic, marital, filial or religious love, nor whether *P*'s question is a request for information, an appeal for advice, an attempt to choose between ways of loving, or quite what. As for the relevance of the other persons, actions and objects named, this is not easy to see. Roses might tie up with the idea of erotic love, but lilies have strong funereal associations. Can *P* be a spoiled youth dithering over betrothing himself to one or other of two maidens who frequent his mother's house, while continuing to enjoy the favours of both the pale *lily* and the more colourful *rose*? Or is *P* a young girl going off to a nunnery, an orphaned beauty renouncing the world as she lays flowers on her mother's grave? The rather ominous line about the bailey and his bell seems to suggest something like the latter rather than the former. But in that case, what about the silver and gold? And the sun? Clearly, mere situational conjecture of this kind might lead us anywhere.

In fact, no attempt to construct a self-consistent inner context of situation for this text is likely to succeed unless we first dispose of the questions about tense and usage mentioned earlier. These involve critical decisions not only about morphology but also about syntax, and so are certain to have fairly important contextual implications. Unlike the situational ones, these grammatical problems admit of only a very limited number of possible solutions. If we survey the possibilities, we should be able to choose those readings which seem most consistent with our impressions about the rest of the text, and thus establish a number of contextual footholds from which we might hope to arrive at an interpretation of the whole. To do this, however, we must keep an eye on the grammatical structure of the whole poem, for such decisions taken purely *ad hoc* could do more harm than good. We shall therefore examine the clause structure of the whole poem, for our questions about tenses involve us in decisions about elements in clause structure. On our decisions about tense, for example, will depend our reading of the grammatical functions of *the lily* and *the rose* in lines 5, 9 and 13, and those of *the robes* and *they* in line 7. Do these function as the Subjects of their clauses, or as the Complements (or Objects), or are some of them appositional elements? These matters are vital to our interpretation of the text as a whole.

CLAUSE STRUCTURE

Table I (see p. 184) shows the details of clause structure throughout the poem. There are altogether fifteen clauses, four of which are repeated as refrain-material (lines 8–9 and 12–13). So in effect there are only eleven clauses in all, of which two are structurally ambiguous, namely those constituting lines 5 and 7. In both these clauses, the function of the verbal element or Predicator is fulfilled by the item *lay*; and in both instances this could be either the simple present of transitive 'lay' or the simple past of intransitive 'lie'. Now if in line 5 we have intransitivity, the verb cannot take an objective (or 'Extensive') Complement, i.e. a Complement which refers to something other than the Subject. The nominal elements, *the lily* and *the rose*, must therefore stand in some appositional relationship to the subject *I*. Contextually this would mean that *P* identifies himself or herself with both flowers, and the time-reference is back to the moment at which the maidens arrived. If, on the other hand, the Predicator is transitive here, then *the lily* and *the rose* can only be

184 ALEX RODGER

TABLE I *Clause Structure*

Clause no.	Clause structure	TEXT (repetitions omitted)	Line no.	Theme N	Theme U
1	SP	||| The maidens | came ||	1	S	
2	AᵇSPA	When | I | was | in [my mother's bower]; ||	2	S	
3	SPC	I | had | all ⟦that I would⟧. |||	3	S	
4	SPCA	The bailey | beareth | the bell | away;||	4	S	
5	XSP (or CSP) *or* Z || Z || CSP	The lily, ׃ the rose, ׃ the rose | I | lay. ||| OR The lily, || the rose, || the rose |I lay. |||	5	Z,Z	X* or C C
6, 7	SPC || CPS	The silver | is | white, || red is the gold; ||	6	S	C
8	S ⟨S⟩ PA *or* CSPA	The robes ⟨they⟩ lay | in [fold]. ||| OR The robes | they | lay | in [fold]. |||	7	S	C
9	A APS	And | through [the glass window] | shines | the sun. |||	10		A
10, 11	A?P(S) || A¹SC	How | should (I) love, || and I so young? |||	11	? || S	

SYMBOLS

S = Subject; usually a Nominal Group.

C = Complement; usually a Nominal Group.

Z = An ambiguous Nominal Group operating neither as Subject nor as Complement.

X = A group in apposition* to S or C.

P = Predicator; a verbal group.

A = Lexical Adjunct; an adverbial or prepositional group.

Aᵇ = Binding Adjunct; has fixed initial position in clause.

A¹ = Linking Adjunct. (*And, but, so, or,* all have fixed initial clause position.)

A? = Interrogative element, normally initial in clause, e.g. *how, why,* and all *wh-* 'pronouns'.

||| = Sentence boundary.

|| = Clause boundary.

| = Group boundary.

׃ = Group 'boundary' between unlinked items in List Complement.

( ) = Enclosure of one element within another.

⟦ ⟧ = A rankshifted or 'demoted' clause. See also Table II.

⟨ ⟩ = Intrusive or 'interrupting' element.

N = Normal theme.

U = Unusual theme.

? = Interrogative theme.

* N.B. The appositional reading of *The lily, the rose, the rose* is not possible unless an additional comma is inserted in the text. See p. 185 and note 7.

Note on Theme

The Theme of a clause is that element in it which occurs first from *choice* and not from grammatical necessity. Linking and binding Adjuncts of the kinds listed above *must* occur initially in the clause, and are therefore discounted in the assignment of this thematic function. *Interrogative theme* is signalled by the presence of an initial interrogative element, which may operate at S, C or A. *Unusual themes* are thus mainly Complements or lexical Adjuncts, i.e. adjuncts giving additional 'information'. Their initial clause-position gives them contrastive meaning in that their content acquires special prominence or emphasis. This is usually marked also by a separate tone-group.

Extensive Complements. Contextually, this gives us a *P* who 'deposits' flowers in some way; and the time-reference is to current action, or there is no specific time-reference and *P*'s *habitual* behaviour is being described. Now there is one snag to the former (i.e. the appositional-intransitive-past) reading of this line. Noun-phrases—or NOMINAL GROUPS as we shall call them—in apposition are invariably marked by commas separating them from the Subject-element proper. The commas graphologically represent the different tone group that marks such phrases in spoken English.[6] Now there is no comma after the second occurrence of *the rose* in lines 5, 9 and 13, in the text as it has been punctuated by modern editors. Furthermore, such appositional noun-phrases most frequently follow rather than precede the subject, but in any case cannot be separated from it by some other element. The absence of a third comma here thus makes it certain that at its second occurrence, *the rose* operates as an Extensive Complement;[7] and since the same item can hardly be both Subject and Complement of the same clause, the first occurrence must likewise operate as Complement. Finally, since two Complements now separate *the lily* from *I*, then it too must operate as Complement, and what we have is a LIST COMPLEMENT unlinked by the conjunction 'and'. Lines 5, 9 and 13 thus have their verb in the simple present tense.

At line 7 we have the 'lie' or 'lay' choice again, this time in the plural. If we have the simple past plus intransitivity here, then *the robes* is clearly the Subject of the clause, but we have an intrusive or pleonastic pronominal element, namely *they*, which can only operate as part of the Subject. We can find plenty of precedent for such structures in the poetry of the period and in the later ballads, e.g. 'My heart *it* grieveth me so', 'The rose *it* is a royal flower', 'The shepard upon a hill *he* satt', 'My love *he* built me a bonny bower', 'The maid *she* went to the well to washe', etc.[8] If, on the other hand, we have simple present and transitivity here, then *the robes* can only be an Extensive Complement, and the Subject of the clause is *they*. What we now have to ask is whether the poem as a whole would gain anything from a 'flashback' in time-reference, linking line 7 to lines 1–3. Since *the robes* are not mentioned again, a reference here to the past, however recent, seems merely to create further confusion. The implication would be that at the time of the maidens' coming, these robes were lying *in fold* somewhere. Why, then, should they be mentioned here, when the rest of the text seems to have moved into the present tense, rather than in the earlier part of the poem?

The assumption of a transitive verb in the simple present here not only gives us homogeneity of time-reference from line 4 on, but helps us to establish a further contextual point. For if the Subject of the clause at line 7 is *they*, we have to identify the earlier set of singular nouns or the plural nominal group which this pronoun presupposes. It might, of course, refer inclusively to all the personages mentioned other than *P*, who seems to be fully occupied with the 'laying' of the flowers. But *the bailey*, too, would seem to have his hands full—or one of them at least. And if carrying off the bell is part of this mysterious dignitary's duties in the situation, and he is already engaged in this, then his *robes*, if any, will be on his back and not being laid *in fold*. So unless participants are cryptically referred to in line 6 as *the silver* and *the gold*, which seems unlikely, the only participants who can be members of the robe-laying party are *the maidens* and *my mother*; and the plural *they*, while it may or may not include the latter, must refer to the former. We may now assume that one reason for, or result of, the maidens' coming was their wish, intention, or obligation to lay the robes in fold. But are they laying them out, or laying them away? And whose are they? Clearly the choice of *robes* (as opposed to 'gowns', 'smocks', 'frocks', etc.) would seem to indicate ceremony of some sort, and the presence of the bailey suggests a civic rather than an ecclesiastical occasion, despite the sombre cadence of the recurrent line in which he figures. We may now be able to make a shrewd guess at the nature of the occasion, but until we can confirm that subjective response by more evidence drawn from objective text, our guess is still only as good as the next reader's.

COHESION[9] 1 *Clause Structure*

Analysis at clause rank has now enabled us to select from the structural possibilities of the ambiguous clauses those readings which seem most probable in terms of both grammar and context of situation. Line 5 (and its recurrences) and line 7 both have a transitive verbal element in the simple present tense. The analysis also reveals a number of interesting features about the text as a whole. The first is that the amount of subordination or BONDAGE between clauses within the same sentence is almost nil. There is only a single BOUND (i.e. subordinate or dependent) clause in the entire text, namely the temporal clause comprising line 2. Within sentences, all other clauses are merely conjunction-linked, as at line 11, or juxtaposed as they are everywhere else in the poem. Furthermore, there is persistent congruence between the grammatical clauses and the metrical lines and half-lines. At lines 6 and 11 we have one clause to each half-line. All other lines contain one clause, neither more nor less. There is a remarkable homogeneity of grammatical MOOD[10] among the clauses, for out of a total of fifteen clauses, fourteen are FREE or independent clauses, and of these all but two are *affirmative* in mood, and function contextually as statements. (The two exceptions form a single sentence—the question at line 11, to which we shall return later.) This congruence between clause and line or half-line, together with the remarkable infrequency both of bondage and linkage-by-conjunction, partly accounts for one major aspect of the poem's elusive impact: its lack of *topical cohesion*. Most of the clauses function as statements, and each statement is 'sealed' into a line or half-line. In fact, simply by removing the binding adjunct (i.e. the adverb *when*) from its obligatory initial position in the clause at line 2, and the linking adjunct (i.e. the conjunction *and*) from its equally obligatory initial position in the clause at line 10, we could punctuate lines 1–10 and 12–13 with full stops at the ends of all clauses. As for line 11, it too really conceals two potentially separate sentences, each consisting of a single free clause. For the question proper really ends at the half-line boundary here. The second half-line, *and I so young*, is a 'moodless' or MINOR free clause, i.e. a complete sentence lacking a finite verbal element.[11] In its given form, it is a sort of suppressed bound clause ('How should I love, *when* I am so young?') but could just as well be written as a major free clause, giving us the line: *How should I love? I am so young!* With this simple transformation, we could then punctuate the text throughout with full stops (including, of course, the interrogation mark) at all the clause-boundaries. The difference in overall meaning would be subtle, but not radical. Essentially the poem consists of separate, single-clause sentences. The effect of this grammatical insulation of each clause within its line or half-line is that each contextual topic tends to be insulated from those on either side of it. We find it difficult to see the situational connections between them for there is very little grammatical COHESION between clauses forming the same sentence, and virtually no cohesion between the sentences forming the whole text.

Cohesion of the latter sort is what gives unity to a piece of discourse by making its sequence of sentences 'hang together' in an intelligible continuity. It operates primarily through three kinds of relationship among features of the text; (*a*) those of PRESUPPOSITION; (*b*) those within LEXIS or vocabulary; and (*c*) those between aspects of LEXIS and aspects of GRAMMAR. Now in this text we have only two examples of presuppositional cohesion. The first is the pronominal substitution of *they* for *the maidens*; the second is the linking Adjunct *And* which initiates the first sentence in stanza III (line 10). When we begin a new sentence with this conjunction, we set up an expectation that the 'content' of that sentence will somehow presuppose or be presupposed by what has gone before (*Genesis* I is the most thoroughgoing example readily available.) In this respect there is something very peculiar about our text, a feature we will have to return to later. For nothing in line 10 seems obviously or necessarily to follow from what has been said earlier, yet line 10 has a curiously climactic flavour that demands explanation.

Lexical cohesion of discourse again seems thin in our poem.[12] This sort of cohesion is closely connected with the notions of topic or subject-matter, for it is in the relations between items of vocabulary that we usually find a strong correlation between the linguistic form of a text and its context of situation. Given a particular FIELD or kind of subject-matter, we expect the lexicon of a text to comprise items having certain kinds of contextual association in common. Thus *lily* and *rose*, for example, belong to the same lexical SET, to which we could go on almost indefinitely adding such items as *tulip*, *daffodil*, *weed* and *poplar*. In the sen-

LINGUISTIC FORM AND LITERARY MEANING 189

tence: '——s grow in my mother's garden', any one of these items in the plural could fill the Subject position. Likewise, we are far from surprised by, and might indeed have predicted, the occurrence in the same context of the items *grow* and *garden*. All these items, that is to say, tend to co-occur or COLLOCATE predictably. Now we have already seen that the collocations *within clauses* in this poem are not intrinsically unusual or puzzling, though the collocation of *bailey*, *bell* and *bear* is admittedly rather obscure situationally. What does strike us as odd and unusual is the clustering within so short and repetitive a text of so many lexical items unlikely to collocate without the presence of additional explanatory matter. We should normally expect to find this in bound clauses, rankshifted[13] clauses, and adverbial and prepositional phrases that would make clear to us the semantic relations among these oddly assorted items of vocabulary. The refrain lines themselves are a striking example of a sentence in which two clauses are simply juxtaposed without discernible lexical relations between the collocates of the one and those of the other. In situational terms, what has P's 'laying' the flowers got to do with the bailey's bearing away the bell?

Apart from this absence of obvious lexical cohesion, there is yet another oddity here. Repetition of the same items is one of the simplest and most obvious forms of lexical cohesion (see *Genesis* I again). But in this poem, apart from the fact that the distribution of the nine occurrences of *I* allows us to assign the whole utterance to P, not even the exact repetition of whole clauses and indeed a whole sentence seems to help us very much. We may no doubt assume that at lines 4, 8 and 12, the *bailey* and *bell* referred to are the same on each occasion, but this does nothing to identify them or establish their situational relevance. And what about the flowers in the second refrain-line? Does P 'lay' the same *blooms* on each occasion, picking them up again between utterances, or are there lots of each kind?

COHESION II *Group Structure*

To understand why the normal kinds of lexical cohesion seem to be absent here, we shall have to consider cohesion by REFERENCE, and this will involve a closer look at the nominal groups that operate as Subjects and Complements in the clauses.[14] Table II shows us that there are altogether thirty-five nominal groups in the poem, of which thirty-two operate at S or C in clause structure. Pronouns and other single-word items account for ten of these thirty-two. One adjectival phrase (*so young*) and one long noun-phrase (*all that I would*) account for two more.

TABLE II   *Nominal Groups*

| Line refs. | MH Groups ||||| HQ Groups with R/S at Q |
	h	dh	dnh	ddh	eh	
1		the maidens				
2	I			my mother's bower		
3	I					all ⟦that I would⟧
4,8,12		the bailey				
4,8,12		the bell				
5,9,13		the lily				
5,9,13	I	the rose				
5,9,13		the rose				
6	white	the silver				
6	red	the gold				
7	they	the robes				
7	[fold]					
10		the sun		[the glass window]		
11	I					
11	I				so young	

Primary structure
M = Modifier.
H = Head.
Q = Qualifier.

Secondary structure
d = Deictic or determiner.
e = Epithet or adjective.
n = Pre-head noun.
h = Headword.

⟦ ⟧ = Rankshifted clause.
[ ] = Rankshifted group.
R/S = Rankshift.*

*Note on Rankshift

Rankshift is a linguistic feature in which a grammatical unit may operate as an element in the structure of a unit of the same rank or of a lower rank. For example, in the sentence 'I said || that I would', *that I would* is a bound clause in its own right. In our poem, however, it operates as part of a Nominal Group: *all that I would*. It has been demoted or downgraded to operate as Qualifier inside a noun-phrase. We may also have group-within-group rankshift, as in *through the glass window*, where the nominal group *the glass window*, which could operate directly at S or C in clause structure, has been downgraded to act as the completive element inside an Adjunct or adverbial group. So also is *my mother's bower*, which contains double rankshift, since *my mother* already constitutes a nominal group demoted to the rank of a deictic or determiner by the possessive morpheme *'s*. (See Table IV.)

All the remaining twenty Subjects and Complements are of the same simple structure, viz. definite article plus noun. Now despite its name, the definite article has no inherent power to *define* the nouns it 'modifies' (i.e. precedes). Where the whole group is self-defining, i.e. where there is no doubt as to the identity of the entity 'named' by the main noun or HEADWORD, then the definite article alone is specific, i.e. sufficient to define that referent, as in 'the world', 'the truth', 'the sky', 'the air', 'the stars', etc. If the headword is not self-defining in this way, then the presence of the definite article in a nominal group merely indicates that something else in the text, or in the implied context of situation, does this work of definition. The identifying elements may be inside the nominal group itself, i.e. in the Modifier, in the Qualifier, or in both.[15] In such cases the definite article is *anticipatory*, presupposing at least one identifying element to come, as in 'The *English* Coast' (= deh, where d = definite article, e = epithet, and h = headword), 'The house *with the green shutters*' (=dh + Q) and 'The *red* rose *of Lancaster*' (=deh + Q). Alternatively, the use of the definite article in a non-self-defining group may have *retrospective* reference to an earlier group in the text where the same headword is specifically defined by identifying elements at M or Q. But if no earlier group with the same headword exists, the identity of a *dh* group may still be clear enough because the earlier context contains one or more items from the same lexical set, or a sufficient number of items likely to collocate with that set, which will make the new *dh* group's reference clear, as in: 'The maidens from our village came to help me tend my mother's bower, and took away all the lilies and the roses to decorate the church.' Here *the lilies* and *the roses* are identified by the earlier group *my mother's bower*, while *the church* is likewise defined by *our village*, which also helps to define *the maidens*. Otherwise, a new nominal group of *dh* structure may simply imply that the headword refers to something we should automatically expect to find in the given situation, as follows:

> The coach plunged off at a frantic gallop toward London. Turpin emptied his hat on the ground and carefully arranged its contents in three piles. All the jewels he stowed

in the pockets of his greatcoat; the other two piles were another matter. He put *the silver* in one saddle-bag, and *the gold* in the other.

Here the italicized groups are the kind of mass nouns for currency that one would expect in a context with eighteenth-century highway robbery as its subject-matter.

Now of the twenty nominal groups of *dh* structure in our poem, only one is self-defining: *the sun*. The remaining nineteen (fifteen of which are accounted for by occurrence of *the bailey, the bell, the lily* and *the rose*) ought either to be retrospectively or situationally defined. Since it is precisely the implied context of situation which is obscure, the latter sort of definition is absent. Nor are there any earlier groups containing these same headwords with identifying elements at M or Q. The one other piece of text that might have made all these groups specific and 'identified' is wanting— namely a *title* of the kind that would clearly label and define the context of situation.[16] The poem's contradictory effects of simplicity and obscurity are thus dependent partly upon the grammatical simplicity of its 'self-contained' clauses, with their homogeneity of affirmative mood and their congruence with the metrical line or half-line, and partly upon this other extreme simplicity and homogeneity of structure in the bulk of its nominal groups. Just how simple these are is obvious when we recall the size and complexity possible in English nominal groups (e.g. '... all the seven large red roses with straight stems that my mother picked last night in her bower for our local bailey...'. We could enlarge this specimen almost indefinitely by continuing to add rankshifted clauses to it in the manner of the nursery rhyme about *The House that Jack Built*). But the simplicity of the *dh* groups in our poem is delusive. Their referents are non-specific, non-identified, except (theoretically) by the situation; which in its turn is obscure just because its main 'topical' nominal groups are of this non-specifying kind.

The verbal groups are not much more helpful. They too show extreme simplicity of structure (see Table III on p. 193), for all are single-item groups except one (*should . . . love*) and there are no non-finite forms, no negatives, no passives and no contrastive

TABLE III *Verbal Groups*

Line refs.	Verbal groups	Transitivity Trans.	Transitivity Intrans.	Modality Modal	Modality Non-modal	Other features
1	came		X		X	
2	was		X		X	No
3	had	X			X	(i) non-finite, (ii) negative, (iii) contrastive, or (iv) passive groups.
3	would	X		X		
4, 8, 12	beareth	X			X	
5, 9, 13	lay	X			X	
6	is	X			X	
6	is	X			X	
7	lay	X			X	
10	shines		X		X	
11	should (I) love		X	X	X	

(i.e. emphatic) uses of the auxiliaries *be, do, have, must*, etc. Also, of the eight verbal items employed, four are lexically rather 'weak', i.e. *come, be* (three occurrences), *have* and *will*—this last being a secondary or 'modal' auxiliary acting for a whole group (line 3, *would*). The four 'stronger' or more specific items likely to provide clues to the nature of the situation are *bear* (three occurrences), *lay* (four occurrences), *shine* and *love*. Three of these more powerful verbal items collocate with prepositional or adverbial groups (see Table IV below) that give us a little additional situational information. The most specific of these is *through the glass window*, collocating with *shine* in line 10; but as we

TABLE IV *Adverbial Groups (or Adjuncts)*

Line refs.	GRAMMATICAL Interrogative	Binding	Linking	LEXICAL Adverbial	Prepositional with R/S completive
2	—	When	—	—	in [[my mother]'s bower]
4, 8, 12	—	—	—	away	—
7	—	—	—	—	in [fold]
10	—	—	And	—	through [the glass window]
11	How	—	and	—	—

have noted, the situational relevance of this line is far from obvious. *Lay* in line 7 collocates with *in fold*. This prepositional Adjunct seems to be equivalent to others in which an unmodified and unqualified headword refers to a generalized location or state (e.g. 'My watch is *in pawn*', 'We've put all our furniture *in store*', etc.). But the implications are insufficient for our purposes. Are the robes being laid *in fold* for wear, or for putting away? *Lay* in lines 5, 9 and 13 takes no adjunct at all, which is rather unusual for this transitive verb. Without benefit of adjunct we normally *lay* roads, carpets, linoleum, foundation stones, charges of explosive, dust, eggs, rumours and ghosts. Lilies and roses, however, are usually laid *on* something, such as a grave, or *at* something, such as feet, or *in* something, such as a basket. The verbal item *love* likewise takes no sort of Adjunct here, but rather more surprisingly is used intransitively. We are not told whom or what *P* should love. So among the verbal groups, too, there is a simplicity which amounts almost to linguistic unhelpfulness.

Our search for cohesion has so far involved analysis at two grammatical ranks. First we looked at clause structure, then went down to the next rank below, that of the groups constituting the clauses. Analysis at both ranks has revealed marked homogeneity and simplicity of structure combined with a notable absence of the normal forms of cohesion that we expect in any kind of discourse, literary or otherwise. If we add to these facts the further observation that the fifteen clauses could, after very slight changes indeed, operate as fifteen separate sentences each of one free clause and each occupying either one whole line or one half-line exactly, we have at least a partial explanation of the poem's self-contradictory effect of 'obscure simplicity'. What, then, gives it its mysterious unity and significance? To answer this question we must first look at the relations between its largest grammatical units, the sentences, and its largest metrical units, the stanzas forming the largest linguistic unit—the whole text (see Table V on p. 196). These 'grammetrical' relations in poetry constitute an important mode of meaning too often critically under-estimated or even ignored entirely. When we have looked at these, we may be in a position to relate them to some form of cohesion not normally found outside poetry.

COHESION III *Sentence Structure and Stanza Structure*

Grammatically, then, we have altogether seven sentences; metrically we have three stanzas, the first of which is slightly anomalous in having one orthographic line (metrically a half-line) more than the other two.[17] The proportion of *sentences to stanzas* runs thus: 2:1, 2:1, 3:1. One of the seven sentences, however, is the refrain, so if we temporarily discount repeated material, the total amount of 'new' text is only five sentences. The ratio of *new sentences to the stanza* runs: 2:1, 1:1, 2:1. Stanza III thus contains the same number of new sentences as stanza I, despite the fact that it has one line less than the latter. Or, if we look at the proportion of *lines per new sentence*, we find a rapidly diminishing ratio, thus: 3:1, 2:1, 2:1, 1:1, 1:1. The new sentences, that is, grow rapidly shorter as the poem proceeds. Also, the proportion of *clauses to the sentence* in the new material is significant, running thus: 3:1, 2:1, 3:1, 1:1, 2:1. We have already seen that the characteristic topic-carrying unit in this poem is the clause (see p. 187), so we can now see that while stanza I introduces five topics, in as many lines, stanzas II and III between them introduce six more in their four lines of new text—three topics each. In other words, new topics are introduced in an even more condensed way in the *new* lines of stanzas II and III than they are in the first three lines of stanza I. Rapid progressive shortening of sentence is accompanied by the rapid introduction of new matter. This clause-to-sentence ratio has a further effect among the new utterances: that of a mounting tension related to the speed with which new topics are introduced. Stanza I, for example, is relatively relaxed and leisurely. It contains, for one thing, the only occurrence of bondage or subordination, and takes five lines to contain five clauses forming two sentences. The new material of stanza II amounts to only one sentence, but into this are squeezed three topic-carrying clauses in two lines. The greatest moment of grammatical 'condensation' in the text comes in the first line of stanza III. Here we have the simplest of the five new sentences, consisting of a single affirmative clause. The acceleration in the introduction of new topics is thus accompanied by a statement whose cumulative effect is in no way diminished by its lack of perceptible relevance to the preceding statements, to which it is linked by that question-begging initial *And*. It is clearly meant to have a cohesive effect on all three stanzas, both by summarizing in some way what has gone before, and by leading us to the final new sentence, the question at line 11. In this last new sentence, we again have the two-clause structure we noted at line 6, only this time the clauses are linked and not merely juxtaposed, and the linkage is of a peculiar kind, for it links a major clause of interrogative mood to a minor free clause, i.e. one with no finite verbal element and indeed no verbal element at all. The minor clause here seems to operate in a way analogous to that of a sentence-tag. These usually work the other way round, converting the contextual function of statement (i.e. a grammatical affirmative) into that of question, e.g. 'I'm very young, aren't I?' In line 11, however, the major clause marks the

TABLE V *Sentence and Stanza Structure*

Clause class and mood	Text	Line no.	Sentence structure and no.
α.	||| The maidens came ||	1	αβα 1.
β	When I was in my mother's bower; ||	2	
α.	I had all ⟦that I would.⟧ |||	3	
α.	The bailey beareth the bell away; ||	4	αα 2.
α.	The lily, the rose, the rose I lay. |||	5	
α.α.	The silver is white, || red is the gold; ||	6	ααα 3.
α.	The robes they lay in fold. |||	7	
α.	The bailey beareth the bell away; ||	8	αα 4.
α.	The lily, the rose, the rose I lay. |||	9	
&α.	And through the glass window shines the sun. |||	10	&α 5.
α?&α–	How should I love, || and I so young? |||	11	α&α 6.
α.	The bailey beareth the bell away; ||	12	αα 7.
α.	The lily, the rose, the rose I lay. |||	13	

Sentence Structure (primary elements)
α = Free (or 'independent') clause.
β = Bound (or 'dependent') clause.
⟦ ⟧ = Rankshifted clause.
& = Linkage.

Free Clause Mood System.
α. = Affirmative.
α? = Interrogative.
α– = Minor or moodless clause.

whole sentence as having the function of a question, and the minor clause tags on as a sort of exclamatory reinforcement of it. Thus, after a sequence of three longer statements, we get a climactic pair of sentences each one line long, the first a statement, the second a question of unusual structure, each of them introducing new topics: the window, the sunshine, love and youth.

However we try, we cannot alter this overall construction of the poem in the smallest detail without damaging, or even destroying the impression it creates. For example, if we imagine the refrain-sentence to be a mere choric convention and try removing it altogether, the semantic connections among the remaining sentences seem slighter than ever:

> The maidens came
> When I was in my mother's bower;
> I had all that I would.
>
> The silver is white, red is the gold;
> The robes they lay in fold.
>
> And through the glass window shines the sun.
> How should I love, and I so young?

So despite its mere juxtaposition of two topically unrelated clauses, the refrain sentence clearly carries vital situational information. But if we try inserting it only once in the poem (either at lines 4–5, or 8–9 or 10–13), an important ingredient of meaning is again lost, despite the presence of the necessary 'information'. The repetition of the refrain at precisely all those points is part of the poem's total meaning. We cannot even reverse the sequence of its clauses, thus:

> The lily, the rose, the rose I lay;
> The bailey beareth the bell away.

This, too, subtly but disastrously destroys the impact of the poem. The same is true for all the other relations. We can alter neither the order of the stanzas, nor the sequence of sentences nor the sequence of clauses within sentences, despite the strong tendency for these to be juxtaposed rather than linked or subordinated.

Even at lines 1–2, where we have a genuinely reversible free/bound sequence (not all such sequences are reversible, e.g. 'They came into the bower, where I was sitting'), we disturb our feeling of the 'rightness' of these lines if we reverse them:

> When I was in my mother's bower,
> The maidens came...

In the true version, the free clause presupposes or predicts nothing necessarily to follow. It is already grammatically complete. Punctuated with a full stop at the end of the line, it would undoubtedly strike us as a rather bald and abrupt statement. Nevertheless, the bound clause comes as a sort of grammatical 'extra', since it is not necessary to the completion of the sentence. Contextually, the result of this is that a greater degree of prominence or weight is given to the coming of the maidens than to *P*'s whereabouts at the moment. The 'occasion' of the poem is in fact marked by the former and not the latter, which is literally a subordinate utterance. The reversed form would throw the weight of contextual importance on *P*'s being in the bower, making the arrival of the maidens seem more casual. So not even the first sentence can be altered. Its final clause, firmly separated from the first two by a semi-colon and so insulated from the temporal clause, thus seems to suggest that its Predicator, *had*, carries a specific time-reference rather than 'habitual' reference, for grammatical sequence is used to suggest chronological sequence, which in turn suggests causality—*post hoc* being used to imply *propter hoc*. P received *all that I would* as a consequence of the coming of the maidens whose function is the folding of *the robes*.

COHESION IV *Foregrounded Features*[18]

If we now look again at Table I, we find something unusual about the structure of the clause that constitutes line 10's strangely cumulative or climactic statement. The sequence of its elements, AAPS, is the exact reverse of that of a normal affirmative clause with an intransitive Predicator, which is SPA. Now we can ignore for the moment the linking Adjunct, since its initial position in the clause is obligatory. But the second A would normally be final:

```
        S         P              A
||| The sun | shines | through the glass window. |||
```

LINGUISTIC FORM AND LITERARY MEANING 199

This reversal of normal structure has a double effect *within* the clause itself. It gives unusual emphasis to the Adjunct, and keeps us waiting for what we should normally get first—the Subject. Stylistically such structures are common in narrative as small-scale suspense-plus-surprise devices, e.g. 'The door opened suddenly, and in rushed Jones', 'Down will come Baby...', 'Here comes the Bride!', etc. Thus part of the contextually climactic effect of line 10 comes from its internal structure, and part from its 'illogical' linking Adjunct. If unusual sequence of elements can produce this sort of effect, we may find others of the same kind in the poem. Since the normal sequence of elements in statements, for example, is SPA or SPC or SPCA, and all our clauses are affirmative, we should expect to find the Subject occurring initially in them all. This is true of six out of the ten 'new' affirmative clauses, but not of the remainder.

The second clause of the refrain-sentence, for instance, is also unusual in its structure, which can be symbolically stated as CSP. The same is true of the second clause in line 6, where the adjectival (or Intensive) Complement is similarly thrust into initial position in the clause: CPS. Likewise, the third clause in that sentence, *the robes they lay in fold*, has the structure CSPA. Outside poetry, such structures are unusually emphatic, and their occurrence tends to presuppose a string of contrasting statements involving items from the same set. Thus 'Treacle I detest' not only gives unusually strong emphasis to the Complement, but presupposes some earlier statement like: 'I like butter/jam/syrup/ etc. on my bread.' Also, such a structure seems to demand contrastive linkage if it comes as the second clause within a sentence, e.g. 'I love Mozart, Beethoven and Brahms, *but* Berlioz I can't stand.' Now we have no such strings of previous statements here. Are all these emphatic Complements therefore simply the results of the exigencies of the rhyme-schemes in the poem? *Away* (lines 4, 8 and 12) demands that *lay* occur in final position in the next line. But on the other hand, the poet could have written:

> I lay the lily, the rose, the rose;
> Away with the bell the bailey goes.

Again, while *gold* (line 6) demands something with the same sound as *fold* as its rhyme-word, it was not necessary for him to place *the robes* initially in the second clause. He could have written:

> The silver is white, red is the gold;
> They lay the robes in fold.

Clearly, the poet has deliberately chosen this unusual and emphatic initial place in structure for *the robes*. In any case, why the emphatic Complement *red*? Surely he could have stuck to normal word-order throughout, and written something like:

> The silver is white, the gold is red;
> They lay the robes upon the bed ...

or whatever else would provide the most contextually suitable rhyme for *red*. We can only assume that the poet felt it meaningful not only to have the refrain-lines in their given sequence, but also for the Complements *the lily*, *the rose*, *red* and *the robes* to have this unusually emphatic position.

In any case, isn't there something a bit odd about that List Complement in the second clause of the refrain? When we use such a structure, we usually list *different* items, as in our sentence about composers, placing a conjunction before the final item. Why, in so short a list, should the poet *repeat* the second item without a conjunction? Why not a third item, e.g. 'The lily, the rose, the rue I lay', or even alternation: 'The rose, the lily, the rose I lay' or 'The lily, the rose, the lily I lay'? Since another item from the flower set is not used, the double occurrence of *the rose* is also presumably deliberate and meaningful, and alternation of the items is also purposely avoided. If we look at the line again, we see there is one further possible structure for it—a three-clause structure of two Minor Clauses followed by a Major Clause with an emphatic (or 'thematic') Complement. Minor Clauses consisting solely or mainly of a nominal group are common enough ('The police!', 'Two four-and-nines, please', 'Stalls, or back circle?' 'Which dress? The green silk or the blue grosgrain?'). Such nominal groups operate ambiguously, having the status and function neither of Subject nor of Complement. In the sort of descriptive grammar we are using here, we label

LINGUISTIC FORM AND LITERARY MEANING 201

them with the neutral symbol Z. What we may have, therefore, in the second refrain-line is the following:

$$\begin{array}{ccccc} Z & Z & C & S & P \\ || \text{ The lily, } || \text{ the rose, } || \text{ the rose } | \text{ I } | \text{ lay. } ||| \end{array}$$

This gives us a half-line that simply names alternatives, each of the Minor Clauses consisting solely of a nominal element. This is in turn followed by an emphatic decision in the second half-line in favour of *the rose*. Alternatively, if we retain the list complement reading, the implication is that *P* is 'laying' two roses to every one lily. Whichever reading we accept, the contextual implication is clear: *the rose* either outnumbers or outvalues *the lily*. We have ambivalent grammar, here, and both meanings are relevant.

Now if we match up the emphatic Complements we find they are the second occurrences of *the rose*, *red* and *the robes*. Structurally, these are equated; and there is an obvious probability of collocation between *red* and *rose*. But *red* is already equated with *gold* by simple predication, i.e. by the verb *be*. A semantic equation is thus set up by means of (*a*) positional equivalence of emphatic or thematic Complements and (*b*) simple predication, such that *the rose* = *red* = *the gold* = *the robes*. The ceremonial dress is thus associated with roses, redness and gold. One term of this equation, however, is already a term in another positional equation with semantic implications. *The gold* shares the highly unusual final Subject position with *the sun*, and there is almost as much probability of collocation between these two items as there is between *the rose* and *red*. These equivalences, set up by contrastive grammatical positioning of Complements and Subjects, establish an extra, *poetic* dimension of cohesion and an emotive-association pattern among these elements as lexical items. In other words, the combined syntactical and metrical patterning of the poem gives it an additional, non-logical mode of meaning by creating an unusual but not impossible lexical 'set'.

As soon as we have seen this set of relationships among the unusually positioned nominal groups, the other set also becomes clear. The Subject-groups which appear in *normal* clause position (i.e. initially) are *the maidens*, *I* (lines 2, 3 and both clauses in line 11), *the bailey*, *the silver*. Furthermore, if we select the Z||Z||

CSP reading of line 5, then the initial group in the first half-line, *the lily*, can be equated with the whole clause forming the first half-line at line 6: *the silver is white*. Here again positional equivalence plus simple predication allows the following equation: *maidens = I = lily = silver = white*. (The only odd man out is *the bailey*, the presumptively masculine legal-cum-civic official.) Again, there is a strong likelihood of collocation between *the lily* and *white*.

Perhaps we can now see the significance of the rather puzzling sixth line of the poem. For if there is clear collocational probability in *the white lily* and *the red rose*, there is an equally probable symbolic relation between the former and *maidens*, in the notion of purity, virginity; and the recurrent *I* is clearly positionally equated with these. Also, there is an equally powerful symbolic relation between *the red rose* and *love*. The flowers in the inner situation are thus not merely 'actual', but also *emblematic* of two highly valued but contrasting states of femininity: maidenhood and womanly fulfilment. Linguistic foregrounding and the special patterning of foregrounded features have provided firm clues not only to the sex of the protagonist, but to the nature of the situation. Also, there is further reinforcement, both in grammar and in sound, for the belief that *P* is a young girl about to be married. The *I* of lines 5, 9 and 13 is positionally equivalent to the *they* of line 7, both lines share the same lexical item as Predicator, and there is strong phonemic congruity between their Complements, *rose* and *robes*:

> The robes *they* lay . . .
> . . . the rose *I* lay.

They and *I* are thus simultaneously equated and contrasted, both belonging to the sub-set *maidens* (i.e. virgins), both busy 'laying', but laying different objects. Grammatically, however, both sets of objects are associated with *love*—the wedding robes and the rose. Now we know, too, why the definite article is used to modify *lily* and *rose*. The reference is not so much specific as *generic*, for the flowers are seen not only as individual specimens of their kind, but as emblems of feminine states of being. This also explains the curious use of the definite article at line 6. For whatever else *the silver* and *the gold* may refer to (her dowry? the traditional loving-cup of silver and gilt?) they refer back, in an unusual but cohesive way, to the emblematic flowers as well. The definite article is thus both specific and generic in both these lines.

Finally, the contrastive structure of the clauses in line 6 (SPC||CPS) implies preference between contending values. In the proverb 'Speech is silver, silence is golden,' the absence of the contrastive conjunction 'but' frequently lures speakers into supplying it. Here the contrastive function is carried by the thematic Complement *red*. Silver, a precious enough metal, is white like the lily; but red is the colour of the more precious gold. The red rose of married love is therefore analogically of greater value than the white lily of virginity. (Now we can suggest a reason why *maidens*, rather than 'women', 'wenches', or even 'lasses', is the first lexical item to occur in the poem.) So, in the choice *P* makes at line 5 and its recurrences, the odds are two to one in favour of *the rose*, whose emphatic initial position in the third clause of the line clinches the matter.

CONTEXT AND INTERPRETATION

We can now see an inner context of situation which is wholly consonant with the linguistic facts as we have found them. The strangely non-cohesive clauses and sentences are given a specifically poetic mode of cohesion and meaning through a grammatical patterning which is itself the major situational clue. A male *P* now becomes grotesquely improbable, since not even the youngest of boys is likely to equate himself with the traditional emblems of femininity and then urgently protest his inability to love. The structure of line 11 clearly suggests anxiety and doubt about the speaker's ability to fulfil an obligation. *How should I love?* certainly implies futurity, but the auxiliary *should* does not seem prosodically to demand stress, as do both *I* and *love*, and the contextual implication is one of sheer incapacity to meet an obligation.[19] We have exact structural, tonal and functional equivalents in modern English for both clauses in this sentence. The first is very close indeed to 'How should *I* know?', our response to a question that baffles or annoys us because we do not feel in a position to answer it. Likewise, the unusual minor clause reminds us of similar linked tag-clauses expressive of resentment, shock, surprise or disbelief, e.g. 'How could *I* dance, and me a *cripple*?' or 'How can *he* gamble, and him a *clergyman*?' It is simply the occurrence of the *I* form (slightly more formal than the modern *me* and *him* of our examples) that enables us to assign to the elements of this second clause in line 11 their functions as Subject and Complement, since the structure clearly implies simple predication. We can therefore paraphrase *P*'s question as: 'How can *I* be expected to love a husband, when I am too young for marriage?'

Our young, feminine, virgin protagonist, then, attended by the maidens who are laying out her wedding robes, is probably strewing with symbolic flowers the floors of those rooms in her home which will shortly be the scene of the wedding-feast and the semi-public consummation of the marriage;[20] for in this line *lay* without an Adjunct suggests the action of strewing rather than the mere making up of posies. These activities suggest an indoor setting which allows us to select the contextual meaning 'bed-chamber' or 'boudoir' for *bower*. The preparation of the bride-to-be is taking place in the appropriate setting, the feminine sanctum of the household. One potential collocate of *bower* within the text is *window*, which is very unlikely to collocate with the 'garden-arbour' meaning of *bower*. But why should this headword be modified by the surprisingly banal epithet, *glass*? This is the only pre-head adjective[21] in the whole poem, and we should have expected something more striking, or no adjective at all—until we recall that in late medieval times, only the feudal aristocracy and the richer of the bourgeoisie could afford glazed windows in their homes. Here we have a girl who uses gold and silver as her measures of value, who has had—on this occasion at least—all that she wished, and whose home has glazed windows and a bower—clearly no mere peasant wench. All is going ahead for the wedding—or is it? The civil and legal official, the bailey, appears to be carrying his bell *away*. The *maidens* may be folding up *the robes* to put them away. Does the girl's question imply withdrawal from the situation, a refusal to wed?

We can best answer this question in terms of the poem's total structure. Before line 11, we have a string of simple assertions of facts, but some of these, as we now know, have an emblematic or symbolic significance. The girl's description of her own actions conforms with her evaluation of the flowers, for in line 5 and its recurrence, she decides, after hesitating, in favour of *the rose*. Why, then, the panic-stricken questions at line 11? And why does she bother even to mention the sunshine? The latter is announced in a clause of climactic structure forming at once the simplest and the most seemingly irrelevant sentence in the whole poem. Yet this 'irrelevant' statement is linked to all those that precede it in a way that suggests that it somehow naturally follows from all that has been said, or adds a finishing touch of some sort. But, for *P*, does the sunshine signify the crowning glory or the last straw? If we now recall our symbolic equations, the *sun* = *gold* (by unusual position). But *gold* = marriage, since *gold* = *rose* and *rose* = womanly fulfilment in love. The sun is *gold* in colour, and colour is the attribute in terms of which her original value-judgment was made. The splendour and richness of the occasion are underlined even by that innocent-sounding adjunct *in fold*, for as the *New English Dictionary* makes clear, the phrase is a 'fixed collocation' of the late Middle English period, a formula often introduced in conventional descriptions of costly garments.[22] Her wedding dress, then, is a splendid affair. She ought to be elated, for 'Happy is the bride the sun shines on ...'.[23] But *the sun* is now clearly established as an emblem of masculinity, and the golden light of this symbolic bridegroom—warm, energetic, life-giving—strikes through the protective *glass* of the rich and comfortable home into what is normally the feminine sanctum, *the bower*. This, however, may well be her bridal-chamber within the hour, as the strewing of the flowers suggests. (For readers or hearers of poetry in this period, the collocation *lily-rose-bower-love* would have powerful romantic-erotic associations.) The whole notion is emotionally ambivalent, both attractive and intimidating to a girl self-avowedly *so young*; and immediately on the heels of the culminative final Subject, *the sun*, comes her outcry of doubt and desperation: how can she be expected to go through with it?

Here, in these last lines of the text, we find yet another reason for its peculiar style of communication. We know its field is marriage, and its precise 'thesis' the speaker's fears, as a very young girl, about her own immediately impending marriage. In its social function, or role, however, *P*'s discourse can hardly be said to be a connected argument of her case. It is clearly *informal*, in its leaping from topic to topic as well as in the tone of its final question, and indeed we can summarize the position by saying that in this poem, *absence of normal cohesion amounts to a deliberately foregrounded device, making the whole structure of P's discourse incompatible with the idea of her actually addressing the other participants.* The retrospective note struck by the simple past tense in lines 1–3 fulfils a double function. In the outer (i.e. performance) situation, it sets the scene for the reader. In the inner situation of *P* herself, it is ambivalent in function. Ostensibly, it has a specific time-reference to the immediate past—the moment of her bridesmaids' arrival. In the 'present' circumstances of lines 4 ff., however, that moment has already acquired a peculiar poignancy. It now represents for her both past and future, for their arrival on this day and for this purpose has brought to an end a whole phase of her life, and is the prelude to a future she hardly dare contemplate. But the simple past tense of lines 1–3 also carries subtle suggestions of *habitual* past action. The maidens (presumably friends) no doubt came on many previous occasions, but merely as girlhood companions. They came habitually when she was in her mother's bower; and during the years spent there she was doubtless indulged, had all that she could wish for. Her memory of the specific moment an hour or so ago thus becomes both a nostalgic retrospective symbol of her comfortable, carefree childhood and a sharp reminder that that way of life is finished for her. Grammar and context of situation support and indeed demand both 'meanings' here. Furthermore, *P*'s use of the simple present tense from line 4 on reinforces this. At lines 5 (9, 13), 6, 7 and 10, the contextual function of this tense is clearly of the 'running commentary' kind. Now not only is this a rare kind of usage, but one in which the speaker's own situation is very seldom the topic. We normally use language to describe situations *other than the one we ourselves are in at that moment*, unless we cannot be seen by our addressees. Even in the latter case we normally use the continuous or expanded present. But in this poem, situation of utterance and 'message' are identical. What in fact we have as text is *P*'s stream-of-consciousness, the sort of 'interior monologue' we think of as being the invention of the modern novelist. If she addresses anyone, she addresses herself, silently. The role and mode of her discourse fully vindicate the paradoxically 'cohesive inconsequentiality' of its form. And that is why the poem ends with the repetition of the refrain. For no one else in the situation, neither *mother* nor *maidens*, answers the young girl's question, simply because no one hears it but herself. In it she interrogatively weighs the unknown splendours and miseries of love against the known certainties of extreme youth and childhood security. She answers herself in the repetition both of words and of action which now have even more poignancy in their weighing of the same issues in the two emblems, *the lily* versus *the rose*. For the choice is by now no choice, but a foregone conclusion. The inevitability of marriage has been implied structurally from the very first utterance of this line.

It is somehow implied also in the parallel reiteration of her description of the bailey's action, and accentuated by its sound and rhythm. (Compare, for example, the wilder and gayer movement suggested by my earlier paraphrase, 'Away with the bell the bailey goes.') Here, however, we are on more difficult ground. What *is* a bailey?—or rather, what was he then? And what was his function at a wedding? If we visualize him walking away from the bride's home ringing a small hand-bell, we may be quite right; but I have found nothing to corroborate this. On the other hand, we do know as a linguistic fact that *bear the bell* and *bear away the bell* were two different but frequently confused proverbial idioms in late Middle English. The first derived from the habit of 'belling' the leader of a flock of sheep or herd of cattle, and came to mean 'to take first place by natural or inherent right'. Thus an outstandingly beautiful woman was said to 'bear the bell for beauty', i.e. to take a natural precedence among beauties, to 'lead' all the rest. In this metaphorical sense, the idiom already implies comparison, or even competition. So it is not surprising that this idiom became fused, and even confused, with another: 'to bear *away* the bell'. This originally meant to win, and thus 'carry off', the prize of a small gold or silver harness-bell awarded to the winning rider in a horse-race. This second idiom likewise acquired purely metaphorical currency, and came to mean simply to prevail, to 'win the day' or 'have the last word' in any sort of contention.[24]

Now the idiom as we have it in our text includes the Adjunct *away*, and despite its being separated from the Predicator through the exigencies of the rhyme-scheme, the probability is that its use here implies the second meaning. For in 'bear the bell' the Predicator is obviously the semantic equivalent of *wear*, whereas in 'bear away the bell' its meaning is clearly that of a fixed collocation *bear away = carry off*. It is, I suppose, just possible that its meaning here is 'The bailey leads away the wedding-procession', and that the simple present tense here alludes to the *habitual* action of such officials in late medieval wedding ceremonies. If we accept this reading, the girl simply reminds herself of the formal order of precedence in the imminent progress to the church. (The simple present is unlikely to be 'running commentary' in this line, for the final stanza closes with the girl still strewing the flowers, and the leader of the wedding-procession would hardly start off without the bride.) In so dramatic a lyric, however, the second meaning is contextually much more appropriate. Despite her panic, there is nothing to be done because the bailey 'has the last word'. She will have to go through with the marriage, whether she feels herself to be too young or not. We know for a fact that child-betrothal and child-brides were common enough at the time. Such classic sources of medieval history as the Paston Letters make it clear that among rich bourgeois families the economic *mariage de convenance* was the rule rather than the exception. The young, especially girls, were regarded as thoroughly marketable property. Parents arranged economic alliances between families for the sake of mutual economic protection. The feelings of the marriage-partners were quite irrelevant, and love matches were very rare indeed. So the bride-to-be of our poem may well represent the child bride of just such an arranged marriage.[25]

The most likely contextual significance of the first line of the refrain is therefore legal. The bailey or bailiff of late feudal times was a municipal magistrate and deputy to the county Sheriff. As such, he would bring the power of the law to bear on the girl herself or on her parents, should she back out of the marriage at the last moment. Whatever these powers may have been (e.g. enforcement of the ceremony, or of restitution in money or goods to the injured parties to the marriage-contract), they make her acceptance of her lot inevitable: 'the *rose* I lay'. Finality and inevitability are phonetically hammered home in the first refrain-line, where alliteration combined with a very narrow vowel-range so reinforces the connotation of *bell* that the line itself seems to mimic a slow and sombre tolling. (This contrasts with the wide disparity of sound between *lily* and *rose*, which underlines the magnitude of the choice for the girl herself.)

We have now arrived at *an* interpretation of the text which is consonant with the linguistic data taken as a whole. Others may be possible, for we have not examined all the data with equal care. Our primary concern has been with linguistic *form*, i.e. with meaning at the levels of syntax and vocabulary, with the relations between these, and with the relation of both to the norms of structure and to the metrical structure of the poem as a whole. The meaning we have arrived at is not some conceptual kernel extracted from a smashed husk of linguistic form, but is coextensive with and inseparable from the patterning of language-patterns which constitutes the complete text. All our critical decisions have been based upon the known facts of usage and the given facts of the text. Only when these have been scrutinized have we moved out, when necessary, to extratextual information. Grammatical analysis revealed an absence of the normal kinds of cohesion of discourse, but simultaneously revealed an unusual pattern of cohesion among the foregrounded features of the poem —a patterning which was the main clue to the overall significance we could feel, but found difficult to pin down. Other poems will reveal other patternings giving additional modes of meaning in similar ways. These too we may at first apprehend intuitively, but in the long run, we can only confirm, reinforce or modify and transform those subjective responses by appeal to the linguistic facts of objective text.

Here I must add a warning. No short text such as we have examined will exhibit more than a handful of the stylistic resources latent in the language. These have been exploited in innumerable different ways by the poets of different epochs, and new poets will create new patterns. Any given text will yield only its own unique 'patterning of the variability of linguistic patterns'.[26] Consequently, this analysis has used only some of the techniques and procedures whereby descriptive linguistics can help to reveal, relate and elucidate those patterns and their meanings. It is offered in the hope that it may show something of the general relevance and desirability of placing a text within the linguistic framework of reference before we proceed to interpret and evaluate it. What matters most is not some particular technique in itself, nor the terminology used, but the value of the basic attitudes and central concepts of linguistics as aids to the proper reading, understanding and enjoyment of poetry.

In the classroom, we shall obviously begin by asking for initial hypotheses about the overall meaning and intention of a a work, i.e. from intuitive attempts to construct a feasible context of situation, whether 'inner' and 'outer' situation coincide or diverge. But instead of saying: 'This is Poet X's great sonnet about Subject Y, expressing the profound sentiment Z. How "apt" or "beautiful" or "moving" is the language of the text?', let us above all encourage a diagnostic approach that takes off from such questions as 'What have we here? What does it mean and how does it convey that meaning? What, as a human utterance, has it in common with other utterances, and how does it differ from them?' Just how far analysis should go will depend upon the text, the age and proficiency of the students. It will also depend upon the teacher's own linguistic knowledge, sense of tactics and literary tact. He has to steer a middle course between the extremes of Literary Humpty Dumpty and Linguistic Alice. Obviously such work must draw upon previous work done in the more functional language classes—on the study of grammar and vocabulary in relation to a wide range of examples from different kinds of social usage, spoken and written. This is perhaps the greatest service we can do, both to our students and to literary studies as a whole. To discover literary meaning for oneself is to discover language and its modes of operation; and to discover those is to enter into the world of literature by its front door, the texts, with a firm sense of possession, not sidelong, with the suspicion or fear that one is peering into the incomprehensible.

NOTES

1 The kind of grammatical description I use in my analysis is part of the general linguistic theory developed in recent years by linguists working largely under the influence of the late Professor J. R. Firth. Extended accounts of the theory will be found in works cited elsewhere in this volume, but for the reader relatively unfamiliar with this approach, conveniently brief *résumés* are available in the early pages of J. C. Catford, *A Linguistic Theory of Translation* (1965) and G. N. Leech, *English in Advertising* (1966). The application of the theory to literary texts has been discussed in general by Spencer and Gregory in 'An Approach to the Study of Literary Style' (see N. E. Enkvist, J. Spencer, M. J. Gregory, *Linguistics and Style*, 1964, Pt. 2), while both theory and practical application may be studied in *Essays on Style and Language* (1966), edited by R. Fowler. I am indebted to colleagues in the University of Edinburgh and elsewhere for general advice, especially to my former colleague, Miss J. N. Ure, who encouraged my stylistic interest in this poem and discussed with me the grammatical interpretation of a crucial point in the text. I also owe my awareness of the stylistic implications of certain points in syntax to Professor J. McH. Sinclair's projected grammar of Spoken English.

2 The modernized spelling and punctuation adopted here are those supplied by Sir E. K. Chambers and F. Sidgwick in *Early English Lyrics, Amorous, Divine, Moral and Trivial* (pub. A. H. Bullen, 1907; republished Sidgwick & Jackson, 1966), p. 82. The stanzaic arrangement is that of Sir A. Quiller-Couch in *The Oxford Book of English Verse* (new edn., 1939, etc.), p. 42. On the contextual significance of this punctuation see pp. 26–7 and note 7.

The original manuscript is apparently unpunctuated throughout. I have not been able to consult MS Harley 7578, but reprint here the transcript first published by B. Fehr, 'Weitere Beiträge zur englischen Lyrik des 15. und 16.

Jahrhunderts', in *Archiv für das Studium der Neueren Sprachen und Litteraturen*, vol. cvii (ed. A. Brandl and A. Tobler, Braunschweig, 1901), pp. 48–61.

Chambers and Sidgwick (*op. cit.*, p. 344) describe the text as 'a short extract from the poem, which is a long one.' Even a cursory reading of the *Archiv* transcript reveals immediately that the MS. contains several poems, of which this is the last. All the others are crude, popular Robin Hood and May Day narratives. They are totally different in subject-matter, style, tone and verse-technique from our present poem, which is clearly the product of a more skilled and sophisticated tradition. Unless MS Harley 7578 is itself defective, there is no reason whatever to see the poem as anything other than complete and self-contained as we have it.

3 E. K. Chambers and F. Sidgwick, *op. cit.*, pp. 281, 303, 344. The poem has been many times re-printed in: *The Oxford Book of English Verse* (New edition, 1939, etc.), ed. Sir A. Quiller-Couch; *The English Galaxy of Shorter Poems* (1934), ed. G. Bullett; *The Oxford Book of Light Verse*, ed. W. H. Auden (1938, 1939); *The Knapsack: a pocket book of verse and prose* (1939, 7th edn, 1947), ed. Herbert Read; *A Treasury of Great Poems, English and American* (1942; rev. edn, 1955) ed. L. Untermeyer; *The Viking Book of English Poetry* (1941) ed. R. Arlington; *The Broadway Book of English Verse* (4th edn, 1946), ed. W. B. Honey; *Poets of the English Language* (vol. i, 1950) ed. W. H. Auden and N. H. Pearson; *A Little Treasury of British Poetry* (1951), ed. O. Williams; *Exploring Poetry* (1955), ed. M. L. Rosenthal and A. J. M. Smith; with a commentary, in Archibald MacLeish, *Poetry and Experience* (1960), pp. 30–33; and with a note on its obscurity and modern popularity in Hugh Kenner, *The Art of Poetry* (New York, 1966), p. 121.

4 See MacLeish, *op. cit.*, p. 33.

5 For a full description of contextual categories, see J. O. Ellis, 'On Contextual Meaning' in *In Memory of J. R. Firth* (ed. C. E. Bazell, J. C. Catford, M. A. K. Halliday and R. H. Robins, 1966), pp. 79–95. For certain aspects of contextual

meaning see also J. C. Catford, *A Linguistic Theory of Translation* (1965), ch. 13, 'Language Varieties in Translation', esp. pp. 84–92.

6 On tone-groups, see Catford, *A Linguistic Theory of Translation*, pp. 5, 13–15, and Leech, *English in Advertising*, p. 21.

7 The complete absence of punctuation in the text as preserved in MS Harley 7578 admittedly makes this point theoretically debatable. In practice, however, insertion of a third comma, making all three nominal groups into appositives, gives us a very improbable clause if the elements are re-arranged in normal sequence: 'I, the lily, the rose, the rose, lay.' It also makes the inner context of situation more obscure than ever, for at lines 5, 9 and 13 we should have to account for a recurrent retrospective time-reference (i.e. to the past as described in lines 1–3). This would oblige us to envisage a *P* who keeps recalling that at the moment of the maidens' arrival, he or she 'lay' in the bower, identifying himself or herself simultaneously with both the lily and the rose. I think the later stages of my explication (pp. 206 ff.) offer a more feasible interpretation than any that might be based on this appositional reading of the second refrain-line. In my view, Chambers and Sidgwick instinctively supplied the correct punctuation, and it is significant that no later editor has punctuated this line to give appositional function to its three nominal groups.

8 See Chambers and Sidgwick, *Early English Lyrics*, nos. lxvii, xxiv, xxvii; and A. Quiller-Couch, *The Oxford Book of Ballads*, nos. 99 and 153; also nos. 4, 103 and 155.

9 On cohesion, see M. A. K. Halliday, 'Descriptive Linguistics in Literary Studies' in A. McIntosh and M. A. K. Halliday, *Patterns of Language* (1966), pp. 56–69.

10 On the mood-system of the clause, see Catford, *op. cit.*, pp. 18, 77–8. Basically, the mood-determining elements of a clause are S and P. Their sequence indicates the mood of the clause,

which frequently defines its contextual function e.g.

> The maidens came = SP = affirmative statement
> Did they come? = P(s) = interrogative = question
> Come! = P = imperative = command

Note, however, that intonation-patterning may give an utterance a contextual function at variance with its grammatical mood, e.g.

> The maidens came? = SP = affirmative = question.

11 On minor or moodless clauses, see G. N. Leech, *op. cit.*, pp. 15–17 and Eugene A. Nida, A. *Synopsis of English Syntax* (second, revised edition, Mouton & Co., The Hague, 1966), pp. 166–8.

12 On lexis, see McIntosh and Halliday, *op. cit.*, pp. 18–23, and 184–99; Catford, *op. cit.*, pp. 10–11.

13 On rankshift see Catford, *op. cit.*, pp. 8–10 and 18, and Leech, *op. cit.*, pp. 19–20, where this type of 'depth-ordered' structure is called *embedding*.

14 On reference-cohesion among nominal groups, see especially M. A. K. Halliday, 'Descriptive Linguistics in Literary Studies' in Halliday and McIntosh, *Patterns of Language* (1966), pp. 57–9, 68–9.

15 On primary and secondary structures in nominal groups, see Catford *op. cit.*, pp. 10, 18; and Leech, *op. cit.*, pp. 13–15.

16 Various editors give titles taken from the text, e.g. 'The Maidens Came', 'The Lily and the Rose'. Louis Untermeyer (see note 3) uses 'Young Girl's Song'. Only Sir Arthur Quiller-Couch seems sufficiently to have grasped the nature of the 'inner context of situation' to entitle the poem 'Bridal Morning' (OBEV, 1939, no. 30, ii).

17 Whatever the *musical* implications of this stanzaic anomaly, it is clearly justifiable in terms of the overall meaning of the poem. There is no reason to think the text defective (see note 2).

18 On 'foregrounding' see, G. N. Leech, '"This Bread I break" —Language and Interpretation' in *A Review of English Literature*, ed. A. N. Jeffares, Vol. VI, No. 2, April 1965, pp. 67–78, and S. R. Levin, *Linguistic Structures in Poetry*, The Hague (1962), esp. pp. 30 ff.

19 On a scale of 0–3, where 0 = unstressed and 3 = maximum stress, the line seems to demand a reading as follows:

$$\overset{1}{\text{How}} \overset{0}{\text{should}} \overset{3}{\text{I}} \overset{2}{\text{love,}} \overset{0}{\text{and}} \overset{2}{\text{I}} \overset{0}{\text{so}} \overset{3}{\text{young?}}$$

20 On the strewing of the bridal chamber and the semi-public consummation of the marriage, see Eileen Power, *Medieval People* (Penguin, 1951), pp. 117–18, 172–3.

21 More precisely, *glass* here is a pre-head noun, not true adjective. We can have a *glass window*, but also clear *glass*.

22 See *N.E.D.*, *fold*, sb[3].

23 I have not been able to trace an earlier date for this proverb than 1607, but M. P. Tilley seems to think it very ancient. See his *Dictionary of the Proverbs in England in the Sixteenth and Seventeenth Centuries* (Ann Arbor, 1950), entry B. 663.

24 For discussion of these two idiomatic usages, see under BEAR or BELL the following: M. P. Tilley, *op. cit.*, entry; *The Shorter Oxford English Dictionary;* Smith & Heseltine, *The Oxford Dictionary of English Proverbs*; Brewer, *Dictionary of Phrase and Fable* (latest edn); *Stevenson's Book of Proverbs, Maxims and Familiar Phrases* (1949). Smith and Heseltine cite as their earliest example Chaucer's use of the phrase in *Troylus and Criseyde*, III, 149. See also Skeat, *Early English Proverbs*, pp. 72 ff., no. 173.

25 On child marriages, the powers of the local bailiff in such matters, etc., see G. C. Coulton, *Medieval Panorama* (Cambridge, 1938) pp. 77–8, 314; P. E. Allen, *The Age of Erasmus*, pp. 197–8; A. Abram, *Social Life in England in the Fifteenth Century*, (London 1909), pp. 96, 170–2; *The Paston Letters*, ed. J. Gairdner 4 vols, (Edinburgh, 1909), vol. iv (Introduction),

pp. 324–6; and H. S. Bennett, *The Pastons and their England* (Cambridge, 1932), pp. 27–50, 195.

26 The phrase is M. A. K. Halliday's. See also his observation that 'all illustrations in linguistics are misleading', in 'Descriptive Linguistics in Literary Studies', *Patterns of Language* (with A. McIntosh, Longmans, 1966), p. 56.